PUNISHMENT AND RESTITUTION

Recent Titles in Criminology and Penology

PUNISHMENT AND RESTITUTION

A Restitutionary Approach to Crime and the Criminal

Charles F. Abel *and* Frank H. Marsh

Contributions in Criminology and Penology, Number 5

Greenwood Press
Westport, Connecticut • London, England

Library of Congress Cataloging in Publication Data

Abel, Charles F.
  Punishment and restitution.

(Contributions in criminology and penology, ISSN 0732-
4464 ; no. 5)
  Bibliography: p.
  Includes index.
  1. Reparation. 2. Punishment. I. Marsh, Frank H.
II. Title. III. Series.
HV8688.A24   1984   364.6′8   83-22837
ISBN 0-313-23717-4 (lib. bdg.)

Library of Congress Catalog Card Number: 83-22837
ISBN: 0-313-23717-4
ISSN: 0732-4464

First published in 1984

Greenwood Press
A division of Congressional Information Service, Inc.
88 Post Road West
Westport, Connecticut 06881

Printed in the United States of America

10 9 8 7 6 5 4 3 2 1

Contents

Preface

Our criminal justice system is beleaguered, and though it has few defenders, it has many apologists. Their apology is that we have no just and practical alternatives; no alternatives true to our principles, ideals, and policies; no alternatives that really solve the problem of what to do about our crime and with our criminals. So we go along with what we have, not really sure of why it is this way or where it is taking us and not really sure if this is really what we should be doing or if we can do anything else. Still, the system is there, undeniable and defacto, and while its attackers are virulent, energetic, and relentless, its apologists are well dug in and well attuned to the advantages of inertia.

In this book we try to describe and justify a workable, efficient, and fair alternative. We begin by reminding ourselves that the criminal justice system is a political institution. This is not meant pejoratively. Political institutions are the way we pursue our policies and secure our values in this particular civilization that we have made. We must recapture our understanding of the fundamental identity of law, politics, and society if we hope to get a clear view of what we should be doing and how it can be done best in our criminal justice system.

The purpose of a criminal justice system from this perspective is to help our society work in the face of certain threats, threats to certain ways of behaving that we must insist upon if there is to be any possibility of a society at all. We are absolutely sure that we have not been doing this in the best possible way, that is, in the way that accomplishes this task most fully. We cannot meet this purpose with an institution that is only coercive, an institution relying only on retributionary, deterrent, and coercive rehabilitative methods. Our institution must be remedial and faciliatory as well; it must, so far as is humanly possible, heal both victims and society and help them to continue in pursuit of social policies and in defense of social principles. This involves broadening the scope of what is legally relevant in criminal law and making courts and penal institutions more flexible tools, tools that can help generate social and economic forces that will help correct both the effects of crime and many of the roots of recidivism that we can track to social and economic factors.

Both the contemporary criminal justice system and the greater part of the studies by social scientists have concentrated on the offender, his socioeconomic background, and his future prospects. Relatively little consideration has been given the victims of crime or the social damage left unaddressed by our courts and penal systems. The results of this neglect have been far from benign, even for the offender. By drawing attention to neglected dimensions of the problem, this book hopes to suggest new questions, open new avenues of approach, and argue effectively for a more efficacious priority of values in this particular area of jurisprudence.

Our approach to the study of the problem is twofold: (1) the analysis and assessment of arguments concerning the proper means of dealing with crime and criminals (i.e., the proper form of punishment), and (2) the proper way of conceptualizing "punishment" so that its institutionalization might work as effectively as possible toward those ethical ends we most reasonably seek through criminal law. Our intention is to consider all that we find persuasive by way of historical argument that a significant dimension of what we understand by "punishment" is restitutionary in nature. We have also attempted to develop a philosophical awareness concerning the purposes of punishment as an institution and to argue that this awareness leads us to consider seriously a restitutionary approach to crime and the criminal as the most viable and most ethical alternative for political action (e.g., in restructuring our priorities) in the area of criminal jurisprudence. We have also dealt, of necessity, with subject matter that requires at some points something other than philosophical analysis. In order to set contexts, parameters, and contrasts, and to support certain points, historical analysis has been employed as well as a modicum of statistical evidence.

When we speak of the "purposes of punishment" or "those ends we most ethically and reasonably seek through criminal law," we are referring primarily to political, social, and economic rationales. It may be that, fundamentally, punishment arises from some dark motive deep in the human psyche. To this possibility, we give no consideration. No political or philosophical writer with whom we are familiar has seriously undertaken to justify punishment or any of its possible forms by reference to such a motive.

The kind of criminal justice system that we envision as restitutionary, of course, requires a society that is willing to make it work, a society with both the resources and commitment to do more with its criminals than simply to oppress them or dispose of them. Our society has been blessed with vast resources. We are rich, educated, technologically advanced, and politically stable. What we need is to be convinced that there is another way of dealing with the problem of crime and the criminal that deserves our commitment. We believe that restitution is just that way.

We are happy to thank those many friends who shared with us the thoughts that the subject of punishment inevitably brings to mind. Several people read all or part of earlier drafts and made many valuable suggestions and raised many important criticisms. We are particularly grateful to Dr. James Glass, University of Maryland, and Justice Luis Rovira of the Colorado Supreme Court. We are also grateful to Linda Smith and Andrea Phillips for their patience with the unfamiliar work of typing and proofreading the final manuscript.

Finally, the portion of the book contributed by Frank Marsh is dedicated to his wife Marty, and to his children John and Molly, for contributions that relate to, but also go well beyond, this book. Charles Abel dedicates his portion of this book to his son with the hope that as he grows to adulthood, there will be a like growth and improvement in the approach to punishment within criminal justice.

PART I
JUSTIFYING RESTITUTION

1

Raising the Questions

Despite ardent attempts to push the question of how to deal with crime and the criminal to the periphery of our political and philosophical concerns, it returns stubbornly to the center. As it is an unwelcome though unsettled question, we have struck upon the device of avoiding it by continually redefining our goals in criminal justice. There is a remarkable consensus, for example, that the problem of crime and the criminal is actually a problem of continually shifting the emphasis our criminal institutions place upon rehabilitation, deterrence, and retribution. Believing that the answer lies somewhere in the simultaneous pursuit of these three objectives, we jump from one to another as the failures of each become obvious in succession. This is an unfortunate mistake. While our social, political, and economic problems and our values, value priorities, policies, principles, opportunities, and costs change, it does not follow that these changes can only be handled by transient and makeshift approaches to the violations of those values, policies, and principles. This is not flexibility but confusion. So what we have to consider is not what to do from time to time about crime and the criminal but what consistent approach is flexible enough to countenance rapid social change and help us make our society a better place to live.

A restitutionary approach to criminal justice is nothing but an opinion we are advancing on this point. It is not necessarily better than anyone else's opinion, and each of us ought to make up his or her own mind on this question. Still, we hope to persuade most people that a restitutionary approach to the problem of crime and the criminal accomplishes the justifiable ends of the deterrence, retribution, and rehabilitation approaches at least as well as they do. Moreover, it is ethically superior to those approaches, at least as practical, more flexible, and much more positive in its social impact.

This last point is very important because our present way of dealing with crime and the criminal has a discriminatory social impact. Every day the problem of dealing with crime and the criminal is addressed in thousands of courtrooms by doling out one form of punishment or another. The different forms of punishment meted out distribute the benefits and burdens of engaging in criminal activity differently. Punishment for white-collar crimes, for example, has traditionally been such that it significantly decreases the burden of engaging in such activities as compared to engaging in street crimes. Similarly, different forms of punishment shift the costs of dealing with crime and the criminal to different sectors of society. It might be thought, for example, that a rehabilitation approach simply costs more in both time and money than a retributionary approach. But while retributionary approaches may be a boon to the average taxpayer, they are a bane to those in the lower socioeconomic strata. It is generally understood that strict retributionary approaches embitter offenders or make them apathetic toward the rights and needs of others. The consequence is a high rate of recidivism, most of which is perpetrated by lower-class individuals against each other (white-collar criminals and corporate criminals seldom experience prison, the central retributionary device in our system). Going from a rehabilitation approach to a retributionary approach, then, does not decrease the burdens of dealing with crime and the criminal; it simply redistributes those burdens to weigh more heavily on a particular social class.

Similarly, victims under our present criminal justice system bear an unrelieved burden. The perpetrator may be punished most severely, but the victim is left with his or her losses intact. When it administers its punishments, the state does nothing to address the loss to person or property occasioned by the crime. Now, you may say, "That is how it should be." After all, the state is not responsible for the act, the criminal is. Moreover, damages might be sought in a civil suit against the offender. But this approach is far removed from the way we live together today. Most people understand that in our highly interdependent society patterns of crime emerge out of the social forces confronting each individual. The level and particular kinds of crime we experience are very much the result of choices made by the state. Decisions to bring down inflation by increasing unemployment, for example, or to cut government spending on social welfare programs in order to decrease taxes, can be traced as fairly direct causes of increased property crime and domestic violence. More broadly speaking, much of the crime in America can be traced to the policy of maintaining the existing distribution of wealth in our society. The state, then, does in fact contribute to our becoming victims of crime and should perhaps help restore us to the *status quo ante*.

Another rationale for state responsibility toward victims derives from the simple observation that in our very close and intricate society we cannot have people engaging in acts of self-help to right wrongs they perceive themselves to have suffered. To live together peacefully, each of us must give up this right to self-help and concentrate coercive power in the state. In return the state promises to keep each of us in line, reduce the overall violence in social interaction, and provide the security to our persons and property necessary for us to go forward with the day-to-day business of making the society work. If the state keeps this promise in the main but fails in individual cases, it does seem that it ought to restore those it has failed (if it fails altogether, of course, we must revert to self-help while we're building a new state).

As far as imagining that damages for criminal activities might be recovered under the civil law, that is stuff and nonsense. Those who most often end up in our criminal justice system are, by dint of the social forces and policy choices we create and pursue, most often living hand to mouth without much prospect of betterment. Moreover, this approach shifts an even greater burden to the victim. He or she must now take on the state's role as prosecutor, detective, and should an award be granted, enforcer of state decrees (i.e., they must legally pursue the criminal debtor to collect that which they have been awarded). Hiring an attorney to perform this task does not soften the burden (quite the opposite). So when you hear this argument advanced, you might shake your head at the naïveté of the speaker, but do not irritate the victims of crimes by repeating it to them.

These arguments and many others will be considered in some detail later. The important point for the moment is not whether the burden and benefits of dealing with crime and the criminal are at present discriminatory and will in the future be shifted to different groups, but how much of the burdens and benefits each group ought to have, and on what conditions certain groups ought to be either alleviated of burdens or allocated benefits.

One plan quite often proposed is to inflict discomfort upon each criminal in direct proportion to the heinousness of the crime. Others say let us dole out punishments in such a way as to discourage certain behaviors and encourage others. Some believe we ought to work with criminals and provide them opportunities so that the industrious and repentant among them might flourish while the weak and dissolute justly flounder. Some say let us treat criminals biochemically or surgically to reduce their desire or propensity for crime. We might even intervene before crimes are committed by screening the genetic material of everyone for indications of criminal propensity. Some believe (though they seldom admit it nowadays) that we ought to have different laws and punishments for different types of criminals; let there be differences among white-collar crimes and street crimes, crimes by political figures, and crimes by corporations. Let some pay fines, others go to jail, and still others be pardoned by executive fiat. Others say let things alone; let us go on quietly as we are.

Those of us who believe in restitution say that none of these plans will work satisfactorily and that the only really ethical, nondiscriminatory, and practical plan is to set the criminal to work repairing the damage done, the courts to work assessing that damage, and the penal system to work administering the process while reintegrating the criminal and society (if possible).

By way of addressing the question of how to deal with crime and the criminal, then, let us take each of these approaches one after another and examine them both for soundness and for the ethical and practical questions that they raise and that must be addressed if we are to argue that restitution is a better solution. Let us begin by noticing, however, that many of these solutions deal with distributing punishments to the criminal and justifying the sort of punishment meted out. Consequently, the first question we should address in our argument for restitution is the relationship between ''punishment'' and ''restitution.'' This will be the subject of our second chapter. The third and fourth chapters will deal in depth with the ethical questions we are about to reopen here, and the chapters in Part II will lay out a practical institutional approach to restitution. That is, we will demonstrate how courts might assess damages from criminal acts, how the criminal might make repayment, and how the penal system might supervise the process.

EUGENICS: THE PERMANENT SOLUTION

The first viewpoint is that of eugenics. Are we really any better off trying to rehabilitate and reintegrate criminals into society by making them repay the damage done, or should we seek a more permanent solution? The first reaction to this question is to say simply that at least the damage is repaired by restitution, including the costs to society of dealing with the crime and the criminal. If this is not an advantage, there is no meaning in the word. Still, restitution does not address the fact that leopards rarely change their spots and similarly that the quality of the individual may be unalterable even by careful socialization.

Some would say that if we want higher quality people, we need to breed them carefully. Failing that, we must screen each person genetically for the propensity to behave criminally and counter these tendencies biochemically. In this way we seek a more permanent solution than those we now have: we sterilize crime out of the population. Perhaps this is right, but there are two difficulties. First, we do not really know what a "criminal propensity" is. No act in the abstract really seems to be criminal. To be criminal, an act must occur within particular social, political, and economic contexts. The same act in different contexts may not be a crime (e.g., killing in a battle as opposed to killing in a grocery store). Propensities to certain acts, then, are similarly criminal only by reference to a context, and we cannot predict that any individual will necessarily either encounter that context or behave the way his or her propensities incline; other propensities and immediate social, political, and cultural forces muddy the water. Moreover, according to what we've said, any propensity anyone might have, given the proper circumstance, could be criminal. In short, depending upon how we look at it, either all propensities are criminal or none are. (We have a similar problem when it comes to finding a "propensity" to counter. "Propensity" is a concept used to sum up a great variety of behaviors, desires, motivations, and inhibitions. It is not a physical thing, nor is it basically identified with particular genetic structures, i.e., a physical genetic structure is not itself the propensity. What counts as a propensity, then, seems a matter of culture and learning rather than physical biology).

The second difficulty is that just as we don't know what a criminal propensity is, we don't know what kind of people we want. Inquisitive, curious, thinking people are forever causing trouble; some very revered people in fact did little else (Socrates and Christ, we must remember, were both put to death for stirring things up). So who decides what people are to be like? And how do they decide? Eugenics, then, is simply misconceived and doesn't really raise any issues of substance once the conceptual problems are dissolved.

RETRIBUTION

Immanuel Kant is a good example of a thoroughgoing retributionist. As he says: "Even if a civil society resolved to dissolve itself with the consent of all its members ... the last murderer lying in prison ought to be executed before the resolution was carried out ... that the blood guiltiness may not remain upon the people."[1]

For Kant, punishment is the infliction of pain upon a subject on account of the crime he or she committed.[2] It is right in and of itself simply because "justice" or the moral order requires it (more specifically, there is a categorical imperative to punish offenders by applying *lex talionis*). However, this approach does not contribute much to any thinking on the justification of punishment. As a categorical duty, or an *a priori* dictate of practical reason, punishment neither needs nor is capable of analysis or proof. It must be accepted as a primitive, fundamental, and final law of our moral nature. But it does raise the interesting question of whether punishment is actually in need of justification and what nature that justification might be. This issue, then, is a primary consideration to be dealt with in considering punishment as restitution.

Besides Kant's suggestion that punishment is a dictate or necessity of practical reason, other retributive writers have variously characterized it as (1) divine law (Aquinas), (2) metaphysical law (Hegel), and (3) an aesthetic requirement (Leibniz).[3] Thus, while sharing the idea that punishment is the "correlate" (Grotius), the "equivalent" (Armstrong), or the "supplement" (Bradley) of guilt and wrongdoing, retributionists disagree about the source of the state's obligation to punish.[4] Is it God, universal natural laws, or internal human needs? Consequently, these retributionists raise (though tacitly) a second important consideration to deal with in considering punishment as restitution: Given the correctness of punishment, by what right does the state arrogate to itself the function of carrying it out?

Overall, the core postulate of the retributionist or punishment as vengeance approach to crime and the criminal is that a cosmic or metaphysical distributive justice must be enforced in this mundane sphere under the auspices of the state. However, it is not self-evident that virtue ought always to be rewarded and wickedness always punished. And given that, exactly what is wicked and what is virtuous is not really evident. What, then, is a state to do when there is serious disagreement on these points within its polity? Moreover, assuming that positive law has definitive social goals and purposes (not all necessarily "moral" in a transcendental sense), how is the state to accommodate simultaneously both these objectives and the diverse moral claims of the citizenry? The point is that in the area of criminal jurisprudence we are concerned with a body of positive rules varying with time and place according to the usefulness of certain conducts toward accomplishing certain ends. Thus, it is not so much the wickedness of certain acts that should concern us, but rather the best way of proceeding after the fact to the tangible benefit of both the society as a whole and the individuals directly involved. What is needed, then, is not a vengeful, retributive process fitted to a "transcendental region altogether separate from the phenomenal world."[5] Instead, we need a system functioning solely to regulate the relationships among people. And since the best people differ in their moral perceptions, we need a process as nearly neutral in moral dictate as is humanly possible. Of course, this is in itself a moral position, but one particularly well suited to the state. A morality is thus impossible to elude, but the content of this particular morality allows for the maxium diversity of doctrine, and is consequently a sort of metamorality. That is, it is a kind of morality about moralities, rather than a special set of directives of principles to follow in being "moral."

The retributionist approach, or punishment as vengeance school, thus presents us with at least four important questions in arguing for punishment as restitution: (1) Does punishment need justifying? (2) What must the nature of that justification be? (3) By what right does the state punish? (4) How can the state both pursue positive social goals and accommodate the diverse moralities of its citizens in the process of punishing? Additionally, it presents a singular challenge regarding our institutional structures and procedures. How do we set up a criminal justice system that functions solely to regulate the relationships among people while remaining as nearly neutral in moral dictate as is humanly possible? We will answer that the state is only justified in punishing if the punishment is restitutionary and that a restitutionary system is better at making these accommodations between moral diversity and practical necessity that a criminal justice system must make.

We need to turn now to more "political" ideas of how to handle crime and the criminal; that is, a consideration of those approaches under which punishment is not an end in itself, but rather a means to ends of the state.[6]

DETERRENCE

The idea that punishment is to be justified by its consequences, and specifically by its effect on the probability of crime, was probably first formulated by the sophist Protagoras.[7] Plato supported this approach, though combining it with the goal of rehabilitation.[8] Fichte writes: "It is to some extent true that punishment serves as an example, namely to convince all of the infallible execution of the law."[9] And Bentham argues that whereas "punishment is an evil ... it ought only to be admitted in as far as it promises to exclude some greater evil."[10] It ought, therefore, to be excluded where "groundless," "inefficacious," "unprofitable," or "needless."[11] H. Rashdall characterizes deterrence as being in the interest of society, but not thereby inimical to the individual and his or her right to be treated as an end rather than a means: "We should never treat humanity *only* as a means, but always also as an end. When a man is punished in the interest of society, he is indeed treated as a means, but his right to be treated as an end is not thereby violated if his good is treated as of equal importance with the end of other human beings."[12] Rashdall then hints strongly that "some good, spiritual or otherwise" will obtain to the punished, particularly if the punishments are "as far as possible reformatory as well as deterrent." Finally, Flugel argues that punishment as deterrence is at least consistent with a great deal of psychological theory. It gives, one might say, support to the superego.[13]

As these citations indicate, punishment as deterrence also raises at least four sets of important questions to consider in arguing for punishment as restitution. First, what is the proper focus of punishment?

Toward whose interests should it be directed? Should it aim at the proscribed act or the individual offender (as retributionists would variously have it)? Should it aim at the "good" of society in a "practical" (i.e., economic or institutional) sense? Should it consider the victim? The victim's family? Second, how should punishment become operative as a social instrument? Should it be relentlessly inflicted or only threatened with great pomp? Should the infliction be of pain? Should it include economic sanctions? Should it be a denial of liberty or property? How might transgressions and punishments be related? Should we severely punish the slightest transgression to insure compliance? Can offenders be equitably treated with regard to each other? That is, should we take into account an offender's economic or educational background in determining punishment?

A third cluster of questions forms around the fact that from Plato through Bentham, Rashdall, and more recently Brandt, there has been a strong tendency to fuse deterrence and reformation.[14] As Brandt puts it:

Traditional utilitarian thinking about criminal justice has found the rationale of the practice, in the United States, for example, in three main facts. (Those who disagree think the first two of these "facts" happen not to be the case.) (1) People who are tempted to misbehave, to trample on the rights of others, to sacrifice public welfare for personal gain, can usually be deterred from misconduct by fear of punishment. (2) Imprisonment or fine will teach malefactors a lesson; their characters may be improved, and at any rate a personal experience of punishment will make them less likely to misbehave again. (3) Imprisonment will certainly have the result of physically preventing past malefactors from misbehaving during the period of their incarceration.[15]

This brings up the question of whether the state should be a positive factor in the area of criminal law. That is, should the state passively await criminal activity before it deals with those involved and its consequences? Or should it take some action to anticipate and preclude criminal activity before it manifests itself clearly? To what extent and in what manner is such positive action on the part of the state justified? Should the state be allowed to "reform" the criminal? Are there ways of deterring without threatening dire consequences? Should we then carry out those threats for the sole purpose of making future threats credible?

The final set of questions centers on Bentham's observation that "punishment . . . ought not be admitted . . . where the mischief may be prevented . . . at a cheaper rate."[16] This is the concept of "economical deterrence": "if the evil of punishment will be unprofitable."[17] What actually is the most "economical" way of dealing with crime and the criminal? Might there be a way of actually increasing the social good through punishment rather than simply producing the least amount of "evil"? Given that we probably cannot deter criminal conduct in every case, is there a form or system of punishment that might nevertheless produce some positive (socially and individually definable) results in every case? Can we establish a set of rules or a flexible procedure concerning punishment which usually or almost always has the effect of either producing the least amount of distress or increasing total satisfaction? If so, then can we at the same time ensure equitable treatment to individuals brought under such rules or procedures?[18]

Those of us who support restitution believe very strongly and will argue throughout this book that the proper foci of the criminal law are the victims and others directly affected by the criminal act as well as the good of society in a practical (i.e., economic or institutional sense), rather than a moral sense. Consequently, we are convinced that punishment should become operative as an award of damages to victims, other injured parties, and society in the person of its political institutions. We also hope to convince most people that restitution is a way of increasing the total social good through punishment (rather than merely reducing the total social evil), since it benefits victims, injured parties, and our political institutions, as well as the criminal, the penal system, and the courts. Consequently, restitution is the most economical and ethical way in which the state can take positive action to secure human welfare (i.e., the benefits of social living) and avoid its opposite.

REHABILITATION

In addition to supporting punishment as deterrence, Plato was one of the earliest writers to see crime as an "evil" in the body or soul of its perpetrator, and one of the earliest to prescribe punishment as a cure.[19] Arguably, Hegel also perceived reformation as a dimension of punishment in his otherwise "transcendental" or teleological approach.[20] "For he says, beyond a possibility of a doubt, that in punishment the criminal is treated as . . . one who is potentially moral . . . and one in whom this potential morality must be called into actual existence."[21] Aquinas was of similar persuasion, arguing that if "the avenger's intention be directed chiefly to some good, to be obtained by means of the punishment of the person who has sinned (for instance that the sinner may amend . . .) then vengeance may be lawful."[22] And both A. C. Ewing and Hans Von Hentig argue, respectively, that punishment in and of itself has a reformative effect on the individual (by emphasizing to a person his or her immorality and by habituating people to legal behaviors), and that it is "educative" in demonstrating exactly the degrees of seriousness among diverse crimes.[23] Thus, there are those who see crime as expressing an illness, those who see it as indicative of a moral weakness, and those who attribute it to intellectual failing.

As we have seen, Bentham included the opportunity to reform criminals in his justifications for punishment, though it is unclear how much this reformation he intends to benefit the individual offender as opposed to the society and its institutions.[24] Consequently, there has ensued a continuing debate over exactly what the effective focus of utilitarian reformation is.[25] The writings of Moore, McClosky, Sprigge, Austin, Rawls, Brandt, and Raphael are illustrative of the fact.[26] Generally, the polemic is defined by the opposition of Moore and McCloskey who argue respectively, that:

It is in this way that the theory of vindictive punishment may be vindicated. The infliction of pain on a person whose state of mind is bad may, if the pain be not too intense, create a state of things that is better *on the whole* than if the evil state of mind had existed unpunished.[27]

And that,

Although the production of the greatest good, or the greatest happiness, of the greatest number is obviously a relevant consideration when determining which punishments may be inflicted, the question as to which punishment is just is a distinct and more basic question.[28]

The former would focus on the effects punishment produces for society *in toto*, and the latter would focus on its effects for the individual punished. The remaining authors argue either about how identical social and individual interests actually are, the possibility that such an identity can be established, or the compatibility of the two foci in practice.

The rehabilitative approach, then, leads us immediately back to the question of punishment's proper focus, the question initially suggested by the punishment as deterrence approach. But punishment as reformation also suggests some particular issues of its own. What justifies the state's attempts to reform the values, priorities, and self-definitions of its individual members? Is it in some sense desirable to do so? Should the state involve itself in the private moralities of its citizens? Might punishment be made a blessing in form as well as substance? That is, with moral, intellectual, or organic regeneration as the end, is pain or discomfort a necessary ingredient of the means? Can we maintain the state and increase the total amount of good for the greatest number without violating individual integrity by involving the state in the individual's mental privacy and self-definition? And finally again, if moral or intellectual improvement is the goal, need there be a violation of an established, preexisting rule before the state can prescribe a remedy?

Of course, rehabilitation has been popular now for about a generation, and though it seems an obvious failure, we have always argued that the reason is that we have never been serious about our rehabilitative efforts. We have always hoped that more rational and better-financed treatment programs would be the answer. Those of us on the side of restitution no longer share this faith. We are honestly convinced that rehabilitation is ethically, theoretically, and practically flawed. The state has no ethical foundation for either reforming the values, priorities, and self-definitions of its individual members, or involving itself in the private moralities of its citizens, though it does have an ethical foundation for seeing to it that those acting on their personal convictions do so in ways that are not harmful to others. Rehabilitation is theoretically flawed because most offenders are not really abnormal. They are making rational decisions, given their social situation, toward gaining those things our society values most. In practice, the abuses of indeterminate sentencing, release time, therapy, and parole for good behavior are well documented. These ethical, theoretical, and practical flaws are obviated by a restitutionary approach as we will seek to demonstrate.

DIFFERENT PUNISHMENTS FOR DIFFERENT TYPES OF CRIMINALS

The idea that punishments ought to be differently formulated for different criminals is in fact a basic premise of the restitutionary approach. Unfortunately, what most people have in mind under this approach is a kind of class differentiation: Different classes in our society should receive different kinds of punishments.

Something like this is actually what works itself out at present in our criminal justice system. Roughly speaking, lower-class people get prison sentences, upper-class people get fines, and the middle classes range between the two. Even when upper-class individuals do get prison sentences, it is no secret that there are different classes of prisons for them, and they are more likely to receive executive clemency than others. Upper classes get better representation, are more likely to make bail, are more likely to be paroled, and are more likely to be diverted into rehabilitation programs than are the poor.

The problem is that no one is willing to come right out and support this idea politically. We do this sort of thing, but we are not happy to have it pointed out to us. So we spend a great deal of time denying this as our purpose and establishing formalities and formal structures hopefully designed to preclude this outcome. Unfortunately, the pattern persists, and it persists because we deal with the problem formally rather than substantively. The substantive reality is that as much and probably more crime is committed each year by the upper classes than by the lower classes, but the opportunities and costs for different types of crime are different for the different classes. Consequently, different classes commit different types of crime, and the crimes committed by the lower classes tend to be those that the criminal justice system is geared to ferreting out and punishing.

All of this ferreting out and punishing is of course done with great solemnity and fanfare, and we are led to believe in the innate evil of the acts being punished and so support the criminal justice system in this mild conspiracy in favor of the upper classes. But as we have argued before, it is very difficult to come up with an act that is justifiable regardless of circumstance, and it does seem more important to ferret out and punish those acts causing the most damage to society rather than those that are somehow abstractly evil. If we want to get rid of the class bias, then our system of criminal justice ought to shift its focus and reevaluate its priorities in allocating time, money, and training so that a more substantive change is effected in the opportunities and costs all classes would face in committing a crime.

THE DO-NOTHING APPROACH

The view that nothing new should be done seems the easiest and most popular plan, but in fact it is impossible. Things simply will not stay as they are, and trying to keep them any particular way is itself a change. Moreover, things in law change quickly but insidiously. The change is barely noticeable because it occurs case by case in widely dispersed courts on different days, and no one, not even the practitioners of law, are really certain about the way things stand now or will stand tomorrow. This is nothing new in the law: Change comes upon us when we think things are just as they were. And the danger of our not perceiving this change is that it is not always directed toward the good of our society but often leaves many people unconsidered and in a worse situation than they might be if there were no law and self-help still ruled. Such is clearly the situation of the victim in our criminal law today, and many would argue that it is the case for the poor generally in our society.

WHAT CONSTITUTES A GOOD APPROACH?

Now we have considered each approach in turn and raised the central questions of this work. We have also suggested how we might answer them should restitution be agreed upon as an acceptable approach to the problem of crime and the criminal. Let us then consider what any approach must do to be acceptable. It is generally agreed that ordinary street crime (burglary, robbery, assault, etc.) is a very uncomfortable misfortune for the victim. It is not so uncomfortable because it hurts (many crimes involve no physical contact between criminal and victim), but because people feel violated. Street crime degrades the victim in a very direct and personal way. White-collar and corporate crimes also degrade, but indirectly. By making everything more expensive for the common person, it leaves less for them to spend on food, medical care, and education, not to mention those requisites for the human spirit like art, music, and dance. Many are encouraged to turn to street crimes to afford the things they cannot otherwise have and thus the degradation is passed on. Similarly, environmental pollution degrades us all, ruining our bodies. Since we believe that it is the quality of our people and the quality of the life they lead that matters, we must take as an indispensable requirement of any approach to criminal justice that everyone be protected from such degradation.

We must also remember that not only crime but also punishment degrades. We should be very honest about this. Prison deprives a criminal not only of freedom but most often of physical security, health, and mental peace as well. If we think this is just, we should say so and acknowledge exactly what we are doing in sentencing someone to prison. However, if we think this is not just, and that is one thesis of this work, it is a second indispensable requirement of any approach that the needs and interests of the criminal are both not abused and actively and consciously considered in forming a punishment.

Finally, we must consider the good of society—what keeps its fabric together, what keeps it functioning. In this regard we must remember that it is the day-to-day working of individuals that accomplishes this task, and the criminal law plays only a marginal role. If any society is to work, people must willingly make it do so. They cannot be coerced into it. You would need one police officer for each civilian and someone watching each officer *ad infinitum*. All societies must ultimately be grounded in some shared values and expectations, however tacit. Police and the criminal law are effective only against marginal individuals, those few individuals acting outside the accepted day-to-day patterns. If many people start changing their patterns of interaction, police will be ineffective in making them follow the rules. The final requisite of an acceptable approach to criminal justice, then, is that its procedure and goals (embodied in the rules of the game) follow from the "form of life" in which the criminal justice system is embedded. That is, the way we deal with crime and the criminal must make sense in terms of the recurrent patterns, regularities, practical behaviors, and characteristic ways of doing things in our society.

Now we are ready to address the really knotty question of doing all this in the best possible way. We believe that restitution is the answer, and let us give a summary argument for why this is so.

RESTITUTION

First of all, restitution has for a very long time been recognized as fulfilling the requisites we have just outlined for any acceptable approach. Jeremy Bentham, for example, stressed the necessity of taking care of the victims of crime through restitution:

Satisfaction is necessary in order to cause the evil . . . to cease, and reestablish everything in the condition it was before the offense; to replace the individual who has suffered in the lawful condition in which he would have been if the law had not been violated.[29]

In this respect, he is supported by Herbert Spencer[30] and Stephen Schaefer.[31] Raffaele Garofolo has pointed out the benefits of restitution to society as a whole:

> If offenders were persuaded that . . . they could in no wise evade the obligation to repair the damage of which they have been the cause, the ensuing discouragement to the criminal world . . . would be far greater than that produced by temporary curtailment of their liberty.[32]

And Del Vecchio has stressed the fact that restitution treats the offender as a dignified human being while pursuing other legitimate purposes of the state.[33]

Regarding the questions raised throughout this chapter by deterrence, restitution, and rehabilitation, we will be dealing with these in detail in the following chapters. Suffice it at present to gather together the points we have made into a summary argument subject to detailed support in the remainder of this work. Broadly, then, our argument will be to the effect that (1) focusing on the victim and the damage done socially by the criminal act, (2) making punishment operative through damage awards, (3) striking a morally more neutral stance (shifting from an ''inherent evil'' idea to a ''damage caused'' idea), and a relatively more ''active'' pose (in terms of awaiting actual criminal activity, but doing more after the fact to ameliorate the social impact of crime), and (4) altering both the structure of our penal institutions and the adversary nature of our criminal procedure, in order to reduce the social isolation of offenders (presently effected through (A) incarceration and its attendant ills including the inability to support the offender's family, (B) social stigma and the failure to reintegrate offenders with the society, and (C) deterrent attitudes in the courts tending to alienate those offenders whose crimes arguably represent rational responses to desperate social situations) is the most effective, equitable, nondiscriminatory, and ethically justifiable approach for the state to take in dealing with crime, the criminal, and the issues just raised.

A restitutionary approach is not only ethically, theoretically, and practically better at securing human welfare and avoiding its opposite than other approaches, but when properly employed it is a punishment, does deter as well as other approaches, can rehabilitate, and even offers a more just form of retribution than that presently meted out. It is punishment because it involves unpleasant consequences for an individual who has interfered with our pursuit or realization of individual and social ends, and those unpleasant consequences are regulated by the state to insure both that they occur and that they do not involve a total forfeiture of rights, property, or life by the offender. Further, it (1) can deter because it involves recognizably unpleasant consequences, (2) constitutes retribution because it involves returning to an offender his or her "just deserts" (they are simply calculated and understood differently than under present approaches), and (3) can rehabilitate and reintegrate an offender into society because it involves the offender working within the functioning economic system and remaining socially responsible for his or her livelihood and the well-being of those injured by the criminal act.

In brief, we believe that the only way out of our present difficulties in dealing with crime and the criminal is by way of restructuring our criminal justice system (from courts to prisons) to embody restitutionary values and goals. But many will say that we simply need to intensify our present approach. We need more prisons, more police, more stringent sentences, less parole, fewer criminal rights, and fewer appeals. Most of us begin with this approach. What changes our mind is the discovery of the terrible array of evils attendant to the present system and the exacerbation of those evils that is likely to occur if we follow the logic of our present system by making it bigger, better, and more thoroughgoing. We may not find restitution very attractive at first. But at least we can see the disasters and inequalities of the present system and come to understand the problems with the values and goals that the present system embodies. And we are now going to make this all as obvious as possible.

NOTES

1. Immanuel Kant, *The Philosophy of Law* (Edinburgh: T. T. Clark, 1887), p. 198.

2. Ibid.

3. St. Thomas Aquinas, *Summa Theologica* (New York: Benziger Brothers, 1947); G.W.F. Hegel, *The Philosophy of Right* (Oxford: Clarendon Press, 1969); G. Leibniz, *Theodicy* (New Haven, Conn.: Yale University Press, 1962).

4. H. Grotius, *The Law of War and Peace* (Washington, D.C.: M. W. Dunne, 1901); K. G. Armstrong, "The Retributivist Hits Back," *Mind* 70 (1961), 481-487; F. H. Bradley, *Ethical Studies* (London: Oxford University Press, 1927).

5. See H. Oppenheimer, *The Rationale of Punishment* (Montclair, N.J.: Patterson-Smith, 1975), p. 227.

6. Other important writers in the retributionist tradition include: G. Del Vecchio, *Justice* (Edinburgh: W. Tait, 1952); J. D. Mabbot, "Punishment and Defeat," *Philosophical Quarterly* 4 (1954), 216-228; K. Baier, "Is Punishment Retributive?" *Analysis* 16 (1955), 25-32; A. R. Manser, "It Serves You Right," *Philosophy* 37 (1922), 298-306.

7. Oppenheimer, *Rationale of Punishment*, p. 235.

8. Plato, "Gorgias," *The Collected Dialogues of Plato*, E. Hamilton and H. Cairns (eds.) (Princeton, N.J.: Princeton University Press, 1967), pp. 262-263.

9. J. G. Fichte, *The Science of Rights* (London: Macmillan, 1884).

10. J. C. Bentham, *An Introduction to the Principles of Morals and Legislation* (Oxford: Basil Blackmore, 1948).

11. Ibid.

12. H. Rashdall, *Theory of Good and Evil* (Oxford: Clarendon Press, 1924), p. 303.

13. J. C. Flugel, *Man, Morals and Society* (London: Oxford University Press, 1955).

14. R. B. Brandt, *Ethical Theory: The Problems of Normative and Critical Ethics* (Englewood Cliffs, N.J.: Prentice-Hall, 1954).

15. Ibid., p. 490.

16. Bentham, *Principles of Morals*, ch. 13, sec. 1.

17. Bentham, "Principles of Penal Law," *The Works of Jeremy Bentham*, J.Brow (ed.) (London: Athlone Press, 1970), p. 397.

18. See S. Wolin, *The Politics of Punishment* (New York: Harper and Row, 1972).

19. Plato, *Dialogues of Plato*.

20. G.W.F. Hegel, *The Philosophy of Law* (London: Oxford University Press, 1969), sections 99 and 100.

21. J. M. McTaggart, "Hegel's Theory of Punishment," *International Journal of Ethics* 6 (1896), 482-499.

22. Aquinas, *Summa Theologica*, II, part 2-2, question 108, First Article.

23. See A. C. Ewing, *The Morality of Punishment* (Oxford: Clarendon Press, 1962) and H. Von Hentig, *Punishment: Its Origin, Purpose and Psychology* (London: W. Hodge & Co., Ltd., 1937).

24. Bentham, *Works of Jeremy Bentham*.

25. See H. J. McCloskey, "A Non-utilitarian Approach to Punishment," *Inquiry* 8 (1965), 239; W. D. Ross, *The Right and the Good* (London: Oxford University Press, 1970); E. Carritt, *Ethical and Political Thinking* (Oxford: Clarendon Press, 1947).

26. See McCloskey, "A Non-utilitarian Approach"; T.L.S. Sprigge, "A

Utilitarian Reply to Doctor McClosky," *Inquiry* 8 (1965), 272; J. Austin, *The Province of Jurisprudence Determined* (New York: Noonday Press, 1954); J. Rawls, "Two Concepts of Rules," *The Philosophical Review* 64 (1955), 3; R. Brandt, *Ethical Theory*, p. 490; and D. D. Raphael, *Moral Judgment* (London: George Allen and Unwin, Ltd., 1955).

27. G. E. Moore, *Principia Ethica*, ch. 6, sec. 128 (Cambridge: University Press, 1971).

28. McCloskey "A Non-utilitarian Approach," p. 239.

29. Bentham, "Political Remedies for the Evil of Offenses," *Works of Jeremy Bentham*, p. 371.

30. H. Spencer, "Prison Ethics," *Essays: Scientific, Political and Speculative* 3 (1892), 165.

31. S. Schafer, *Compensation and Restitution to Victims of Crime* (Montclair, N.J.: Patterson Smith, 1970).

32. R. Garofolo, *Criminology* (Boston: Little, Brown and Co., 1914), p. 419.

33. G. Del Vecchio, "The Problem of Penal Justice," *University of Puerto Rico Law Review* 27 (1957–58), 419.

2

Restitution as Punishment

The first question we have raised is whether or not requiring criminals to make restitution is really a form of punishment. After all, we have come to think of "punishment" as nearly synonymous with various forms of mental and physical abuse. It is not at all clear that gainfully employing felons and integrating them into our society and economic system is an acceptable use of the term. We will demonstrate in this chapter that restitution has actually always been considered a form of punishment and is, in fact, a necessary (if not sufficient) element in any definition of the term.

There is another reason for delving into the proper conceptualization of "punishment" at this point. It is interesting to note that in spite of many centuries of thought and effort, our understanding of punishment has become much more elaborate but not significantly more profound. Much interesting and stimulating material bearing on the implications, ramifications, and motivations of punishment can be found in the literature; but generally speaking, our fundamental concept of the essence and the nature of punishment remains largely untouched. Generally, the following have been considered necessary and sufficient conditions for the proper use of the term:

1. Punishment must involve pain or unpleasant consequences;

2. It must be for an offense against a rule;

3. It must be visited upon an actual or supposed offender;

4. It must be intentionally administered by others than the offender; and,

5. It must be imposed and administered by a duly constituted authority under a legal system against which the offense is committed.

We will argue that none of these constitute a necessary condition for punishment, and that together they are insufficient to define the nature of punishment. We will offer instead a reformulation of "punishment" that, we believe, better captures the meaning of that term as we understand it socially. This reformulation, we will argue, opens the way for understanding why restitution is the most justifiable form of punishment.

Now, in the process of reformulating "punishment," it will be important to distinguish clearly the definition or idea of punishment from its justifications. There is a persistent tendency in much of what is written to define "punishment" in terms of its justifications, and to justify its imposition in terms of its definition. Hobbes, for example, includes in his *definition* the fact that punishment is addressed "to the end that the will of men may thereby be better disposed to obedience," a phrase clearly cast in justificatory form. Yet, he then writes: "evil . . . inflicted without intention or possibility of disposing the delinquent, or (by his example) other men, to obey the laws, is not punishment." Thus, he means deterrence to be part of punishment's definition and does not include that final phrase by way of justification.[1] Similarly, Anthony Quinton defines punishment as the "infliction of suffering on the guilty and not simply the infliction of suffering,"[2] and H. M. Hart writes "it is the expression of the community's hatred, fear, or contempt for the convict which alone characterizes hardship or punishment."[3] Justification and definition are in this way confounded, so that punishment is both justified by definition and defined through its justification. To avoid this problem, we will try to reformulate "punishment" in such a way as to separate its meaning from its justifications.

Finally, we will investigate the congruence between our reformulated concept of punishment and the judicial definition of punishment as found in the written decisions of appeals courts. We will argue that a restitutionary understanding of "punishment" comports well with precedent and can be understood as an improved technique for doing exactly what courts have traditionally understood to be the end of punishment in our society. In brief, we will demonstrate the reformulated concept of punishment is functional within our system of law as it has developed according to precedent.

PREHISTORIC, ANCIENT, AND CLASSICAL CONCEPTS OF PUNISHMENT

The first part of our task in this chapter is to argue that restitution has *always* been considered a form of punishment and a necessary element in any definition of the term. Consequently, some brief enquiry should be made into the view taken of punishment historically. Many philosophers, social theorists, and psychologists have tried to reconstruct human social, psychological, and economic origins and therewith the origin of punishment.[4] Unfortunately, the psychological, social, and material origins of punishment are so shrouded in time that the most we are able to reconstruct are some mis-laden speculations as to punishment's original forms and conceptualizations.

Some of the more widely known and interesting speculations on the roots of punishment include: (1) the intoxicating joy of cruelty stimulated by an offending act, (2) the desire for self-expansion after the "self" has been humiliated by the infliction of injury, (3) an ambiguous human nature expressing a combination of cruelty and compassion, and (4) a reflexive action to pain modified by reason and calculation. In short, punishment is some act (usually painful) reasonably calculated to appease the desire for vengeance excited in victims or other private individuals with interests in the victims. It should be noted in passing that there is a kind of restitutionary aspect to these speculations. Victims or people interested in them are seeking appeasement for their loss, pain, or humiliation. The concept of punishment as an institutionalized restitutionary process would thus not be inconsonant with these speculations.[5]

The important question for our purposes is how these very private and individual sorts of reactions were transformed into public processes, thereby becoming punishments as opposed to vengeance. An excellent survey of the literature and analysis of this subject is given by H. Oppenheimer in *The Rationale of Punishment*,[6] wherein he states:

Never do we find the individual, either expressly or impliedly, deputing society to exercise his rights or his remedies on his behalf. History fails to supply the missing link in the chain of that theory according to which the state punishment of crime originates in, and has to be regarded as the continuation of, private revenge. Criminal law has a different origin. With the rise of the power of the state it gains its strength and expands and begins to claim joint ownership in large tracts hitherto held by the civil law alone. As the weapons of which it disposes are so much more powerful, the individual is content to rely on them more and more for the protection of his vital rights.[7]

This, of course, provides a very strong foundation for a restitutionary view of punishment (that is the public act of punishing). In becoming "punishment," private vengeance merged into civil law, the essence of which is restitutionary. In our own courts of justice we "merge the tort into the crime," thus exactly inverting what Oppenheimer argues to be the original process. The particular historico-cultural reasons for this turnabout will not be considered here, as what we are dealing with is restitution's conceptual consistency with punishment's original meaning (as well as we can make it out) rather than whether punishment or restitution (once they are made conceptually distinct) has been the historically dominant theme.

A second set of speculations on the roots of punishment and its original conceptualization includes (1) a common compassion for the individual sufferer, (2) a safety valve for violent indignation of the community, and (3) an expression of the "group instinct" to hate one violating the rules of their organization. In short, punishment is some act (usually painful) reasonably calculated to incarnate the compassion, social hatred, and demand for vengeance (as opposed to a private hatred and demand for vengeance) excited by the commission of a crime. The same argument, however, that Oppenheimer used to criticize the idea of punishment as private vengeance is applicable here:

When in the long run, the state came to interfere, it did so not in order to lend its aid to the offended party, as we should expect if the latter's were the arm entrusted with the sword of punitive justice; on the contrary, it imposed restrictions upon his right to vengeance and prescribed conditions with which he had to comply before he was allowed to enforce his claim.[8]

The state, in other words, did not seek to take over or put itself in the place of those hotly desiring vengeance; nor did it become an agent of social vengeance. Rather, the state sought to control and impede the expression of such drives for its own purposes. It only became involved civilly (not criminally) to the extent that it saw some profit for itself in doing so. Moreover, the same sort of "translation" problem exists for "social vengeance" as existed for "private vengeance." How does a wrong done such an abstraction such as "the state" call forth individuals seeking vengeance on its behalf? In most instances few of the total number in a society experience any harm from the crime, and the notion of harm to the state as a whole involves a great deal of abstraction and would probably not impel many individuals to seek a public vengeance.

Since these speculations prove generally unprofitable, it is advantageous to look elsewhere for some hint of the view taken of punishment by prehistoric peoples. One obvious notion is that the prehistoric view might be echoed to some extent in the criminal codes of ancient civilizations. Many studies of these codes indicate that at an early stage the payment of damages as a salve to vindictive feelings became a customary institution.[9] Eventually, graduated scales of compensation were established for most offenses.[10] These payments were considered restitution to the victim and neither compensation to society as a whole nor punishment of the criminal.[11]

While these studies emphasize the restitutionary aspects of punishment at the inception of human society, it is nevertheless clear that certain classes of crimes were thought too generally threatening to be assuaged by monetary compensation to a single, immediate victim. Usually these crimes were limited to treason, witchcraft, sacral offenses (sacrilege, etc.), sexual offenses (especially incest and bestiality), poisoning, and breaches of the hunting rules.[12]

Here we might ask: Is the existence of such crimes necessarily at odds with a restitutionary conceptualization of punishment? Probably not. If we take a close historical look at the enumerated offenses, an interesting pattern emerges. It appears that each of these offenses was thought to be fraught with serious supernatural danger. Gods identified with and sometimes thought to be embodied in certain communal groups were understood to be abused either physically (through treason or breaches of the hunting rules), or supernaturally (through poisoning, sacrilege, or witchcraft).[13] The immediate effect of such an abuse was to leave the offender "unclean" and to introduce a "polluting" substance into the society at large and consequently into the body of the deity:

The magic material sends forth effluvia which are absorbed both by living creatures and by inanimate objects, and which, if of sufficient virulence, consume and destroy everything with which they are brought into contact. By reason of their great penetrating power, they may act at a distance from the original focus of infection and thus produce results in remote quarters, and where least expected.[14]

Of course this makes things quite uncomfortable for the god in question, and every effort is made by the group in propitiation, even to the point of sacrificing the offending party, both to purge the evil and to appease the god.[15] Hence, punishment of these crimes can be seen as sort of social rehabilitation accomplished by making restitution to the offended deity, a restitution which involves cleansing of the social (and sometimes the god's) body and the infliction of suffering upon the offender.[16]

The dual theme of an abused deity and an infectious effluvia persisted through the classical period as did the idea of rehabilitation through restitution. Plato, for example, speaks of punishment as a cure for the evil infecting the wrongdoer, and characterizes those seeking to avoid punishment as ignorant of the meaning of health: "those who escape punishment . . . are blind to its benefit and know not how much more miserable than a union with an unhealthy body is a union with a soul that is not healthy but corrupt and impious and evil."[17] Punishment to Plato, then, was meant to restore health and comfort to the individual rather than to the community or deity.

The Romans did not have a well-developed system of criminal law; most offenses were dealt with through private redress. When public authority did intervene, it did so because an offender refused to make restitution. A fixed fine was sometimes levied, but the most common procedure was the confiscation of the offender's goods and property and their proportional transfer to the victim.[18] These ideas from the classical period persisted through the Middle Ages. As John of Salisbury writes, "all law is, as it were, a discovery and a gift from God." When God's laws are broken and punishment is called for, a prince's "love of his brethren should not prevent him from correcting their errors with proper medicine." Thus John combines the idea of an offended deity with the need to heal the offender in order to preserve the "justice of God, whose justice is an everlasting justice and his law is equity . . . being impartially disposed toward all persons, and allotting to each that which belongs to him."[19] This is certainly a restitutionary end though it is becoming clouded as is the idea of a medicinal effect. The point is, however, that restitution remains a dimension of the term "punishment." Historically, then, at least one of the things people thought they were doing when they punished was restitutionary in nature.

Even in more modern times, it would be a mistake to suppose that either the idea of an abused deity or of "unclean" offenders infecting the social body are without supporters. Today there are clear-headed people seeking to support the present means and ends of our criminal justice system through just such arguments. F. H. Bradley, for example, has argued for "the principle of social surgery" according to which punishment is "a reaction of the whole community against conduct that weakens it."[20] And the high esteem Lord Devlin has for the place of morals in criminal law is clearly an echo of the divine nature of moral law so undisputed in antiquity.[21] This view persists because however decidedly the sympathies of those taking a dispassionate look at punishment might incline against accepting any such beliefs, the fact remains that explaining and justifying punishment in terms of deterrence, incapacitation, and rehabilitation simply prove unsatisfying. We take a little bit of the humanity from ourselves and from the other person when we punish and we do it consciously. Cost/benefit calculations always seem inadequate in such situations, and we need to believe we are acting as we must because either God or survival demands it.

Arguably, then, prehistoric, ancient, and classical views of punishment, persisting to this very day, are quite in harmony with the idea that restitution is both part of the meaning of the term "punishment" and part of what the state does in punishing. Moreover, those views take into account the community benefits in terms of the reduced tension, the reintegration of productive members into society, and the maintenance of internal security that could be realized through a restitutionary approach.

We believe that this brief consideration of the ancient view of punishment is sufficient to establish the legitimacy of considering restitution as an important form of punishment from the inception of that practice, and at the very least an important dimension of the meaning of the word. In fact, there are certain historical indications that restitution was the primary understanding of the term in early times.[22]

It is now time to turn from the question of whether or not restitution has always been considered punishment to the task of reformulating our modern concept of punishment in order to gain greater insight into exactly what punishment is and exactly how we understand it socially. It should be made clear, however, that we are not trying to define punishment in a new way. We are not saying that the common definition is incorrect; it simply masks certain very important things about the nature of punishment that we are trying to draw back into the light. Once these things are illuminated, the desirability of a restitutionary approach should become clear.

We will go about this task by first considering exactly how each of the conditions which the generally accepted definition of punishment lays out as necessary is lacking in some way, and how a restitutionary approach would obviate these difficulties. We will then offer certain reperceptions of punishment derived from our critique and draw out their implications both to derive our reformulation of "punishment" and to demonstrate exactly how this idea of punishment accords with judicial precedent.

PUNISHMENT AS INVOLVING PAIN OR UNPLEASANT CONSEQUENCES

The idea that punishment must involve some pain, harm, hurt, or injury is prevalent from Hobbes to Hart.[23] As an objective definition, however, this idea runs into certain difficulties. For one thing, there seems to be a large subjective component to pain. According to some psychological definitions, "Pain is a subjective and personal experience, actively created by the self, rather than a sensation passively undergone and endured."[24] This idea is bolstered by numerous studies of ancient cultures.[25] The most that can actually be said on an objective level is that the application of certain measures is generally agreed to cause discomfort and that we might infer from that that punishment actually occurs in specific cases. To avoid this difficulty, we may simply say that what counts is not the actual discomfort experienced but either the intent in fact to cause pain or the reasonable assumption that pain would be caused in the normal course of events. In any case, the idea of punishment becomes one step removed from the statement that it must involve pain or discomfort. It becomes a question of perceptions or intentions among the actors involved and therefore does not necessarily involve any indisputable or obvious pain in the definition.

Another tack we might take would be to define punishment in terms of the intent or purpose for punishing at all, rather than in terms of the intent to inflict pain. Indeed, this may be a more fruitful way of going about the definition of punishment altogether. Rather than seek a set of necessary and sufficient conditions to which the label "punishment" might be attached, we might define punishment in terms of ends sought, rules followed toward those ends, and techniques employed under those rules.[26] Thus, if we have certain ways and means of deterring people from breaking moral or legal injunctions, we might call that complex of purpose, rules, and techniques "punishment." It might also be called "deterrence," however, and that's the rub. To call it punishment might require some means of differentiation from all the other things we might call it and that might return us to the necessity of requiring the infliction of pain as the means. This seems then to lead in a circle, so that we might simply equate the two words of punishment and deterrence to avoid this logical difficulty. Deterrence, in other words, might become punishment when it is taken as a socially defined goal and equipped with rules (socially defined) for its pursuit. Similarly, we might define punishment in terms of education, disablement, rehabilitation, restitution, or any combination thereof.

Defining punishment in this manner has two interesting consequences. First, it implies that punishment may be an instance of that not-so-rare phenomenon, the "essentially contested concept."[27] There may be different groups of people in our society with fundamentally different ideas of the exact makeup of the complex of purposes, rules, and techniques called punishment. There may be an irresolvable disagreement about the proper use of "punishment" because none of the possible complexes can be set up (agreed upon) as the generally accepted and, therefore, standard use.[28] We will return to this possibility when we consider the judicial definition of punishment and its implications for restitution. Secondly, this view of punishment implies that it is a social institution and not simply a behavior occurring under certain necessary and sufficient conditions. In social terms purposes, rules, and techniques describe an institution, and in the case of punishment might well imply an institution with diverse purposes stemming from the "essentially contested" nature of the concept being institutionalized.

We are a far cry now from identifying punishment with the occurrence of pain or discomfort. Neither seems at all necessary to our definition—in fact, quite the opposite. Inflicting pain or insisting upon discomfort may positively get in the way of certain socially defined goals set up as the proper standard for "punishment's" use. And at this point, some difficulties arise. For one might in fact say that some social purposes sought under rubric of "punishment" might better be obtained by giving pleasure or simply doing nothing, for example, withdrawing the protective or facility arm of the law from one violating established rules.[29] But somehow, the positive infliction of pleasure does not agree with our understanding of "punishment," and we draw back from this extension of our logic. We feel that punishment must be more than the mere infliction of pain, but less than the purposive infliction of pleasure regardless of our purposes. Certainly, then, there are some means (rules) to the socially desired ends of "punishment" which cannot reasonably be included in the standards chosen for the proper use of the term.[30]

Still it seems that there must be some way of incorporating all of the diverse purposes traditionally associated with the meaning of punishment, while maintaining that balance between pain and pleasure which allows us to pursue effectively our purposes without extending our logic too far. We feel that a restitutionary approach fits these requirements neatly. Enforced restitution is hardly a pleasurable experience, and yet it is not just painful either. Arguably, there are definite advantages to all concerned.[31] For example, the public must presently support through taxation the maintenance of the court system and the convicted offender, in addition to bearing the effects of the crime itself. Under a restitutionary system the social effects of crime are ameliorated and the costs of dealing with the criminal repaid. Furthermore, to the extent that crime reflects social alienation, restitution provides reintegrative opportunities. It may have the effect of reconciling offenders with their victims as well as putting offenders in a better light with society at large. It may also help to develop a sense of responsibility and self-worth in offenders who at present often perceive themselves as the helpless victims of forces beyond their control.[32] Insofar as deterrence is a goal of punishment, it is as likely to be realized by the swift and sure imposition of a restitutionary requirement as by the threat of imprisonment.[33] Insofar as punishment is meant to educate or to express the community's condemnation or contempt,[34] a graduated scale of restitutionary requirements would be both expressive and elucidating.[35]

We have tried to demonstrate in this section that not only is the identification of punishment with pain or discomfort not necessary, but that "punishment" defined in restitutionary terms comports much more exactly with all we are trying to achieve through the concept of "punishment" than does "punishment" defined in terms of pain or discomfort. In this same light, let us move to the second consideration in the common definition of punishment.

PUNISHMENT AS INVOLVING AN OFFENSE AGAINST A RULE

The idea behind this second condition of the definition is simple enough. To say that people have a legal obligation to do or to forbear doing something is to say that there is a readily identifiable and formally promulgated rule already alerting them to their responsibilities. This requirement is, of course, born of the positivists and is open to all of the usual objections to that philosophy of law, that (1) it is difficult to identify a single sovereign promulgating rules in a pluralistic and shifting political environment, (2) many (if not most) laws are not orders to do or forbear, but means of facilitating social arrangements, and so on. These objections need not concern us here, though, because it is possible to say that although the position does not hold in general, it nevertheless holds in the particular case of crimes and punishments, that is, all of the positivist requirements *should* be fulfilled in order to "punish." Our inquiry here must be to whether or not we have "punishment" in the absence of formally promulgated rules, not to whether we have "law" in such a case.

The first thing we should notice, of course, is that court cases are often the occasion for the first formulation of a particular rule. Very often cases make it to the trial stage just because there is no readily identifiable rule that comfortably fits the factual nuances of the situation being litigated. After the case is decided, we may say it stands for a certain rule, but the rule does not exist before that final decision, though offenders may know in some vague way that they are probably committing some sort of unspecified transgression. Perhaps they arrive at such a conclusion through a process of generalization from sets of other rules, but formally promulgated rules are often not the case and punishments flowing from rules enunciated through the case cannot be said to depend upon the preexistence of a formally promulgated rule.

A second thing to notice is that while situations may be underdetermined in that there is no rule directly *apropos*, they may also be overdetermined. There may be some conflicting rules that can cover the situation. Under this circumstance the decision as to which rule prevails can be made only by appealing to something beyond the rules themselves. That decision must also be made through cases so that punishment flowing from overdetermined cases can also be considered independent of preexisting rules.

Another way of looking at what is going on when punishments follow from cases rather than rules, is to consider the policies (economic, social, or political) set out as goals to be fostered through and by the legal system.[36] One source of the vague feeling of wrongdoing transgressors may have in doing an act later characterized by a court as illegal may be their understanding, as parts of a larger social order, of the values, goals, and priorities of their society. Whatever they might do to disrupt the orderly pursuit of those values and ends might reasonably be expected to call forth some reaction. Thus, it is ultimately the policies (not the rules) that are an intricate element of punishment's definition, and it is the disruption of the order required by the policies (not the transgression of the rules) that is the occasion of the punishment.

From this perspective, restitution once again provides great promise. The immediate problem would not be to deter (that has already failed) nor to reform or educate (these look to the future) nor even to express indignation or provide retribution (these look to the past). The immediate problem is to readjust the disrupted pattern of things in continuation of the pursuit of social policies, ends, values, and goals. Moreover, restitution would do this in a way calculated (as argued above) not to preclude the benefits of reform, deterrence, education, public condemnation, or retribution.

One final thing should be noticed regarding punishment as requiring an offense against a rule. For slightly more than 130 years strict liability has been recognized in both criminal and civil law.[37] Since then the scope of strict liability has steadily increased. It is presently applied to felony-murder, the sale of narcotics, misdemeanor-manslaughter, negligence, bigamy, sexual offenses, the sale of adulterated food, the transportation of intoxicating liquor, the sale of liquor to minors or habitual drunkards, violations of building regulations, and traffic offenses.[38] Strict liability involves liability to punitive sanctions (punishment) despite the lack of *mens rea* (traditionally a necessary condition for an "offense"). In many cases, then, punishment does not require an offense in the traditional meaning of that term.

Historically, the growth of strict liability paralleled the development of industrialized society. As the primary purposes and values of social policies became economic in nature, the stability and welfare of the society itself increasingly became dependent upon the economic welfare of the total population. The paramount concern shifted from individual responsibility and fault to distributing losses as widely as possible. Thus, most cases holding a defendant strictly liable make reference to the reasonableness of imposing the risk upon him or her rather than the victim. Most often, strict liability statutes apply to classes of offenders economically well situated to bear the burden. The important point for our argument here on restitution is that the recognition inherent in the strict liability doctrine is the paramount consideration to be given an intricate economy, an impersonal market, and the apparent inevitability of interpersonal conflict and damage in a highly integrated industrial society. Strict liability is meant to promote social policy in the only practical manner under those circumstances—without the necessity of showing fault and with a view toward reestablishing the *status quo ante* in the least disruptive manner possible.

Clearly, strict liability is not concerned with deterrence, retribution, education, reform, or expressions of public indignation.[39] In many cases the convicted defendant's high degree of care is irrelevant,[40] as is his or her moral rectitude. But strict liability *is* concerned with restitution, as we have defined it above, and punishment serves to secure that end and the subsequent benefits to social policy. Consequently, we can once again argue that restitution is more to the point of what we are after in punishing than is the infliction of pain or discomfort for an offense against established rules.

PUNISHMENT AS APPLICABLE ONLY TO A SUPPOSED OFFENDER FOR HIS OR HER OFFENSE

Applying the considerations of the immediately preceding section, this element translates into a requirement that only those socially considered responsible for punishable acts actually be punished. Now, as we have just said, sometimes people are punished (held socially responsible) under strict liability rationales though they committed no act and even though they took express action to preclude any harm.[41] What punishment is after here is the general public welfare in an economic and social sense rather than in a moral sense. Thus, questions of fault become secondary. At one time the moral rectitude of individuals may have more directly affected the total social welfare than in the modern state where people are more insulated from one another by their political and economic institutions. At present, however, individual moral rectitude does not so directly affect the person and property of others that it should be made the primary concern. This is not to deny that the integrity and rectitude of people in general does not affect the functioning of the social enterprise. Theft, tax evasion, and white-collar crime, for example, clearly raise the individual costs of products. But the burden is spread out over everyone buying the product so as to reduce substantially the burden that any one purchaser experiences. As another example, it is possible that the theft of an animal (say a horse) in an agricultural or nomadic society could have profoundly damaging results, particularly for the individual owner. But theft of a car in industrial societies like our own, with insurance spreading the risk around, is not so damaging and is handled as a matter of course.

Restitution, of course, fits well with this condition, regardless of whether the person considered socially responsible is a wrongdoer in the strictest sense. Both restitution and strict liability recognize that what gives any physical act its criminal character has nothing to do with the intrinsic nature of the act, but with the framework of social relationships within which it occurs. For example, "the physical act of stealing merely involves moving a piece of matter from one place to another. What gives it its immoral character is the framework of property rights in which it occurs. Only the violation of these rights transforms an inherently harmless movement into the iniquitous act of stealing."[42] Since it is the violation of the social framework that is punished, it is only the reparation of that framework which the society, through its authoritative structures, has a right to demand. Disruption of the socioeconomic framework gives rise to a claim on the part of those affected. But it is not a claim on the comfort of the person punished. It is a claim to be made whole. Similarly, an obligation arises on the part of those benefiting from the violation of the framework, and there is no necessity that he who benefits need only be the actual agent of disruption. Often (if not usually) the benefiter and the disrupter will be identical, but this will not invariably be the case. Strict liability recognized this most directly. The obligation of the state is to the injured members of society, to protect them from the adverse consequences of the disrupting act, and therefore, to provide a mechanism through which reparation might be efficiently realized.

Finally, let us always remember that the state has a duty to treat offenders as ends, and not merely as a means to reparation. Both strict liability and restitution perceive justice as the adjustment of competing interests. But such adjustment must take place according to the principle that no person is to be treated only as a means. Given that "social life would not be possible without the constant subordination of the claims of some to the like claims of many,''[43] some mechanism must be devised as punishment which will not only subordinate the rights of offenders, but also treat offenders as ends in themselves.[44] The state, in other words, has the moral duty to offer an opportunity to an offender for rehabilitation or reconciliation. Restitution, it has already been suggested, is well suited to fulfill this duty simultaneously with the state's duty to the injured; as well as its duty to the society at large to maintain the viability of social policies in the face of criminal activity.

PUNISHMENT AS REQUIRING AN INTENTIONAL ADMINISTRATION BY HUMAN BEINGS OTHER THAN THE OFFENDER

The act of restitution itself is not an act of the state, but of the responsible party. Restitution may be overseen or facilitated by the state (in the sense that it is imposed by public authority), but it is the responsible party who actually performs the act here considered to be punishment. Can we speak in a meaningful way of responsible parties punishing themselves? Is it required that "punishment" be inflicted by a significant other?

On one theoretical level, both Hegel and Beccaria agreed, at least in part, that punishment was based on the self-determination of the criminal.[45] Hegel's theory is more radical than Beccaria's, all punishment inflicted on the wrongdoer being self-determined, while Beccaria believes the criminal to will only certain punishments, never including death. As one writer puts it:

Having maintained against Beccaria that the externalized will of the criminal is both a particular and a "universal" will, and that it is the attributed or constructive "universal" will to punish crime, the "universal" will of the criminal wills and justifies his own punishment, (the present writer has said). Thus, for Hegel the will of the criminal externalized in the criminal act is self-directed against the criminal. It seems to have turned against him and to dominate him. Here the externalized particular will of the criminal is appropriated or alienated as an Hegelian "universal" which wills and justifies the punishment. What has been criminal will-for-self, realized in the world, becomes repressive will-against-self, that is a will-for-other, will-for-the-state.[46]

One might argue that this transference from the particular to the general and back to the particular is institutionalized in representative governments and put in practice as they prescribe penalties for violations of their laws which are then enforced. Marx and Engels adopt this line of thought:

Under *human* conditions punishment will *really* be nothing but the sentence passed by the culprit on himself. There will be no attempt to persuade him that *violence* from *without*, exerted by others, is violence exerted on himself by himself. On the contrary he will see in *other* men his natural saviours from the sentence which he has pronounced on himself; in other words, the relation will be reversed.[47] (emphasis added)

This view, however, is a unique approach in the general field of criminal theory. Ordinarily criminals are considered the object, not the subject, of punishment.[48]

Historically, something very similar to self-punishment was required of feuding parties at the early stages of tribal involvement in private disputes. At that stage some historians argue that "courts" were alternatives to violent self-redress and their determinations took the form of suggested resolutions to be carried out by the disputing parties. These suggestions could be ignored, yet they were often carried out voluntarily to win public favor and the practical aid of kinship groups. There was, in other words, a social pressure for self-punishment at one point in the growth of criminal justice systems.[49] Presently, something of a return to this idea has been suggested by many writers supporting the self-determinate prison sentence.[50] Under this approach, criminals are not totally responsible for their own punishment, but the length of their sentences is to the greatest possible degree their own responsibility. Actual length of sentence is determined both by the courts on the basis of the seriousness of the offender's crime and by the criminal's own efforts during his or her sentence to compensate the victim and society at large. The nature of "restitution" under such systems is often broadened to include at the extreme "any creative act" of the offenders by which they give "something of themselves" in a "constructive effort" as recompense to society or the victim.[51]

We might conclude now that the idea of self-punishment imposed by public authority, particularly in conjunction with punishment as restitution, is not all that unfamiliar. Yet there is another dimension to this element of punishment's definition. Is it necessary to the idea of punishment that it be intentionally inflicted? There is at least one sense in which it is not. At least since 1867 it has been authoritatively recognized that the denial of the right to engage in one's calling is a punishment.[52] Somewhat later it was also recognized that the state in the proper exercise of its police power might establish certain criteria for the practice of certain professions, which have the effect (though not the purpose) of denying particular members of affected professions the right to practice their calling.[53] Thus, the state may punish, though its intent is to regulate. Of course, one might argue that exactly because the intent to punish was not predominant in the latter case, the state's act did not constitute punishment. Yet, in that same case all the other elements of the classical definition of punishment being considered were present,[54] along with at least the realization on the part of legislators that their regulatory act would have the effect of depriving some of their calling. Are we then to make intention in the sense of purpose the single hallmark of punishment? It seems that intent is certainly not a sufficient condition, and arguably it is not a necessary one either. Unintentional punishment in the sense considered here is justified by the facilitation it provides for public policies and as a preventive measure (it precludes, in grossly obvious cases, an almost certain future need for restitution).

PUNISHMENT AS REQUIRING IMPOSITION AND ADMINISTRATION BY AN AUTHORITY CONSTITUTED BY A LEGAL SYSTEM AGAINST WHICH THE OFFENSE IS COMMITTED

In discussing whether or not punishment required the violation of a set of rules, it was suggested that in fact what punishment required was the interference with social policies and principles. Rules were thought to proceed from cases considering certain violations of those policies and principles, and to exist only after their enunciation by the court in its decision. Similarly, it was argued here that offenses are not committed against the legal system *per se*, but against the policies and principles that the system of rules is constituted to pursue and ensure. That such offenses are more effectively answered through restitutionary forms has also been argued.

Finally, it was argued above that self-punishment is both theoretically and practically conceivable. With this as an extreme, we might argue here that there is no reason for all punishment to be directly administered by authoritative (governmental) agencies. Administration by something very like a credit agency with recourse to governmental authority might work just as effectively. For example, at present, restitution for many juvenile offenses is overseen by parents or a respected member of the community.[55]

A REFORMULATION OF "PUNISHMENT"

We seem now to have disposed of all the conditions usually thought necessary and sufficient for the existence of punishment. The central points of our analysis have been (1) that restitution has always been an important (if not *the* important) element in what "punishment" has meant historically, (2) that the conditions usually laid down as necessary and sufficient conditions for the proper modern use of "punishment" are neither necessary nor sufficient, (3) that punishment might better be understood as a social institution with social purposes rules for properly pursuing those purposes, and acceptable and unacceptable techniques for following those rules, than as a label describing certain types of behavior, and (4) that the idea of restitution seems to go hand in hand with looking at punishment in this way.

Let us then consider for a moment a small number of writers who have considered punishment according to this last understanding. These writers include, for example, Kurt Baier in "Is Punishment Retributive?" G. E. Moore in *Principia Ethica*, and H.L.A. Hart in "Prolegomenon to the Principles of Punishment." These writers respectively suggest that punishment is (1) a total social process, (2) an element of an organic social whole, and (3) a social institution with numerous, varying, and even contradictory purposes. Punishment is thus seen as something more integral to the social structure and more involved in the social dynamic than the mere intentional infliction of "harm," "evil," or inconvenience, even if done by an authority having clearly social ends in mind. These viewpoints, we believe, constitute the beginnings of a fundamental reperception of exactly what we are doing when we "punish" and, therefore, exactly what "punishment" is.

In the first case, the act of punishment is seen to include more than, say, throwing a switch on the electric chair. The act of punishment is broadened to include the total process leading up to that final act. In the second, the form that the particular part of the social and political structure we call punishment takes is understood to vary with the "organic" nature of the structure in question. In the final case, punishment is an institution vying for position and influence in a total system of institutions. Success in this endeavor may well require the pursuit of multiple ends, each of which might necessitate different and even contradictory forms of punishment for its realization. All of these views perceive punishment as an institutionalized, dynamic (i.e., changing) social process aimed at furthering social goals and the most fundamental of these goals is to make possible orderly social intercourse.

What do these reperceptions imply about the nature of punishment? To begin with, these perceptions suggest that those responsible for punishing want some return from the punishment and they may want it both from the person punished and the society at large. Whether they seek to deter, rehabilitate, or strike some moral balance, there is some expectation that social behavior will be affected and hopefully encouraged in some particular direction.

This, of course, suggests that punishment involves some reciprocity. Those responsible for punishment must figure out exactly what will work to produce the desired effect. What will deter? What will rehabilitate? What will satisfy the community's moral conscience? In this way both the person punished and the society guide those responsible for punishing. There is an interaction, an exchange of influences.

This last implication further suggests that punishment involves a measure of freedom both in the person punished and the society at which the threat of punishment might be directed. For example, what will the people punished really consider painful enough to deter them from repeating the act? Similarly, what price might others be willing to pay for committing similar crimes? Punishment, in other words, involves more than the unilateral imposition of a sanction. It involves calculation on the part of both the immediate person punished, and others in the general populace disposed to similar criminal behaviors. Such people are always free both to gamble on paying this price and to accept this price as a cost of realizing some criminal aim.

Fourth, these perceptions suggest that the pain, discomfort, or deprivation involved in punishing obtains in a reduction or limitation of alternatives for social action. But these limitations or reductions must not frustrate the expectations or return sought by punishing in the first place and since the most fundamental of these goals is to make possible orderly social intercourse, complete deprivations of rights, property, or life might be precluded. Such complete deprivations take at least one person totally outside the social network and can severely affect economically, socially, and psychologically others with whom he or she is intimately connected. Furthermore, it may make other desirable side effects more difficult to realize. Reform and rehabilitation could be expected to suffer, as might deterrence. Offenders themselves might be more disposed to further criminal acts following complete forfeitures, as might others in the society who sympathize with their plight.

Finally, we should recognize that since punishment is a policy aimed at social goals, there are different social benefits and different social burdens distributed to different people not only by the realization of punishment's ultimate ends but by the process of punishment itself. Punishment, then, is nothing more nor less than one way of distributing social benefits and social burdens in order to accomplish certain social ends. The social ends, of course, change. They are changed every day by Congress because none of us is ever satisfied with them. They are changed moment to moment in thousands of courts all over the country to make them fit local conditions or because they address local conditions too well and nobody likes what they require. Laws are made, altered, and repealed to make people do things they've never done or to stop them from doing things they've always done. We should keep this fickleness in mind when deciding how the benefits and burdens of punishment ought to be distributed.

What distinguishes punishment is the source and nature of the benefits and burdens. Certain policies are considered too important to be left to the private anarchy of markets or the private authoritarianism of family, church, school, or big business. Public authority is needed, and this authority must be truly "public," that is, not a facade for any of the private authoritarianisms. This public authority must have a set of benefits and burdens at its disposal that can, to the greatest extent that is humanly possible, be so distributed as to realize completely these socially necessary goals.

At this point we must be very careful, for what we have just said sounds very ominous, and it might be concluded that ominous means are required for profoundly important ends. So, for example, we might require that the burdens distributed be by nature the most ominous we can imagine and slip into a behavioral definition of punishment (e.g., execution, imprisonment, levying a fine) rather than sticking to a social one. In view of all we have said about punishment so far, what counts as a punishment socially does not depend upon some particular objective behavioral criteria. Rather, punishment is socially defined as any limitation or burden overseen by public authority upon the social action of individuals who have disrupted or frustrated in any socially significant way the orderly pursuit of what are socially defined as necessary public goals.

Now, we must avoid the temptation of adding that the burdens imposed be directed at reestablishing the effective pursuit of public goals by restoring (so far as humanly possible) the *status quo ante* of those groups and individuals injured by the criminal act (with reasonable modifications for the way the situation was changed). This would sound too much like a justification of punishment, and we would be guilty of the same confounding of definition and justification we have criticized in others. However, by reformulating punishment in this way, we think restitution will emerge as comparatively the most justifiable form of punishment. That is, we will demonstrate in the next chapter that all other forms of punishment (1) fail to address the values and interests of society to the most effective extent humanly possible in devising forms of punishment, (2) violate our social principles in pursuit of legitimate social goals, and (3) themselves frustrate the realization of our social policies.

THE REFORMULATION OF "PUNISHMENT" AND THE COURTS

What difference will this reformulation of "punishment" make as the courts go about the day-to-day business of doling out punishments? This question is important for two reasons. First, the judiciary defines "punishment" in practice. The policies it most diligently pursues, the priority it gives to the purposes it seeks to fulfill, the principles it most protects and enhances, and the techniques it uses in its everyday practice, incarnate the meaning of "punishment" in our society. How might these change under the reformulation? Second, our courts are thoroughly committed to the idea of precedent. This does not mean they will not go against precedent. Nor does it mean they will not use precedent rather creatively when they believe policy or principle so require. It does mean that courts are more likely to try to make restitution work on a day-to-day basis if they perceive it as fitting neatly with the way they have punished in the past. That is, if they can see restitution as a new technique of punishment rather than a whole new set of rules or an entirely new philosophy, they will be more likely to make it work in practice. No one likes to think that what they've been doing day in and day out for most of their professional careers has been entirely wrongheaded. But an improved technique is something else. It is progress. The right idea has been employed all along, we have simply learned how to apply it more effectively. Restitution is just such a new technique as we will soon demonstrate.

First, what difference will this reformulation make in day-to-day practice? It will broaden the scope of the possible forms punishment can take. Under this reformulation of punishment courts might find the imposition of debt, forced sales of property, receivership, providing opportunities for rehabilitation and reform, deprivation of privileges, enforced work routines, and others all useful techniques under the proper circumstances to attain restitutionary purposes. At first glance this might be expected to create even more widely varied sentences for the same ostensible act than are presently inflicted.[56] In practice, however, a convergence of sentences may occur, since judges would have to make some calculations of the actual damage done in order to impose a sentence. Thus, there would be some standard outside the judge's personal discretion against which his or her final decision might be evaluated. If more convergent sentences do not occur, at least some justification for the variations that do result will be provided. This in itself would go a long way toward increasing the overall credibility and dignity of the court. Of course, this expected converging of sentences would be a convergence more in substance than in form. The amount similar offenders one could be expected to be similar while the ways and means employed to pay it off could be very different.

Second, to what extent can restitution be seen as a new technique? To what extent does it conform to court precedents on the means of "punishment"? At present, neither the state nor federal courts have given extensive consideration to the definition of punishment. Usually the question is not directly an issue, and a few sentences on "punishment" are provided only to tighten an argument or fill in a gap in the reasoning process. Consequently, the definition tends to be descriptive in the sense of offering what the court sees as necessary and sufficient conditions for the proper use of the term. Thus, "punishment" is defined as pain, suffering, loss, confinement, or "penalty" inflicted on a person for an offense by the authority to which the offender is subject,[57] any evil or inconvenience consequent of crime or misdemeanor[58] the taking of life, liberty, or property[59] and any "liability."[60] The words "penalty," "liability," and "forfeiture" can be used synonymously with "punishment,"[61] but it has also been held that "forfeiture" is beyond the congressional power to "punish."[62]

This descriptive approach has led to certain problems of definition, which the Supreme Court has simply resolved by fiat. Thus, for example, while the deprivation of any right, civil or political, such as the removal from office, or the deprivation of the right to hold office or pursue a lawful avocation is a "punishment,"[63] it has also been held that disqualifications on conviction of a crime are not punishments.[64] Nevertheless, such disqualifications seem to fit the descriptive definition quite well and therefore would be considered "punishments" in a practical sense despite the court's unwillingness to apply the term. The problem is that if the court admits these disqualifications to be punishments, they would be open to constitutional challenge as bills of attainder, and this would very seriously affect states in the exercise of their constitutionally recognized "police powers." For political and social reasons, then, these disqualifications cannot be treated in the same manner as other punishments. Rather than taking this tack, however, the court for these policy reasons simply cast disqualifications outside the purview of what they would call punishments.

This tendency to un-define things as punishment has been taken to some interesting lengths. According to some courts, for example, when an accusee is convicted and fined, commitment to jail until the fine and costs are paid is defined as a "mode of executing the sentence but not a punishment."[65] This is a classic case of a distinction without a difference, and it is the kind of thing, necessary for policy reasons, which is an inevitable result of the descriptive definition of punishment.

When we begin to look at punishment as a reciprocal social dynamic aimed at realizing social purposes, we find quite another state of affairs. It is quite well established that neither vengeance nor retribution is part of punishment's purpose so far as the judiciary is concerned.[66] Overall, judicial statements of purpose fall into three categories: deterrence, rehabilitation, and what we shall call "restoration." Interestingly, deterrence is often not cast in terms of preventing certain acts because they are *malum in se*, but because public safety and the continued smooth functioning of the social system require it.[67] Deterrence itself, then, is not seen as the ultimate purpose, but as a means to the more important end of an integrated society smoothly pursuing its policies. Similarly, the idea of rehabilitation is not primarily meant to profit the offenders but to reintegrate them into society so that they might contribute to its growth and development. Both deterrence and rehabilitation are ends that can very effectively be pursued through restitution as argued above. Moreover, the ultimate ends of deterrence and rehabilitation as defined judicially are completely compatible with the ends restitution has historically been effective in pursuing: facilitating the pursuit of social policies and encouraging the development of new policies by providing some assurance of their accomplishment. Consequently, restitution as punishment should not be too drastic a conceptual shift from the present judicial idea of punishment when it focuses on deterrent and rehabilitative ends.

The third type of purpose that judicial definitions look to, "restorations," is one of which the courts may not be fully conscious. Yet some of their pivotal decisions employ this end. *Mapp v. Ohio* is a clear example.[68] *Mapp* announced the applicability of the exclusionary rule to the states. Explicitly, the court thought of the exclusion of evidence as a "punishment": "Since the 4th Amendment's right of privacy has been declared enforceable through the due process clause of the 4th Amendment, it is enforceable against them by the same sanction of exclusion as is used against the federal government."[69] But what is not immediately clear is the purpose served by exclusion. We do not think it can seriously be argued that it sought to deter or rehabilitate the police (the violators of the constitutional guarantee). It is rather common knowledge that "the source of an officer's power is not so much the possibility that he can bring about a conviction, but that he can subject a person to arrest, delay, a night in jail, frantic calls to relatives and lawyers, the expense and trouble of a trial, and the undeniable uncertainty about whether a local magistrate's court might in fact convict."[70] None of this is at all affected by the exclusionary rule. Not only can the police accomplish all of the above through an illegal arrest, but they may never be called on it, and if they are, they suffer no deprivation. The criteria most often used to evaluate police performance is not how many cases are thrown out for insufficient evidence. Rather, they are more often evaluated on their "clearance rate": the proportion of all their cases that are "solved."[71] Once the case is "solved," the nonconviction of the offender can hardly be considered a punishment in the sense of deterring or rehabilitating the police officer.

In fact, the ineffectiveness of the exclusionary rule as a deterrent to police has been explicitly recognized by the court in another landmark decision on that rule, *Terry V. Ohio*.[72]

As an alternative explanation, you might say that it is the "system" that is being deterred from similar acts or that is rehabilitated through the exclusionary rule. But the meaning of this is hard to grasp. At any rate, it is difficult to think of "punishing a system." The whole suggestion is too obscure.

We believe what is actually going on with the exclusionary rule is both a kind of restitution to the victim of police abuse and a restoration of (or reaffirmation of) the policies and principles of our criminal procedure. The accused are in many cases being given their freedom, and in all such cases they are given some advantage in the defense of their case, to make up in some way for the deprivation of their rights by a police officer's illegal act. Moreover, both the principles of the Fourth Amendment and the formal policies of the criminal justice enforcement establishment are legitimated and the adherence to them is encouraged by the demonstration that their violation will come to naught. Briefly stated, the exclusionary rule is intended to repair damage, facilitate the attainment of policy goals, and encourage the development of those policies through an act of restitution to the victim of a crime. It is a restitutionary punishment.[73]

It is still possible to see deterrence, rehabilitation, and restoration as divergent purposes rather than convergent on the goals of restitution.[74] One can easily imagine different groups of people disagreeing about the proper use of "punishment" in a judicial sense depending on which of these purposes they see as paramount. Since our justices have never authoritatively ruled any purpose predominant, we are justified in thinking that no use of "punishment" is generally accepted and, therefore, "correct." Judges might hold these purposes to be equally important or never consider possible contradictions. This could return us to the idea of "punishment" as a social institution striving to meet several purposes simultaneously, and to the argument that this is best done by adopting restitution as a primary goal. But it need not feed back in this manner. There could simply be a head-on clash, centered on the concept of "punishment," by perfectly respectable arguments and evidence, and not resolvable by argument or compromise of any kind. Each group may simply see its definition as the "true" or "real" meaning of the concept.

Are we, then, simply at an impasse? Must genuine disputes of the kind just mentioned lead to stagnant policies and preclude defining punishments as restitution for policy purposes? To begin with, we must ask ourselves why the dispute perseveres in practice. There must be important aspects of the term which each group captures, but which is not captured by any other group. Thus, to obtain an optimum expression of what we seek by punishment in our institution, a continuous competition among the enumerated purposes must continue. Only the re- alization of such an optimum justifies the continued competitive uses of the term. However, if continued use of two of the rivals has the effect of frustrating the attainment of that optimum, or if the costs of sustaining particular versions and developing them competitively be- comes too high in light of their general effects, then there is practical justification for choosing certain versions over others, though they may remain theoretically equal.

At present there are innumerable studies suggesting that imprison- ment, institutionalization, and other forms of punishment for deterrent and rehabilitative purposes both frustrate those very attempts at deter- rence and rehabilitation, and are extremely costly ways of attaining the deterrence and rehabilitation that does occur.[75] Under these circum- stances, choice of restoration as the paramount purpose of punishment would seem to be indicated. At any rate, there is a strong case on its behalf, and as its primary aim is restitutionary in nature, there would also seem to be a strong case for stressing the restitutionary aspects of punishment over its deterrent and rehabilitative aspects.

CONCLUSION

Requiring criminals to make restitution, then, is really a form of punishment. In fact, we might argue that restitution is at the core of our notion of what punishment is all about. Moreover, in coming to this conclusion we have discovered some sound practical reasons for choosing restitution as the best form of punishment in highly complex industrialized societies, where many ends are simultaneously sought by punishment and where the costs of stressing certain other forms of punishment can be prohibitive. Finally, we have argued that restitution is an improved technique of punishment completely compatible with judicial precedent defining punishment and offering a solution to the generally recognized problem of widely divergent sentences for similar crimes.

We have also separated the definition of punishment from the justification of punishment. This requires that we now address the second set of questions we have raised: First, is punishment in need of justification or is it simply a primary directive of our moral nature? Second, how do we justify punishment? What is the nature of such a justification? Third, if punishment is justified, what form should it take (i.e., what form is justified)? Finally, given that punishment is justified and that we know what form it ought to take, what justifies the state in acting as the agent of punishment? We will, of course, argue that punishment is not justified unless it is restitutionary in nature, and that the state is not justified in punishing unless the form of punishment it metes out is restitutionary. But as a failsafe position we will also argue that restitution is the best and most moral way of attaining any justifiable ends other forms of punishment might have.

NOTES

1. See Thomas Hobbes, *Leviathan* (New York: E. P. Dutton and Co., 1950), pp. 266-269.

2. A. M. Quinton, "On Punishment," *Analysis* 14 (1954), 512-517.

3. H. M. Hart, "The Aims of the Criminal Law," *Law and Contemporary Problems* 23 (1958), II, A.D.

4. See, for example, A. Montagu, *The Nature of Human Aggression* (New York: Oxford University Press, 1976); E. Fromm, *The Anatomy of Human Destructiveness* (New York: Holt, Rinehart and Winston, 1973); S. Freud, *Totem and Taboo* (New York: W. W. Norton Co., 1961); E. Durkheim, *The Division of Labor in Society* (New York: The Free Press, 1922), Chapter 2, pp. 70-110; J. Piaget, *The Moral Judgment of the Child* (New York: The Free Press, 1965). Freud's construction in particular has been severely criticized by A. L. Kroeber, *The Nature of Culture* (Chicago: University of Chicago Press, 1952); and C. Levi-Strauss, *Totemism* (Boston: Beacon Press, 1962).

5. This view of revenge or retaliation as primarily restitutionary in motive is argued by S. Schafer in referring to the blood feud as the earliest form of "compensation" to the victim. See S. Schafer, *Victimology: The Victim and His Criminal* (Reston, Va.: Reston Publishing Co., 1977), p. 8.

6. H. Oppenheimer, *The Rationale of Punishment* (Montclair, N.J.: Patterson-Smith, 1975).

7. Ibid., p. 35. This view is reinforced by studies of primitive cultures such as the Eskimo, the Ofugao, the Comanche, Kiowa, Ashanti, and Trobriand

Islanders. Some interesting studies in this regard can be found collected in E. A. Hobel, *The Law of Primitive Man: A Study in Comparative Legal Dynamics* (Cambridge, Mass.: Harvard University Press, 1954).

8. Oppenheimer, *Rationale of Punishment*, p. 46.

9. See for example, L. T. Hobhouse, *Morals in Evolution* (London: Chapman and Hall, 1951), pp. 71-120.

10. Examples can be found in the Torah: A. Diamond, *Primitive Law* (London: Methuen, 1971); in the code of Hammurabi: A. Wolfgang, "Victim Compensation in Crimes of Personal Violence," *Minnesota Law Review* 50:223 (1975); and early English codes: F. Pollock and F. Maitland, *The History of English Law* (London: Methuen, 1966).

11. Pollock and Maitland, *English Law*; H. Holdsworth, *A History of English Law* (London: Oxford University Press, 1963); S. Schafer, *Restitution to Victims of Crime* (Reston, Va.: Reston Publishing Co., 1978); G. Holland, *Elements of Jurisprudence* (London: Methuen, 1963); and C. Chilores "Compensations to Victims of Crime is as Old as Civilization," *New York University Law Review* 39:444 (1964), to name just a few sources with this opinion.

12. See H. Maine, *Ancient Law* (New York: E. P. Dutton and Co., 1960); H. Oppenheimer, *Rationale of Punishment*, and A. Diamond, *Primitive Law*.

13. See Oppenheimer, *Rationale of Punishment*, pp. 71-91.

14. Ibid., p. 80.

15. Ibid., p. 83.

16. An interesting twist to this has been identified by B. Read, "Crime and Punishment in East Africa: The Twilight of Customary Law," *Howard Law Journal* 10:164 (1964). In East Africa restitution is forced by the tribal council in an express attempt to *avoid* punishment. The rationale is apparently that one party might be a witch, in which case there may be some form of supernatural retaliation. How prevalent this consideration was historically does not surface in the literature. But it is interesting to speculate that perhaps primitive and ancient people had a definite aversion to simple retaliation, deterrence, and incarceration for just this sort of reason and therefore thought of punishment in primary restitutionary terms. Also *Lex Talionis* may be looked on as a *restrictive* rule keeping things restitutionary to avoid continuing reprisals.

17. Plato, "Gorgias," *The Collected Dialogues of Plato*, E. Hamilton and H. Cairns (eds.) (Princeton, N.J.: Princeton University Press, 1967), p. 263.

18. W. W. Buckland, *A Textbook of Roman Law from Augustus to Justinian* (Cambridge: Cambridge University Press, 1963).

19. John of Salisbury, *The Statesman Book* as reprinted in W. Ebstein, *Great Political Thinkers* (New York: Dryden Press, 1969), pp. 198-211.

20. F. H. Bradley, "Some Remarks on Punishment," *The International Journal of Ethics* 4 (1894).

21. P. Devlin, *The Enforcement of Morals* (New York: Oxford University Press, 1959).

22. Some examples include: A. Flew, "The Justification of Punishment," *Philosophy* 29 (1954), 291-307; H.L.A. Hart, *Punishment and Responsibility* (Oxford: Clarendon Press, 1968), pp. 4-5; and *Corpus Juris Secondum*, Criminal Law Section 69, for a survey of judicial definitions agreeing with the one put forth here.

23. Thomas Hobbes, *Leviathian* (New York: E. P. Dutton and Co., 1950), pp. 266-269; H.L.A. Hart, *Punishment and Responsibility*, pp. 4-5.

24. T. Szasz, *Pain and Pleasure* (New York: Basic Books, 1975), p. xiii.

25. R. Kraft-Ebing, *Psychopathia Sexualis* (New York: F. J. Rebman, 1925); G. R. Scott, *The History of Torture Throughout the Ages* (London: Luxor Press, 1938).

26. See L. Wittgenstein, *Philosophical Investigations* (New York: The Macmillan Co., 1968), for a complete explication of this method of definition.

27. For a complete explication of "Essentially Contested Concepts," see W. Gallie, *Philosophy and Historical Understanding* (London: Chatto & Windus, 1964), Chapter 8.

28. Of course it might be objected (as Gallie points out in a different context) that there is no real disagreement in this situation, only a failure to delineate properly the two individual concepts. To all appearances different concepts of punishment with different purposes and rules would identify different acts, reasons, and strategies as within the definition according to the different schools of thought on the proper use of the term. Is there, then, any ground for maintaining that punishment has a *single* meaning that is in contest? Actually this reduces to a request that one or another of the complexes of purposes, rules, and techniques be chosen over the others, and it is exactly that choice that is in question when a concept is "essentially contested." The point is that all groups involved in any such debate necessarily consider their own definitions to be controlling and better than (more accurate or "truer" than) the others in contest with it.

29. Which brings us to the question of why punish at all, an issue which will be examined in depth in the following chapter.

30. Notice that if purpose is not included in the definition of punishment, quite another situation obtains. J. Mabbitt, "Punishment," *Mind* 48 (1939), 150-167, for example, does not so define punishment and therefore concludes that reform and deterrences are continuances, side effects of punishing which might be taken into account in determining the nature of the punishment inflicted, but are no part of the punishment *per se*. This leaves him, however, with no choice but to justify punishment by an inferential lead: "One fact only can justify punishment . . . and that is a *past* fact, that he has committed a crime." Certainly the mere fact of committing a crime implies nothing necessarily. But if punishment is not defined in terms of purposes, rules, and techniques, no other standard than a *past* fact immediately presents itself as a tool for evaluation

of the propriety of punishing. This is always a problem with primarily descriptive definitions (labels put on a set of necessary and sufficient conditions). There is never any way of evaluating the institution even to the point of deciding whether what we are looking at is, in fact, the institution it is supposed to be.

31. Some of the following ideas on the social benefits of enforced restitution draw from R. Garofolo, ''Enforced Reparation as a Substitute for Imprisonment,'' *Criminology* (Boston: Little, Brown and Co., 1914), pp. 419-435.

32. A sense of helplessness and worthlessness can stem from both his social situation and his treatment subsequent to arrest. Regarding the former, many criminals are generally known to conceive of themselves as the victims of social prejudice and economic discrimination beyond their control. Regarding the latter, it seems that the more involved an offender becomes in the criminal justice system and the more serious his crime, the less he is permitted to take an active part in the procedure determining his fate. This is strikingly true, for example, in the case of parole. He must await the considered judgment of a panel before which he might prove his case. See as illustrations of the helplessness of offenders within the system J. Mill, ''I have Nothing to do with Justice,'' *Life Magazine*, March 12, 1972, and P. Sanford, ''Model Clockwork Orange,'' *The New York Times Magazine*, September 17, 1972.

33. For research suggesting that certainty and swiftness of penalty imposition are more important in deterring than is the severity of the punishment inflicted, see J. P. Gibbs, *Crime, Punishment and Deterrence* (New York: Elsevier Scientific Publishing Co., 1975); C. R. Tittle and C. H. Logan, ''Sanctions Deviance,'' *Law and Society Review* 7 (1973), 371-393; and F. E. Zimring and G. J. Hawkins, *Deterrence: The Legal Threat in Crime Control* (Chicago: University of Chicago Press, 1973).

34. J. Feinberg, ''The Expressive Function of Punishment,'' *The Monist* 49:3 (1965), 397-408.

35. Hans Von Hentig, *Punishment* (Montclair, N.J.: Patterson Smith, 1973), p. 1.

36. This point of view is dealt with in depth by R. M. Dworkin, *The Philosophy of Law* (New York: Oxford University Press, 1977), pp. 38-65.

37. The original English case was *Reg. v. Wilson* 153 Eng. Rep. 907 (1946). The original American case was *Commonwealth v. Earren*, 91 Mass. 489 (1864). Both involved the sale of adulterated substances to the public for consumption.

38. As example, see *U.S. v. Baunt*, 258 U.S. 277 (1922); *Hobbs v. Winchester Corporation*, 2 K.B. 471 (1910); *State v. Kelley*, 43 N.E. 163 (1896); *People v. Boxer*, 24 N.Y. Supp. 2nd 628 (1940); and, *Commonwealth v. Mixer*, 93 N.E. 249 (1910).

39. R. Wasserstrom, ''Strict Liability in the Criminal Law,'' *Stanford Law Review* 12 (1959-60), argues (1) that it is at least plausible to suppose that the

knowledge that certain consequences ensue might induce a person to engage in that activity with much greater caution, and (2) it is reasonable to believe that strict liability might keep a relatively large class of persons from engaging in certain kinds of activity that may lead to offenses. But consider (1) that in cases like *Faulkes v. The People*, 39 Mich. 202 (1878), a high degree of care and caution was ineffective and held irrelevant, and (2) that the activities mentioned to which strict liability often applies, building, driving, banking (in fact, one of the landmark cases in strict liability, *State v. Lindberg* 215 P 41 (1933), dealt with the strict liablity of bank directors) and not the sorts of things we want to discourage in our present society (the auto and housing industries especially are at the foundation of our economic structure), and Wasserstrom's arguments are less convincing as explanations of the purpose for strict liability.

40. *Faulkes v. The People*, 39 Mich. 202 (1878); *Laird v. Dobell*, 1 K.B. 131 (1906); *Groff v. State*, 15 N.E. 769 (1908).

41. An extreme case of this last sort is *Cappen v. Moore*, 2 Q.B. 306 (1898) affirming an employer's liability though his employees violated his express order.

42. B. Wooton, *Crime and the Criminal Law* (London: Stevens and Sons, Ltd., 1963), p. 55.

43. H. Rashdall, *Theory of Good and Evil* (Oxford: Clarendon Press, 1924), vol. 1, pp. 303-304.

44. Looking at Kant's principle in this way helps satisfy competing *prima facie* duties which those in authority are often required to face, without violating well-understood precepts of justice. As W. D. Ross puts it, "The interests of society may sometimes be so deeply involved as to make it right to punish an innocent man 'that the whole nation perish not.'" *The Right and the Good* (Oxford: Clarendon Press, 1965), p. 568. Here the *prima facie* duty of consulting the general interest has proven more obligatory than the *prima facie* duty of respecting the rights of those who have respected the rights of others. Restitution does not require such an ordering of priorities. It allows both to be accomplished, in the case of punishment at least, to the extent that the offender is willing to be rehabilitated.

45. G.W.F. Hegel, *Philosophy of Right* (Oxford: Clarenden Press, 1973); C. Beccaria, *On Crimes and Punishment* (Indianapolis: Bobbs-Merrill Co., 1965).

46. A. Franklin, *On Hegel's Theory of Alienation*, Tulane Studies in Philosophy, 9, no. 55 (1960).

47. K. Marx and F. Engels, *The Holy Family* (Moscow: Foreign Language Publishing House, 1956), p. 238.

48. It is interesting to consider the possibility that the Fifth Amendment is to some extent a recognition of the individual as the subject of criminal law and its punishments rather than its object. Under this view, the Fifth Amendment

would embody some recognition of Hegel and Beccaria. Historically, Adams and Jefferson at least are known to have studied Beccaria; C. K. Wroth and H. B. Zobel, *The Legal Papers of John Adams* (Cambridge: Harvard University Press, 1965), vol. 3, p. 16; G. Chinard, *The Commonplace Book of Thomas Jefferson* (New York: Arbor House, 1926). At one time, Justice Douglas explicitly recognized Beccaria's influence: *Ullman v. U.S.*, 350 U.S. 450 (1956), dissenting opinion.

49. L. T. Hobhouse, *Morals in Evolution* (London: Chapman and Hall, 1951), pp. 71-129.

50. A book blocking out exactly how such a system of self-determinate sentences would work in relation to various sorts of crimes is K. J. Smith, *A Cure for Crime: The Case for the Self-Determinate Prison Sentence* (London: G. Duckworth Co., Ltd., 1965).

51. See A. Eglash, "Creative Restitution—A Broader Meaning for an Old Term," *Journal of Criminal Law, Criminology, and Police Sciences* 48 (1958), pp. 619-622. This is done so that society might purchase the victim's right to restitution from the victim and enforce his claim on the offender. This is most useful where an offender may for various reasons require special handling to exact restitution. The state in effect acts as an insurer, compensating the victim and seeking full restitution from the offender. By being able to vary the form of restitution, the state makes its collection more certain.

52. *Cummings v. Missouri*, 71 U.S. 356 (1866).

53. *Hawker v. New York*, 170 U.S. 1002 (1897).

54. Specifically, (1) they involved the unpleasant result of denial of the pursuit of one's choice, (2) such denial was based on a set of rules prescribing requirements for practice within each state, (3) application of punishment was to supposed offenders of these rules, (4) those enforcing the rules never denied an understanding that the intentional execution of the rules would work a hardship, and (5) the rules were imposed by the general state legislatures and enforced by the state attorneys general.

55. R. E. Laster, "Criminal Restitution: A Survey of Its Past History and an Analysis of Its Present Usefulness," *University of Richmond Law Review* 5 (1970).

56. G. Mapes, "Unequal Justice: A Growing Disparity in Sentences," in *Before the Law*, Bonsignore et al. (eds.) (Atlanta, Ga.: Houghton Mifflin Co., 1974), pp. 304-311.

57. *Bearden v. Attalla*, 117 So. 603.

58. *Thomas v. Bunton*, 22 S.W. 863.

59. *Brown v. Wilemon*, 139 F 2nd 730, certiorari denied 64 S. Ct. 1151.

60. *U.S. v. Veric*, 28 F. Cas. No. 16, 544.

61. *U.S. v. Roe Reisinger*, 128 U.S. 480; *Jones v. State*, 136, p. 182.

62. *Trop v. Dulles*, 356 U.S. 86.

63. *Cummings v. Missouri*, 71 U.S. 356.

64. *Hawker v. New York*, 170 U.S. 1002.

65. *Ex Barte Arnett*, 775 P. 2nd 281.

66. *Williams v. New York*, 377 U.S. 241; Sauer v. U.S., 241 F 2nd 640, certiorari denied 354 U.S. 940.

67. Examples: *Edwards v. State*, 319 F 2nd 1021; *State v. Wojang*, 282 F 2nd 675. This aspect is also brought out through the Supreme Court case of *Williams v. New York*, 377 U.S. 241. Some states, however, still see deterrence of certain acts as an end in itself. These courts perceive deterrence as retribution which can also rehabilitate. *State v. Newman*, 152 S.E. 195.

68. *Mapp v. Ohio*, 367 U.S. 643.

69. Ibid. at 647.

70. C. A. Reich, "Police Questioning of Law Abiding Citizens," *Yale Law Journal* 72: 1161 (1975).

71. J. Skolnick, "The Clearance Rate and the Penalty Structure," *Justice Without Trial* (New York: Wiley, 1966), Chapter 8; also J. R. Isenstein, *Politics and the Legal Process* (New York: Harper and Row, 1972), pp. 50-95. A person whose rights are violated by police procedures does have civil recourse, *Rivens v. Six Unknown Named Agents of Federal Bureau of Narcotics*, 703 U.S. 388. This is clearly restitutionary.

72. *Terry v. Ohio*, 342 U.S. 1.

73. Other instances of this sort of restitution can be seen in cases like *State v. Arizona*, 171 N.W. 605, where a severe delay in the constitutional right to a speedy trial is sanctioned by dismissal of the charge operating as a bar to further prosecution for the same offense.

74. What follows is an application of Gallie's theoretical analysis of essentially contested concepts, Gallie, *Philosophy*, note 30, Chapter 8, pp. 162-168.

75. See, for example: J. Andenaes, "Does Punishment Deter Crime?" *Criminal Law Quarterly* 2 (1978), 76-93; E. Olin Wright, *The Politics of Punishment: A Critical Analysis of Prisons in America* (New York: Harper and Row, 1973); N. Morris, *The Future of Imprisonment* (Chicago: University of Chicago Press, 1974); M. E. Alexander, *Jail Administration* (Springfield, Ill.: Thomas Press, 1957); R. A. Goldfarb and L. R. Singer, *After Conviction: A Review of the American Correctional System* (New York: Simon and Schuster, 1973); R. Hood and P. Sparks, *Key Issues in Criminology* (New York: McGraw-Hill, 1970).

3

Restitution as Comparatively the Most Justifiable Form of Punishment

The problem of justifying punishment is different under our reformulated definition than it would be under the traditional definition. Traditionally, punishment has been *hypothetically* justified. That is, most authorities on the subject have argued that *if* punishment deters, or *if* punishment rehabilitates, or *if* punishment advances the moral good in some other way, *then* it is justified. This approach follows easily from thinking of punishment as a specific behavior (i.e., as a label for a given event).

Thinking of punishment as a social process defined in terms of its purposes, rules, principles, and acceptable techniques, requires that we do much more. First, we need to justify the purposes themselves regardless of whether or not we can attain them. Then we need to justify the rules and techniques (the means to the ends) and the distribution of burdens and benefits punishment works on society. If no acceptable purpose can be found, or if that purpose can be better served without punishing, or if no acceptable means of punishing can be developed, or if the burdens weigh too heavily on some, or the benefits to others are too great, then punishment is unjustifiable and we may need to drop the practice altogether.

Our purpose in this chapter is to suggest that punishment (insofar as it is justifiable at all) is justifiable only in terms of restitutionary goals or techniques. Basically, this reduces to the task of showing (1) that retribution is unjustified except when the concept of "desert" is defined in restitutionary terms, (2) that certain aspects of rehabilitation can be interpreted as justifiable purposes under very rigorous assumptions, but for modern societies these assumptions do not hold, and (3) that deterrence is not justifiable at all. This argument, of course, first necessitates some speculation on what is meant by "justification," as well as some argument that whatever "justification" is, "punishment" is in need thereof.

THE NEED FOR AND NATURE OF THE JUSTIFICATION OF PUNISHMENT

The need for justifying punishment seems to arise from three considerations. First, whether we perceive punishment as the positive infliction of suffering or the deprivation of some right, privilege, or immunity (i.e., some restriction on social action), some one individual or group is singled out to experience suffering or denial. Secondly, others besides the specific person punished (spouse, family, business partners, etc.) are usually affected by the suffering or denial even though they may be innocent of any wrongdoing in all relevant respects. Finally, our general quality of life (reflected by the nature and quality of our public and private institutions) is fundamentally affected by the existence of such an institution as punishment, regardless of the goals it may have and the technique it may employ.[1]

To establish any form of punishment (deterrence, retribution, restitution, rehabilitation) as justified, then, its purposes, rules, and techniques need to be themselves justified in terms of the individual punished, those directly affected by the punishment, and the way that form of punishment affects the general quality of our life. The question now arises as to what extent the traditional justifications of punishment in fact justify that practice in these terms. We will begin by looking at each justification separately. This procedure has the advantage of allowing the justification of restitution to arise naturally out of a criticism of the other forms of punishment. We shall end by explicitly considering the compatibility of the concept of punishment as restitution with the generally recognized concept of "just" or "balanced" distribution of social benefits and burdens. In this manner we will suggest that punishment as restitution succeeds where the traditional concepts of deterrence, retribution, and rehabilitation fail in securing the reasonable ends of criminal jurisprudence.

Incidentally, as we have hinted, none of the traditional justificatory theories of punishment require *theoretically* that their supporters necessarily support any punishment at all. The commitment to punishment in all cases assumes that punishment does, in fact, deter, rehabilitate, or satisfy retributory requirements. But this need not concern us here. What is at issue is not the ability of punishment to effect certain ends, but rather the justification for punishment even assuming the accomplishment of those ends.

THE JUSTIFICATION OF RETRIBUTION

Justification for retribution seems always to begin on a very high plane and to remain there, though we see to it that retribution's effects are earthly with a vengeance. In much of the early literature on punishment, for example, retributionary theory holds that we are not merely justified, but obliged to punish in order to "annul" wrong and "restore the right." Transgressions are understood not as harms to particular individuals, but as denials of "the right" and establishments of "the wrong." Punishment in this regard may be talked about as "restoring the good,"[2] "ratifying morality,"[3] or erasing bad effects on the "general mind."[4] In any event, punishment establishes or reestablishes a moral principle regardless of its implications for people. The cancellation of wrong is the only justification necessary for punishment according to this view. As presented by Hegel:

It is not merely a question of an evil (i.e., retribution) or of this or that or the other good (i.e., deterrence and rehabilitation): the precise point at issue is wrong and the righting of it. If you adopt (those) superficial attitudes to punishment, you brush aside the objective treatment of the righting of wrong, which is a primary and fundamental attitude in considering crime."[5]

This is retribution on the most metaphysical of levels, and it raises the question of whether this sort of sublime thinking justifies the more mundane act of punishing. Certainly it does not concern itself in any immediate way with serving human welfare or distributing social benefits and burdens in any balanced fashion. As far as indirect effects are concerned, the focus still seems directed elsewhere, that is, to the offending party. Punishment is pain inflicted to force recognition of the "good" by offenders, and it is their right to be so treated:

punishment is regarded as containing the criminal's right and hence by being punished he is honored as a rationale being. He does not receive his due . . .

if he is treated whether as a harmful animal who has to be made harmless, or with a view to deterring or reforming him.[6]

Now, this is all very obscure. "Ratifying morality," "annulling evil," and "erasing bad effects" are peculiar phrases at least. "Erasure," for example, is something one does in the physical sphere. It is used in discourse about physical markings, and trying to cross over with it into the area of discourse about principles without completely redefining the use of that term is to create obscurity at best and illusion at worst. Similarly, "annulment" and "ratification" are ordinarily used in an area of discourse on laws, decrees, edicts, court decisions, established rules, and contractual agreements. "Annulling" an "evil," then, makes little sense unless "annul" is somehow used in a new and metaphysical sense. Trying to keep its "legal" implications in a moral sphere is nothing short of conceptually puzzling. "Ratifying" morality, on the other hand, might well make sense on a mundane level. Thus attempts to weave "higher" law into American law through statutes and court decisions can be sensibly talked about as giving authoritative approval to that "higher" law. But what does it mean to "ratify" on a metaphysicl plane? Surely a mundane authoritative pronouncement would have little effect on the sublime. Yet, punishment is somehow meant to be directed at the "higher" plane according to the Hegelian justification.

Finally, there is no necessary relationship between a punishment and a "ratification." Punishment may or may not express approval of certain principles. Minor sorts of punishments might not be expressing anything at all. Parking tickets are generally looked upon primarily as revenue-producing devices by local authorities, and as "price tags" for parking in certain places at certain times by most of the populace. When punishment *is* meant to express something, there is a host of possibilities. Punishment may simply be a condemnation of the criminal: "It is the expression of the community's hatred, fear or contempt for the convict which alone characterizes physical hardship as punishment."[7] In fact, various forms of punishment have been used to express very specific attitudes: "Note the difference, for example, between beheading a nobleman, and hanging a yeoman, burning a heretic and hanging a traitor, hanging an enemy soldier and executing him by firing squad (loosely speaking, these differences are part of their 'meaning')"[8] Moreover, anything that can be looked upon as a "ratification" can also be seen as a disavowal. Ratifying one set of actions inherently disavows a set of contradictory acts, and it might be the point of punishment to express that disavowal rather than to ratify the complimentary principles. As J. Feinberg explains:

Suppose that an airplane of nation A fires on an airplane of nation B while the latter is flying over international waters. Very likely high authorities in nation B will send a note of protest to their counterparts in nation A demanding, among other things, that the transgressive pilot be punished. Punishing the pilot is an emphatic, dramatic, and well understood way of condemning and thereby disavowing his act. It tells the world that the pilot has no right to do what he did, that he was on his own in doing it, that his government does not condone that sort of thing. It testifies thereby to government A's recognition of the violated rights of government B in the affected area, and therefore to the wrongfulness of the pilot's act. Failure to punish the pilot tells the world that government A does not consider him to have been personally at fault. That in turn to claim responsibility for the act, which in effect labels that act as an "instrument of deliberate national policy," and therefore an act of war.[9]

Finally, punishment may be a purely political act. Selective enforcement of drug and homosexual laws, for example, may be aimed at oppressing certain groups of people rather than ratifying "higher" law. Alternatively, punishment may simply be intended to reestablish or "ratify" statutes that have fallen into disrepute or obsolescence through lack of enforcement. All in all, the justification for this very sublime retribution is obscure at its foundation, and even if it were not, it probably would not function in the manner it must in order to be justifiable.

At the core of less sublime retributionary theories lies the concept of "desert." As Kant expressed it:

Even if a civil society resolved to dissolve itself with the consent of all its members ... the last murderer lying in prison ought to be executed before the resolution was carried out. This ought to be done in order that everyone may realize the desert of his deeds, and the bloodguiltness may not remain upon the people.[10]

What is most important (most central) here is neither that legal obligations exist nor that we may be morally obligated to support existing laws. Rather, it is necessary that we arrange things (laws, duties, obligations) to ensure the realization of just deserts. It is important to notice, however, that Kant uses the term "ought," suggesting that desert is a necessary but not sufficient condition of a just punishment. A just punishment must also conform both to the categorical imperative (never treat anyone merely as a means) and to the principle of "equality."[11] In essence, everyone (victim and victimizer) should be made equal in suffering. A balance between moral turpitude and suffering must be restored. This to Kant is in some sense what is deserved. But this idea does not rest easily with certain intuitions we have about justice. Why must people be made equal in suffering rather than well-being? Why not restore some balance between well-being and righteousness? Moreover, it does not comport very well with what we actually do in our society when we punish.

Many vices, cruelties, and selfish exploitations of one person by another are in fact punished in our society but many others are exalted or ignored. It is a matter of policy; it depends upon our social purposes. But you might say that if punishment is not distributed according to desert in our society, it ought to be; in keeping with Kant, we should set about immediately writing our laws to insure that good people are rewarded and bad people punished. Unfortunately, this may be impossible. Perhaps we cannot measure anyone's desert in terms of suffering or the restriction of their alternatives for social action. Consider, for example, a politician and a member of the clergy, both of whom have embezzled, one from the public trust and one from the church. How are you going to ensure that each gets what he or she deserves? Is it worse to steal from God or from the state? Is it worse to betray those who pay taxes or those who pay tithes? Do we expect more of one who has chosen either of these vocations than we expect from the other?

We must begin with a clear view of what it means to "deserve" a punishment. From this we may arrive at some idea about exactly what sorts of "punishment" might be called "deserved." Now the claim that a person deserves a punishment can be taken to mean a number of things, each of which is open to different objections. Let us begin with the simplest rendering of that concept to the effect that in saying that a person deserves punishment we are simply saying that he or she is morally or socially culpable. He or she has done the wrong thing, and there is an essential connection between this and his or her desert. Of course, this cannot mean that culpability and desert are the same thing. If it does, it is simple fallacy to say that punishment is deserved *because* of culpability. The statement reduces to tautology. Perhaps it is meant instead to convey the idea that one should be punished for certain acts, but this really begs the question, since this is exactly what we are trying to elucidate. What does it mean that he or she should be (deserves to be) punished?

Kant seems to think that desert describes a sort of boomerang effect that "evil" actions are meant to have. Hence, as he puts it: "the undeserved evil which anyone commits on another is to be regarded as perpetrated on himself."[12] In fact, Kant argues that legislators have a duty to incorporate this boomerang effect into the law to ensure its realization. A slight but important modification of this approach is that the *distress* caused by a morally or socially culpable act is to be returned to the offender. This gets us away from the necessity of inflicting exactly the same evil on offenders as they have inflicted on others, but it leaves us with three other problems. First, how does one exactly balance evil effects without creating (or constantly being in danger of creating) another imbalance requiring redress? Moral turpitude and evil are not quantifiable concepts, and to talk about them in this way is to create a mythology of punishment rather than to justify it in terms of desert. Secondly, our ideas of justified punishments include considerations of excusing conditions.[13] But the notion of desert as a reaction or boomerang would exclude such considerations. Finally, there is what J. D. Mabbott calls "the Question of Status."

It takes two to make a punishment, and for moral or social wrongs I can find no punisher. We may be tempted to say when we hear of some brutal action "that it ought to be punished"; but I cannot see how there can be duties which are nobody's duties. . . . For a moral offense, God alone has the status necessary to punish the offender; and the theologians are becoming more and more doubtful whether even God has a duty to punish wrongdoings.[14]

In short, what justifies the state in assuring the boomerang effect?

The view of the state in which it does have such a duty is an old one, identifying the state with the whole organization of the community rather than viewing it as a subunit of the community organized for a particular purpose. Under the latter view the state functions to protect fundamentally necessary or important social rights. It does not concern itself with questions of morality and evil outside the scope of those rights. That function is left to other social groups (churches, learned societies, professional associations, etc.).

The latter view is, we think, more consistent with our own view of the state. It is more consistent because the former view is more consistent with fascism than pluralist democracy. There does seem to be a practical tendency to fascism in our democracy and thus a practical tendency to view the state as justly having the duty to punish moral offenses. We flirt with fascism now and then when the more obvious abuses of our existing order become apparently widespread and government seems capable of nothing more than playing politics, talking, and churning out more of the same in such situations. Criminal and social reformers seem to be getting away with things, the moral order seems to be in disarray, and a leader ineluctably emerges promising to set things aright. Part of the inevitable popular mandate to put things right involves debilitating those reformers, minorities, revolutionists, and seditious cranks conspiring against the existing social (i.e., moral) order. The state is thus called on to interfere energetically in every aspect of social life where change has reared its head. Change being inevitable, this is everywhere, and the state, the society, and the traditional morality become all in the same.

Now, since the state is directly involved, the criminal justice system becomes the primary means of debilitating these threats to the moral order of society (i.e., the state). Crime, then, is suddenly recognized to be saturating every aspect of social life (if you are involved in any change whatsoever, you are immoral and undeniably criminal), and the demon that has been called up cannot be put down (if you try, you are criminal). The state runs rampant, and this does not comport with justice even as we understand it. In self-defense we must return to Mabbott and the view that the state has no right to punish moral offenses, and relegate the state once again to the status of a social subunit organized for particular, well-defined practical purposes.

Now it might be argued against Mabbott's view that though the state has no *right* to punish moral offenses, it does have a "prima facie *duty* to injure wrongdoers to the extent that they have injured others."[15] More exactly, an injury to the rights of others gives the state the necessary status to punish. But actually the requisite status here is in those citizens whose rights were invaded, and it really seems more like a right to restitution than to the punishment of the offender. Since, in fact, the injured parties seem the only ones in this situation with any status at all, it is reasonable to argue that the boomerang cycle should be focused on them rather than on the criminal. An injuring action should occasion a mitigating reaction. The evil should be made to boomerang in such a way as to leave the victim in a state as close to being untouched as possible. Kant's conceptualization of desert, then, seems misdirected.

A slightly different viewpoint than Kant's would say that desert refers to the relationship between the "innate evil" of the act and the distress to the offender caused by the proposed punishment.[16] Unlike Kant's approach, even if an act had no detrimental consequences, the perpetrator would still deserve punishment. Several problems with this approach suggest themselves immediately. First of all, how much physical or mental distress is enough?

No one can say. As our consideration of the concept "punishment" has argued, "distress" or "pain" is too highly personal and subjective to be quantifiable. Similarly, it is difficult to say of almost any act that it is "innately evil." It is most persuasive to consider evil as a function of the particular established relationships and social expectations within which any given act occurs, rather than something inherent in the act itself. Finally, the "innate evil" of something is just as difficult to measure precisely as is pain or distress. Consequently, the two can hardly be compared and struck off against each other.

Taking as our cue the idea that evil is a function of our social relationships, we might find a way out of our difficulties by saying that desert refers to the relationship between the extent to which a person acted responsibly against a known set of rules and social expectations, and (given our definition of punishment) the extent to which we restrict his or her alternatives for social action. This actually involves three subsidiary claims. First, it is often claimed that offenders "deserve" punishment because they knowingly undertook to act in a manner they knew or should have known society had undertaken to punish, and they had an option to act in a penalty-free manner.[17] Secondly, it is often claimed that offenders "deserve" punishment because others guilty of similar breaches of the rules have been treated similarly.[18] And finally, it is often claimed that offenders "deserve" punishment because their acts produce a "debt" to those following the rules and fulfilling or acting upon the expectations necessary for society to function properly.[19] In short, focus shifts from conceptualizing "desert" in terms of a relationship between offenders and the nature of their acts (inherently evil, productive of evil effects), to the relationship between offenders and others in society.

Of course, there is a second way out of our difficulties. We might also avoid the problems we've been discussing (particularly the commensurability problem) by stressing the idea that deserts have solely to do with the satisfactions punishment brings to others.[20] Punishment, in other words, is a "conventional symbol of public reprobation" through which public authority can to some extent assuage the feelings of insecurity and abuse taking place in the injured person and other empathetic members of society. Punishment is in this sense a symbolic act, but nevertheless quite effective to its purpose. Once again, it is the knowing and free violation of established rules and social expectations that can be assumed to have caused the public and private feelings of insecurity. What is important regarding commensurability is that the equivalence of the harm or evil and the punishment is not of particular concern. That punishment *does* provide such a satisfaction is sufficient; that alone may be enough to say that it is "deserved."

However, using punishment to assuage social fears really seems more like a purpose for punishing than a way of getting at what is deserved. And, of course, there is no immediate reason for assuaging only fears. It seems just as sound to address the physical and social as well as the psychological damage done. In fact, if we take this last idea together with our definition of punishment and our explication of desert, we arrive at a rather clear idea of what it means to deserve a punishment. Briefly, that punishment is deserved which so limits the freedom (alternatives for social action) of those who have knowingly and with other options acted in ways society has undertaken to punish, that those injured by that action are assuaged to the greatest extent that is humanly possible. We have, then, through a process of seeking ways out of certain difficulties in our understandings of "punishment" and "desert" arrived at what is clearly a restitutionary understanding of the terms.

Something of a commensurability problem remains, however, and in addition it seems somewhat arbitrary to punish a person in a particular manner simply because we have always punished people that way. What's more, the justification for originally punishing in any particular manner is never addressed. But the incommensurability here is in some ways less bothersome. The degree to which we are restricting the freedom to choose among alternative social actions is something much more concrete than the amount of pain we might be causing an offender. Similarly, the extent to which people are violating established rules or social expectations (duties) of which they were or should have been aware given the regularities and configurations of our social lives, is more concrete than the "innate evil" of an act. We seem, then, to have arrived at one way out of our difficulties. We can sensibly talk about "deserving punishment" in terms of the relationship between people who knowingly and with other options act in ways they know or should have known society undertakes to punish, and the extent to which we restrict their social freedom (alternatives for social action). We can also talk sensibly about exactly what is deserved when we punish. Indeed, it is an idea that can be concretized fairly well through a scheme of restitution involving monetary damages to victims. Victims can translate their monetary rewards into whatever they perceive as commensurable pleasures, and the party held responsible can be put under various restrictions resulting in monetary return to the court or the offended parties. Maximum possible scope is thereby provided for both the nature of the restriction of the criminal and the form of pleasure for victims. Offenders are deprived, both of their absolute liberty (freedom under the law) and the right to use the proceeds of their endeavors in any legal way they wish. Victims are made whole again, at least as far as is humanly possible.

What is most interesting is that we can now see how "desert," the core concept in retributionary theories of punishment, is most meaningful and sensible only when defined in restitutionary terms. What this means is that as we now turn our attention to whether or not retribution can be justified given this understanding of desert, we are really saying that if retribution is justified at all, it is only justifiable in restitutionary terms.

Now, it is immediately apparent that we have already justified retribution in the abstract by coming up with a restitutionary concept of desert which avoids the objections we initially raised to retributionary theories. Punishment is justified if we can meaningfully and sensibly say that it is deserved. However, we still need to justify retribution in concrete terms. That is, given this new understanding of "desert," is the state justified in punishing? Let us recall all that we have said over the last few chapters about the nature and function of states. First, to avoid fascism, states should be subunits of the community with defined purposes. Generally, their main purpose ought to be the securing and insuring of necessary social rights. What social rights are "necessary," of course, depends upon the nature and development of the particular community the state finds itself a part of. But for purposes of criminal law the phrase "necessary social rights" refers to rights embodied in principles and policies often formulated in rules "so fundamental that if our system didn't have them there would be no point in any other rules at all."[21] Specifically, we are talking about rules such as those "forbidding the free use of violence and insuring the minimum form of property—with its rights and duties to enable food to grow and be retained until eaten ... above this minimum the purposes men have for living in society are too conflicting and varying to make possible much extension of the argument that some fuller overlap of legal rules and moral standards is 'necessary' in this sense."[22] We have also pointed out that in the process of securing and insuring necessary social rights, the state inevitably becomes involved in distributing some of the benefits and burdens of social living. So long as the state sticks to these purposes and does so in what the community accepts as an equitable fashion, its activities are justified.

Under a restitutionary retribution approach, the state is directly and explicitly involved in insuring fundamental rights. The state guarantees to return people whose fundamental rights are violated to the *status quo ante* so far as is humanly possible. Moreover, it promises to do so in a most equitable fashion. It promises to consider explicitly the impact of each particular crime on the human welfare of those directly involved, and to take a hand in redistributing or reestablishing the proper distribution of social burdens and benefits. Retribution understood in restitutionary terms thus fulfills the state's mandate to further human welfare and avoid its opposite by helping to balance the benefits and burdens of social living in some recognizably just fashion.

On the other hand, retributionary approaches not having the restitutionary understanding of desert at their core can be seen to be unjustified. If desert is defined in terms of the nature of the criminal act rather than its impact on society or the individuals directly affected, retribution is not concerned with human welfare and its just distribution. Arguments that retribution also benefits the offender are rehabilitory, while arguments that society indirectly benefits from retribution are deterrent (i.e., the offender will think twice before doing it again as will others who might be considering similar behavior). Similarly, retributionary theories defining desert only in terms of the boomeranging of evil upon the offender also evince an insensitivity to human welfare and its just social distribution. Hence, under any but the restitutionary concept of desert (focusing as it does both on the impact of crime on the welfare of victims and other directly affected parties, and the securing of re-establishment of a just distribution of social benefits and burdens), we cannot say that retribution is justified.

It should be noted briefly that this restitutionary approach also avoids some of the traditional objections to the retributionary theory. One such objection has been that it is inconsistent to "injure" or deprive offenders because they have committed a wrong by injuring another. The social act of punishing, it is argued, brings society down (morally) to the level of the offender for the proclaimed purpose of producing a moral good. If the offender's act is wrong, so is the society's. Under the restitutionary approach to retribution, of course, the focus and point of the punishment is not harm to the offender, but to satisfy those injured. This end is not inconsistent with producing moral good, and it can be accomplished through methods of restitution (as explained in the first chapter) not necessarily resulting in the infliction of pain. Similarly, it is often argued that to determine the responsibility of offenders for retributive purposes, it would be necessary to understand their whole past history and be privy to their innermost thoughts and feelings. This sort of objection again derives from conceiving of "desert" in terms of the nature of the criminal act. A profound understanding of an offender is necessary to characterize his or her behavior fully. But all that is minimally necessary to characterize an offender as deserving of punishment when you focus on the social impact of a crime is a knowing transgression and an injured victim. The history of transgressors and their peculiar psychologies are not necessarily relevant, though such benevolent considerations can be included in any equation meant to satisfy grievances by providing satisfaction.

It seems, then, that retribution in any but its restitutionary form is not a justifiable purpose of social action, and this is the first thing we set out to argue. The second thing we set out to argue is that deterrence is not justifiable at all, and it is to that argument that we now turn.

THE JUSTIFICATION OF DETERRENCE

The classical statement of deterrence theory is generally attributed to Jeremy Bentham, the founder of utilitarianism.[23] Like retribution, deterrence looks to the consequences of punishment. But unlike retribution its classical formulation focuses neither on the nature of the offender's act, nor on any sort of boomerang effect, nor on the satisfactions provided to victims and others. Instead, it focuses on the probability of repeated criminal behavior. Bentham suggests that punishment decreases the probability of repeated offenses by (1) making it difficult or impossible for an offender to break the law again (through incapacitation), (2) by increasing the fear or prudence of others so as to keep them from performing the same or similar acts, and (3) by opening an avenue for rehabilitation.[24] Others have added to these suggestions the idea that offenses can be prevented by "unconscious inhibitions" created, reinforced, and transmitted socially and historically by punishment.[25] Usually, such "socio-pedagogical influences"[26] or "educative and habituative effects of our penal sanctions,"[27] are used as long-term justifications for punishment as opposed to incapacitation, fear, and prudence, which are of relatively short duration and must be reinforced periodically. For the moment we will ignore Bentham's point about rehabilitation and concentrate on the other two, plus the morally educative function as constituting deterrence theory. Bentham's final point will be considered in the next section.

Bentham explains the justification of punishment as deterrence in the following way:

The end of law is to augment happiness. The general object which all laws have, or ought to have, in common, is to augment the total happiness of the community, and therefore, in the first place to exclude, as far as may be, everything that tends to subtract from that happiness: in other words to exclude mischief.[28]

Punishment is justified because it decreases the probability of unhappiness by decreasing the probability of future offenses.

General prevention ought to be the chief end of punishment as it is its real justification. If we could consider an offense which has been committed as an isolated fact, the like of which would never recur, punishment would be useless. It would be only adding one evil to another.[29]

This rationale, of course, directly justifies only the threat of punishment. Actually inflicting a punishment ought only to follow to the extent it is necessary to make the threat credible enough to decrease the probability of an offense. "General prevention" does not require (imply) punishment. There is no necessary connection between the "evil" of punishment and the reduction of the offense. Punishment itself is only indirectly justified and characterizable as a desperate act of last resort. Only if we take its primary function as the educative-habituative one does punishment as a regular event seem directly justified. Let us begin with a closer look at this function, then, and consider the indirect justifications later.

Is the state justified in punishing for educative, moralizing, and habituative purposes? Is it justified in engaging in a purposive program of deterrence through inculcation of unconscious controls or habits in the general populace? At least one well-known argument has been made that the state is so justified. Lord Devlin has argued:

society means a community of ideas; without shared ideas of politics, morals, and ethics no society can exist. Each one of us has ideas about what is good and what is evil; they cannot be kept private from the society in which we live. If men and women try to create a society in which there is no fundamental agreement about good and evil they will fail; if, having based it on common agreement, the agreement goes, the society will disintegrate. For society is not something that is kept together physically; it is held by the indivisible bonds of common thought. If the bonds were too far relaxed the members would drift apart. A common morality is part of the bondage. The bondage is part of the price of society; and mankind, which needs society must pay its price.[30]

If society has the right to make a judgment and has it on the basis that a recognized morality is as necessary to society as, say, a recognized government, then society may use the law to preserve morality in the same way as it uses it to safeguard anything else that is essential to its existence. If therefore the first proposition is securely established with all its implications, society has a prima facie right to legislate against immorality as such.[31]

Lord Devlin is not, of course, directly addressing the question of punishment in these passages. But he is dealing with criminal law, and it is at least implicit in this argument that punishment is justified as a means of establishing a "community of ideas" or the moral unity he describes as necessary to preserve society.

A number of objections to this train of thought have been raised, all addressed to the sufficiency of Lord Devlin's premises or the logical implications of his argument.[32] But what seems more important to notice is that Devlin is advocating the active manipulation of "personhood." Given that personal identity is profoundly shaped by the social environment, we can still speak of some personal autonomy in choosing the kind of person we want to be (particularly vis-à-vis governmental entities embodying a monopoly of legitimate force) when all we must contend with are the systematically occurring constraints that shape all of our lives and for which no person or group can be held responsible. But active attempts by governments to "program in" certain moral codes through the application of penalities deprives individuals of the right to self-definition and their own concept of "being human."

Now, coercive conditioning by government (governmental efforts to produce mental conformity) by requiring affirmative participation in behavioral or electrochemical therapies has generally been limited by law to persons who have caused some considerable harm and who have been incarcerated for antisocial behavior or mental illness.[33] Less coercive, but no less direct techniques needed to promote mental conformity, have been rather systematically held unconstitutional since *West Virginia State Board of Education v. Barnette*.[34] In that case the state asserted, by way of justification for coercing participation in flag-saluting ceremonies, the interest of the state in instilling national unity. The court held that though the state interest was legitimate, such "officially disciplined uniformity" and "compulsory unification of opinion" would lead to "the unanimity of the graveyard."[35] As Justice Jackson put it:

Freedom to differ is not limited to things that do not matter much. That would be a mere shadow of freedom. The test of its substance is the right to differ as to things that touch the heart of existing order.

If there is any fixed star in our constitutional constellation, it is that no official, high or petty, can prescribe what shall be orthodox in politics, nationalism, religion or other matters of opinion or force citizens to confess by word or act their faith therein.[36]

This principle was confirmed and extended in *Wooley v. Maynard*[37] where the Supreme Court held that a state may not "constitutionally require an individual to participate in the dissemination of an ideological message by displaying it on his private property in a manner and for the express purpose that it be observed and read by the public."[38] Direct governmental coercion, then, even of a relatively minor sort is not considered justifiable when its end or purpose is "social solidarity" through enforced moral unanimity. Such activity interferes with our constitutional principles and our policy of securing human welfare through individual choice in self-definition. The state is justified in doing what it can to foster this process of individual choice, but it is not justified in securing itself from criticism or change when individual "personhood" is made to suffer.

But what has been discussed so far is really a limiting case. What about indirect attempts to shape individual identities, which are mostly what Devlin is talking about? Few members of the populace actually experience punishment directly under Devlin's scheme. They are provided with useful knowledge and inculcated with habits and socially acceptable patterns of behavior before they ever confront coercive authority. Some steps have been taken to indicate the unacceptability of oblique intrusions into individual mental processes in cases like *Meyer v. Nebraska*[39] and *Pierce v. Society of Sisters*.[40] These cases dealt with the state's power to determine the content of the knowledge imparted through the educational system. Thus, there was no direct confrontation with coercive power, but a structuring of inputs to children's minds. In both cases the court held the state powerless to "standardize its children" or to "foster a homogeneous people."[41]

Another way of "homogenizing" people is to screen certain things out of their experience, and some of this sort of thing has been held unconstitutional. Thus, in *Stanley v. Georgia*[42] the court held that states could not punish the possession of obscene material. Yet, there is still a recognized governmental power to ban the commercial distribution of pornography,[43] and governmental bans on drugs affecting mental processes are still upheld. Arguably, the latter might be justified as the state's legitimate power to secure human welfare. However, the state still tolerates wide use of alcohol and tobacco which have well-known and extensive harms associated with their use. At the moment, courts are divided as to whether governmental prohibition in this area is justified or not.[44]

What is clear, however, is that even subtle governmental attempts to inculcate citizens with a homogeneous morality are looked upon suspiciously by our society, while more blatant forms of moral education are considered absolutely unjustifiable purposes of state action. What is justifiable in a situation of competing moral systems is a neutral arbiter adjusting each to the other for their mutual benefit. As such, courts and legislators could seek to accommodate interests and facilitate an ongoing social exchange and development among those with different ideas of the right and the good. It would be a question of coordinating groups with differing, divergent, and even contradictory (but equally valid) interests in different social goals. As each pursues contradictory interests in particular, some amount of socially unacceptable damage is likely to be done. The state would then be justified in acting both to reestablish the smooth functioning of the social order and to return damaged individuals to their *status quo ante* (at least to the extent that is humanly possible).

Since the educative-moralizing function of punishment appears an unjustified end for punishment as deterrence, we need to take a critical look at the other suggested functions: incapacitation and the engenderment of fear or prudence in others. To begin with, incapacitation is not in itself deterrence. While it does keep individuals from committing certain kinds of crimes for the duration of their incapacitation, it does not accomplish this feat by discouragement, but by disablement. Potential offenders are confined within rigid limits and have no choice. The deterrent aspect of incapacitation derives from the implicit threat in its execution that future offenses by this same individual and others will result in similar or worse treatments.

Bentham's justification for this sort of deterrence was based on his idea that "to augment happiness" meant "to exclude ... everything that tends to subtract from that happiness."[45] Hence, total human happiness would be increased if wrongdoers were excluded from society (imprisoned) for certain periods of time. Unfortunately, this is neither logically or empirically the case.

Logically, removing the causes of unhappiness may simply leave one feeling neutral. Some other action may be necessary to increase happiness positively. Empirically, total happiness is often decreased as a direct result of imprisonment in at least two ways. First, on the individual level imprisoned offenders are subjected to well-documented and extensive acts of dehumanization.[46] Following imprisonment, the offender's career chances are severely affected. Felony convictions usually preclude the practice of most professions, and any position requiring some trust (cashier, night watchman, sales clerk, etc.) is usually denied as well. Police tend to focus their suspicions on past offenders, and this generally implies increased harassment. Finally, many offenders become more disposed to committing future crimes while in prison. Many writers on prison reform, for example, conclude that prisons (and juvenile facilities) socialize and educate prisoners into criminal patterns of behavior.[47] Beyond the individual level, the imprisoned offender's family often ends up on relief, and this factor alone has far-ranging effects on the future socioeconomic status of each family member. Often the young in welfare families are "structured" into crime by the sorts of options available for improving their situation. Bentham's justification for incapacitation would seem weak at best in light of these considerations.

But more fundamentally, Bentham's justification is weak because it is based on two conceptual confusions. First of all, he applies an arithmetic language to an emotional sphere. Happiness is nothing like a number, say six, from which you might subtract a negative (unhappy) number, say minus three, and be blessed with a totally greater amount (in this case $6 - (-3) = 9$). Secondly, assuming that one could exclude unhappiness in the manner just described (i.e., when speaking in the special context of abstract speculation) one cannot conclude (as Bentham does) that we can simply identify a person with a certain quantity of unhappiness and exclude him or her in the same manner from the concrete context of society.

Let us assume, however, that none of the above objections to incapacitation could be made. Deterrence as incapacitation would still not be logically and empirically the most justifiable form of punishment. Given that our standard for justifying state action involves the securing of human welfare and avoiding its opposite (and distributing welfare in some balanced fashion), it can be seen that logically incapacitation at its best only provides for half of this formula. It merely avoids the opposite of human welfare and precludes its distribution. Now, this may be a justifiable end, but it is not necessarily the best that can be done. And if there is an alternative social action which might fulfill more of the formula, we might say that incapacitation is unjustified relative to that alternative.

Restitution is just such an alternative. First of all, it is a positive state action seeking to secure human welfare (that of the victims, their families, and other directly affected individuals including the criminal if he or she is so disposed), and seeing to it that its balanced distribution (such as it was at the time of the offense) is reestablished. This is not meant to suggest of our society that there is anything like a balanced distribution of welfare. But the imposition of punishment need not exacerbate the situation as it often tends to do at present. Empirically, punishment as presently institutionalized not only leaves the victim and others worse off than they were prior to a crime, but criminals themselves are effectively sentenced, in many cases, to nutritional deficiency, physical brutality, substandard living conditions, and mental deterioration.

Secondly, in the positive act of securing welfare, restitution seeks to avoid the obvious ramifications of the crime which would have negative effects on the victim and other affected parties. Thus, it seeks to avoid family and business problems, for example, that could arise from the loss experienced because of a theft. In this manner restitution might be said to fulfill logically and empirically more of the formula justifying state action and, therefore, be a more justified end than incapacitation at its best.

If the idea that we can increase total human happiness by incapacitating offenders is based on conceptual confusion and can be seen as logically and empirically false, is there any other basis on which we might justify deterrence as incapacitation? One suggestion has been that society has a legitimate claim to protection from recidivism. The "dangerousness" of offenders thus provides the justification for their incapacitation. The problems with this are twofold. First of all, as Norval Morris has pointed out:

In relation to the second principle that "dangerousness" as a prediction of future criminality is an unjust basis for imposing a sentence of imprisonment, we move from the broadly accepted to the highly contentious. "Dangerousness" must be rejected for this purpose, since it pre-supposes a capacity to predict future criminal behavior quite beyond our present technical ability. Further, it is clear that in a world of even remote resemblance to our present social organization such predictive capacities will continue to elude us.[48]

Secondly, "dangerousness" is a very elastic concept. This is nowhere more clear than in Supreme Court decisions on the question of abridging free speech when it threatens the foundation of established order. In the cases of *Gitlow v. New York*[49] and *Whitney v. California*[50] the court upheld convictions for publishing a pamphlet called *The Left Wing Manifesto* and participating in the Communist Labor party convention, which adopted a platform urging revolutionary unionism. Statutes under which the convictions were made were upheld against First Amendment challenges as legitimate means to securing the safety of the state. In other words, advocacy of particular political viewpoints was considered so "dangerous" to the state as to justify punishment.

Current doctrine on this point requires that any such restrictive statute be limited to advocacy which is (1) directed to inciting imminent lawless action, and (2) likely to incite or produce such action.[51] Yet, it has been persistently difficult for the Court to keep from misperceiving the facts as to imminency and likelihood, particularly in times of social unrest. Thus, in *U.S. v. Obrien*[52] there was a conviction for violating a recent amendment to the draft laws which made it a felony knowingly to destroy or mutilate a draft card. The conviction was upheld against First Amendment challenges on the theory that draft-card burning interfered with the government's interest in a smoothly functioning draft, an interest the government presumably has because of the state's need for an army to defend its existence. Through this tortuous reasoning, draft-card burning (a particularly expressive means of dissent) was found "dangerous" to the national interest, even though the Selective Service had never prosecuted anyone for not carrying a card and testified that it functioned quite well whether people had their cards in their possession or not. The concept of "dangerousness," then, has been so expanded as to include almost anything our government might wish to discourage. Such a vague, ambiguous, and demonstrably elastic concept cannot reasonably be considered a justification for any form of deterrence, let alone incapacitation.

So far, neither incapacitation nor the educative-moralizing function of punishment seem up to the task of justifying deterrence as the proper form of punishment. The third end usually attributed to punishment as deterrence is the engendering of fear or prudence in either the offender or those not punished who might otherwise be disposed to commit an offense. Is this a justifiable end for punishment? We might begin by examining exactly what we mean by "engendering prudence." Either we mean the development within the person of a certain set of priorities (in which case the end is recognizably unjustified as argued above), or we mean the inculcation of a persistent low-level anxiety, engendering the greatest hesitancy to wander from "ordinary" or "normal" behaviors. If the latter, we might ask ourselves by what right the state engenders fear and anxiety in its citizens. What could possibly justify such a program? Hobbes justifies punishment to the end of "disposing men to obedience" through "terror" in the following way:

Before the institution of Commonwealth, every man had a right to everything and to do whatsoever he thought necessary to his own preservation; subduing, hurting or killing any man in order thereunto. And this is the foundation of the right of Punishing, which is exercised in every Commonwealth.

For the subjects did not give the sovereign the right; but only in laying down theirs, strengthened him to use his own, as he should think fit, for the preservation of them.[53]

Briefly, one preserves through terror, and state-instituted terror is thus justified as a means of preserving the commonwealth. But is a terrorizing commonwealth justified in preserving itself? Its central concern has clearly shifted from securing human welfare and avoiding its opposite, to securing its own survival and avoiding demise. Furthermore, it is less interested in distributing welfare than in distributing terror as necessary for its own preservation. Unless we are willing to say that human welfare is identical with the preservation of a terrorizing state (that the former is defined in terms of the latter), we cannot conclude that such a commonwealth as Hobbes suggests is justified in its existence, and hence neither is it justified in its inculcation of the populace with fear.

Deterrence, then, does not provide us with any better justification for punishing than did retribution. None of the ends sought by either of these theories can justify state action unless translated into restitutionary terms. This might lead us to recognize restitution as the emerging justifiable purpose of punishment (particularly given the contractual and insurance-oriented character of modern society). But we have one final end to consider which is often put forward as a justification of punishment.

THE JUSTIFICATION OF REHABILITATION

The fundamental argument for punishment as rehabilitation is that punishment can be so structured that it either reforms in and of itself, or provides an excellent opportunity for reforming offenders. According to this theory, rehabilitation through properly structured punishments is to be expected because (1) criminal behavior is determined largely by factors outside the control of the individual; therefore, (2) retribution and deterrence are impractical and unjustified; however, (3) new factors might be introduced into an offender's life which affect "the natural causes of the phenomenon of social pathology which one can call crime,"[54] and thus provide effective remedies; consequently, (4) penalties can be tailored to each unique offender so as to "effect changes in the characters, attitudes, and behaviors of convicted offenders, so as to strengthen the social defense against unwanted behavior, but also to contribute to the welfare and satisfaction of offenders."[55] Reforming offenders in this way is justified as a humane way of reducing offenses and thereby avoiding their unpleasant social consequences. Ostensibly, rehabilitation involves at least one positive act—increasing the welfare of offenders by reforming them—in addition to avoiding the opposite of human welfare (embodied in particular criminal acts). Once again, however, it does nothing for victims or those indirectly affected, and so it does not provide as much in the way of securing human welfare and avoiding its opposite as does restitution—though it is certainly meant to do more along both these lines than is either deterrence or nonrestitutionary retribution.

In general, the ethical objections we raised to the educative-moralizing purpose of deterrence are equally sound with regard to rehabilitation. For the reasons outlined in our analysis of deterrence, we are convinced that the state has no ethical foundation for reforming the values, priorities, and self-definitions of its individual members; although, as we have argued in our analysis of retribution, there is an ethical foundation for the state's duty to see that those acting upon their values and priorities do so in ways not harmful to others. Because of our society's persistent opposition to both blatant and subtle forms of "programming," we feel that this purpose of rehabilitation is simply unjustified.

Now, there is one situation in which an attempt at rehabilitation avoids these ethical problems. An individual who basically and fundamentally agrees with or is committed to the existing consensus as to wrongfulness or undesirabilty of certain kinds of behavior might be "reformed" by punishment without being reprogrammed.[56] If individuals (1) "recognized the punishing authority as one which embodies the moral law, and which has a right to enforce it," and (2) they violate the law because "indolence or prejudice" has prevented them from seeing its application to a particular case, or (3) they "systematically failed to see that the law applies in certain cases" for any other reason, the "punishment may lead to repentance; but not otherwise."[57] Given this total situation, the state may be justified in punishing, assuming that punishment is, in fact, a

striking way of bringing home to him, so far as external symbols can, the wickedness of his conduct. It is generally admitted that recognition of one's sin in some form or other is a necessary condition of real moral regeneration, and the formal and impressive condemnation by society involved in punishment is an important means toward bringing about this recognition on the part of the offender.[58]

Of course, this rationale also justifies punishment regardless of *mens rea*. In fact, it suggests strongly that in exactly those cases where violations occur unintentionally, punishment should be most assured. It is there that the most education is needed.

The important thing to notice here, however, is that such a case as the one just described is certainly conceivable, but somehow questionable as to its concreteness in modern society. Imagining logically possible worlds other than our own can lead to all sorts of justifications for state action. But whether or not such action is justified in the tangible situation we actually face is another question altogether. As J. E. McTaggert explains:

When are these conditions realized? . . . the crimes which a state has to deal with may be divided into two classes. The first and smaller class is that in which the state, for its own welfare, endeavors to suppress by punishment conduct which is actuated by conscientious convictions of duty. Examples may be found in high treason and breaches of the law relating to vaccination. Now in these cases the criminal has deliberately adopted a different view of his duty to that entertained by the state. He is not likely, therefore, to be induced to repent of his act by a punishment which can teach him nothing except that he and the state disagree in their views of his duty—which he knew before. His punishment may appear to him unjust persecution or may be accepted as the inevitable result of difference of opinion, but can never be admitted by him as justly deserved by his action, and cannot therefore change the way in which he regards that action.[59]

In the second, and much larger, class of criminal offenses . . . by the time a man has become subject to the criminal law for any offense, he has become so far callous, with regard to that particular crime, that his punishment will not bring about his repentance.[60]

Finally, why should the modern citizen regard the state as expressing the moral law? He does not regard it as something morally superior to himself, as the ancient citizen regarded his city, as the child regards his parents, or the religious man his God. The development of individual conscience and responsibility has been too great for such an attitude. As between adult human beings, it has become in modern times impossible for man to yield up his conscience into the hands of any other man or body of men.[61] In short, it may be that none of the conditions necessary for justifying punishment on the ground that it rehabilitates in and of itself is present in modern society.

Other objections to the idea that punishment in and of itself can rehabilitate include (1) an objection to the implication that offenders are "sick" or "abnormal"; this approach argues that social reform, not individual reform, is the solution to the problem of crime and the criminal,[62] (2) the idea that the necessary social skills cannot be learned in the highly structured and often brutal prison environment,[63] and (3) that the very nature and structure of a prison socialize people in exactly the opposite way sought by rehabilitation.[64] In addition, critics argue (1) that the indeterminate sentence that theoretically goes along with a rehabilitative approach in seeking the best cure for individual offenders is more often used to coerce offenders into playing the prison game according to the dictates of particular wardens,[65] (2) that a rehabilitation ideal fosters "the medicalization of deviance" and allows the use of chemical, biological, and psychological rehabilitative techniques that would be constitutionally questionable if offenders were considered normal rather than sick, and (3) that judges dole out widely divergent sentences for similar offenses not because of the individual needs of offenders, but because of the judge's particular set of biases.[66]

A restitutionary approach, of course, would obviate each of these objections. Restitution begins with the idea that offenders are not abnormal in any abnormal way. That is, they are no more abnormal than the rest of us. It proceeds to require that offenders work either in the community or in prison environments which have been altered to the extent necessary to make them economically productive (this will all be detailed later). Sentences would not be indeterminate; they would be as long as necessary to repay the damages. As a result, both the medicalization of deviance and the abuse of judicial discretion (no matter how subtle) would be curtailed.

Now, there have been recent attempts to reaffirm rehabilitation despite the clamor against it from both the political left and the political right. These attempts are founded on the premise that abandoning rehabilitation leaves us at the mercy of deterrence and retributionary approaches, which are by their nature insensitive to human needs, repressive, and dehumanizing.[67] We, of course, agree with these characterizations, but we are not left with choosing the lesser evil. Restitution is clearly a workable fourth alternative which accomplishes all that we might presently wish for in sensitizing and humanizing our criminal justice system.

To make this more clear, let's consider each of the points generally advanced by those seeking to reaffirm rehabilitation[68] and argue that their concerns are met equally well by the restitutionary approach we have already shown to be free of the difficulties inherent in a rehabilitative approach. First, reaffirmers argue that "rehabilitation is the only justification of criminal sanctioning that obligates the state to care for an offender's needs or welfare."[69] Certainly, this is inaccurate. Restitution, as we have formulated it, clearly concerns itself directly with the humane punishment of offenders, prison reform, and the social (not just the personal or individual) nature of crime. What we might add is that restitution is the only justification of criminal sanctioning that obligates the state to care directly for the needs or welfare of victims and other injured parties as well. It is an approach that conveys the message that society has an obligation and is willing to do good not only for offenders but for others who are under a disadvantage because of a criminal act.

Second, reaffirmers argue that "the ideology of rehabilitation provides an important rationale for opposing the conservative's assumption that increased repression will reduce crime."[70] That rationale is simply that "social and personal circumstances often constrain, if not compel, people to violate the law."[71] Efforts to repress individual criminal behavior will therefore not be successful; broad structural transformations of the social order is the only true solution to the problem of crime and the criminal. This may very well be true, and restitution is not inconsistent with this rationale as nonrestitutionary retribution and deterrence often seem to be. But broad structural transformations of the social order cannot happen quickly. Neither violent revolution nor immediate, rapid legislative reform can by themselves create a new order. New orders are created only when people change the way they live together. The present social order is a way of living together in which everyone has made many investments of many different kinds. In addition to economic interests in the *status quo* there are emotional and religious attachments to the way things are. There are psychological and social obstacles to change as well, such as fear of the unknown, loss of status, loss of personal identity, and a sense of not understanding where one belongs or how things go together. Change, then, which is of course inexorable, must also be inevitably gradual. We must content ourselves at present with transforming the broad structure of the criminal justice system and wait for its effects to ripple through our social order. The best that we can hope for is that restitution is a step toward social transformation, an important step that will change the patterns of our social interactions and help clear the way for a more equitable distribution of social benefits and burdens in the society at large.

Another point in rehabilitation's favor, argue reaffirmers, is the fact that "rehabilitation still receives considerable support as a major goal of the correctional system."[72] More specifically, they argue that "the rehabilitative ideal . . . is deeply anchored within our correctional and broader cultural heritage."[73] Rehabilitation "makes sense to the electorate as well as to criminal justice interest groups and policy makers."[74] We can only say that this support is not unanimous or there would be no need for reaffirmers: Rehabilitation is always being attacked at one point or another by spirited reformers from both the right and the left.[75] But taking the problem more generally, we should say that faced with the prevailing alternatives (retribution and deterrence), most people, being fundamentally humane, want the system to do something positive for the good of society in some direct and tangible way. Because restitution is not part of our "correctional heritage," the general public is not aware of how it might better facilitate that most desired end. Part of the function of this book is to help restitution make sense to both the electorate and criminal justice interest groups and policy makers. We are aided to some degree in this endeavor by the fact that restitution is part of our cultural heritage as we have demonstrated in Chapter 2 (i.e., it has always been an important part of what we meant when we said we were punishing). It has therefore been tested by long experience (Greece, Rome, the feudal states, etc.) and is quite possible and practicable. It is also simple and understandable. It gets rid of all the hubbub over all the questions we have been addressing as they are raised by all the other approaches. And it is already in operation in most juvenile justice systems and therefore familiar to many people in our society.

The final point raised by reaffirmers of rehabilitation is that "rehabilitation has historically been an important motive underlying reform efforts that have increased the humanity of the correctional system."[76] Disaffirming rehabilitation may deter "potential reformers from attempting to do good in the correctional system."[77] This argument reduces to the suggestion that it is a positive good to do the right thing for all the wrong reasons. Perhaps so, but then it must be even better to get the reasons right as well. Making the system function more humanely is clearly right, but how humane we can make it depends upon our getting started correctly. It depends upon our getting it right at its foundation. So when reaffirmers ask, "Should rehabilitation be forfeited . . . what will remain as the medium through which benevolent sentiments will be expressed and instituted into meaningful policy?"[78] We can answer that there will be no vacuum here, just the advent of a clearer, simpler, more understandable way of making the system more humane for criminals and victims as well.

Restitution, then, seems an altogether better way of going than rehabilitation. We must be careful to point out, however, that we do not support the idea that rehabilitation should be altogether abandoned. It should only be abandoned as the justification of punishment and a central goal of our criminal justice system. Rehabilitation might remain an opportunity provided by the state to offenders who more or less fit the description given at the beginning of this section or those likely to benefit from noncoercive rehabilitative techniques. After all, if government is engaged in an otherwise legitimate and justified activity, there is no reason why it should not take any opportunity that presents itself to persuade (rather than coerce or brainwash) an individual or the public to certain values and priorities (moral systems). If punishment is defined as restitution and justified on the basis that it seeks (1) to secure the welfare of the victim and other directly affected individuals, (2) to reestablish the smooth functioning of the social mechanism, and (3) to encourage mutual trust and reliance (through a kind of insurance against loss), then there is no reason why we should not simultaneously try to win offenders over to certain points of view.

CONCLUSION

So far, we have considered all the questions and problems in our opening chapter regarding retribution, deterrence, and rehabilitation and found those approaches unsatisfactory when compared with restitution. If we have not yet convinced most people that there are overwhelming reasons for abandoning retribution, deterrence, and rehabilitation as both the justifications of punishment and the central goals of our criminal justice system, then we probably never will.

Besides, it is now time to get on with the positive justification of restitution. Specifically, we have demonstrated that only punishment as restitution both justifies the state in punishing and enables the state to fulfill its mandate to further human welfare and avoid its opposite while helping to distribute benefits and burdens of social living in some balanced or just fashion. We have accomplished this latter demonstration by showing (1) how retribution does not at all address the question of advancing human welfare and balancing the distribution of the social benefits and burdens of crime, (2) how deterrence also either ignores human welfare and the balance of benefits and burdens, or violates our constitutional principle of self-determination in the pursuit of human welfare, and (3) how rehabilitation not only violates that same principle but works in practice to counter the very policy goals it is instituted to effect.

By focusing on repairing the individual and social damage caused by criminal acts, restitution brings punishment back to a direct concern with human welfare and the distribution of social benefits and burdens. Moreover, it does so in a way that is not only respectful of our constitutional principle of self-determination, but supportive of it. Restitution allows both victim and criminal some opportunities to define more effectively what will happen to them after a crime is committed.

Now we will argue that punishment through restitution not only does better by comparison but better fulfills our expectations of a criminal justice system in some absolute sense. This, we believe, can best be accomplished by going into detail on exactly what constitutes a just and balanced distribution of social benefits and burdens. We have been using this idea consistently and critically (if somewhat loosely) since Chapter 1, and it is now time to make ourselves very clear on this point.

NOTES

1. Of course, claiming these three as a basis for the claim that punishment needs justifying involves a moral judgment to begin with. But here, we think, we are at rock bottom. It simply seems that what we do in justifying social action (in the moral sense at least) is to concern ourselves with (1) securing human welfare and avoiding its opposite, and (2) distributing welfare, social benefits, and its opposite, social burdens, in some balanced fashion. This seems not to be something that itself needs justifying; it seems simply to be a persistent pattern in the fabric of human existence.

Occasionally it is argued that certain moral codes or the state of affairs they insure have intrinsic value beyond the securement and distribution of human welfare. State punishments are then justified as preservations of such moralities, proper in themselves, though individuals necessarily suffer in consequence. The purpose is neither the avoidance of harm nor the securing of welfare, but rather commitment to a particular dogma.

Besides the discomfort this sort of argument usually brings (just because it does relegate human welfare to a relatively subordinate position), and besides the obvious point that punishment in no way assures the moral commitment sought, there is a third difficulty tending to lead the state back to the task of distributing welfare and securing its necessities. There does not seem to be (in any modern and good-sized society at least) anything close to a consensus on the nature of a moral code with intrinsic value. A state may, of course, simply choose one of the competing moral codes and enforce it against all others. This was, in fact, the approach taken at one time in many American courts. See *Reynolds v. U.S.*, 98 U.S. 145 (1878); *Joyner v. Joyner*, 54 N.C. (1862); and *State v. Black*, 60 N.C. 262 (1864). But the theory of social stability and progress upon which our own society presently rests (liberal pluralism) assigns a central role not to the common possession of a single morality, but to the mutual toleration of different if not radically opposed moralities. Insofar as this theory is correct, the state is faced with both the task of being neutral arbiter among competing moral systems, and with the provision and distribution of what this kind of diversity needs to flourish. Thus, we must return again to justifying social (state) action in terms of securing and distributing the necessities of human welfare.

2. G. W. Hegel, *Philosophy of Right* (Oxford: Clarendon Press, 1973), p. 69.

3. Attributed to James F. ****(Victorian Judge) by H.L.A. Hart in *Law, Liberty, and Morality* (London: Oxford University Press, 1963), p. 63.

4. B. Bosanquet, *Some Suggestions in Ethics* (London: Macmillan, 1966), p. 190.

5. Hegel, *Philosophy of Right*.

6. Bosanquet, *Suggestions in Ethics*.

7. H. M. Hart, "The Aims of the Criminal Law," *Law and Contemporary Problems* 23:2 (1958), 4.

8. J. Feinberg, "The Expressive Function of Punishment," *The Monist* 49:3 (1965), 401.

9. Ibid., p. 403.

10. I. Kant, *Philosophy of Law* (Edinburgh; T. T. Clark, 1887), p. 198.

11. Ibid., pp. 194-198.

12. Ibid., p. 195.

13. H.L.A. Hart, "Prolegomenon to the Principles of Punishment," *Punishment and Responsibility* (Oxford: Clarendon Press, 1968), pp. 17-18.

14. J. D. Mabbott, "Punishment," *Mind* 48 (1939), 152-153. In the first chapter, we argued that it doesn't necessarily take two to punish and that

theoretically, historically, and practically, people can and have punished themselves. Despite this, we feel Mabbott's point still holds. In some societies this was probably recognition of the status problem. As the Tao Te Ching says: "The earth in its patience carries both the good and the evil." But it also might point up the justificatory problem in another way. Many instances of self-punishment can be traced to subtle social pressures on the offender or to internalized values resulting from the socialization process. The question then runs to a justification of these pressures and processes, and Mabbott's point would thus hold in self-punishment situations.

15. F. W. Bradley, *Ethical Studies* (London: Oxford University Press, 1927).

16. W. D. Ross, *The Right and the Good* (Oxford: Clarendon Press, 1965).

17. H. Morris, "Persons and Punishment," *The Monist* 52:4 (1968), 476.

18. Ibid.

19. Ibid.

20. This is our own reinterpretation or reapplication of ideas in J. Feinberg's "The Expressive Function of Punishment," pp. 397-408.

21. H.L.A. Hart, "Positivism and the Separation of Law and Morals," *Harvard Law Review* 71: 593 (1958).

22. Ibid., p. 612.

23. J. Bentham, "Principles of Penal Law," *The Works of Jeremy Bentham*, J. Brown (ed.) (New York: Hafner Press, 1948), p. 383.

24. Ibid., p. 396.

25. J. Andenaes, "The General Preventive Effects of Punishment," *University of Pennsylvania Law Review* 22:114 (1966).

26. Ibid., p. 50.

27. M. Morris, "Impediments to Penal Reform, *University of Chicago Law Review* 22:631 (1966).

28. J. Bentham, *An Introduction to the Principles of Morals and Legislation* (Oxford: Basil Blackwell, 1948), ch. 13, Sec. 1.

29. Bentham, *Principles of Morals*.

30. P. Devlin, *The Enforcement of Morals* (London: Oxford University Press, 1959), p. 10.

31. Ibid., p. 11.

32. R. Dworkin, "Lord Devlin and the Enforcement of Morals," *Yale Law Journal* 75:486 (1966); H.L.A. Hart, "Social Solidarity and the Enforcement of Morality," *University of Chicago Law Review* 35:1 (1966); F. Schorman, "The Enforcement of Matters of Custom and Morals," *Philosophical Studies* 30 (1976), 341.

33. *O'Connor v. Donaldson*, 422 U.S. 563 (1975); *Rouse v. Cameron*, 373 F. 2nd 451 (1966); *Welson v. Likins*, 373 F. Supp. 487 (1974); and *Yatt v. Stickney*, 344 F. Supp. 387 (1972).

34. *West Virginia State School Board of Education v. Barnette*, 319 U.S. 624 (1943).

35. Ibid., p. 641.

36. Ibid., p. 642.

37. *Wooley v. Maynard*, 97 S. Ct. 1428 (1977).

38. Ibid., p. 4381.

39. *Meyer v. Nebraska*, 262 U.S. 390 (1923).

40. *Pierce v. Society of Sisters*, 268 U.S. 510 (1925).

41. Ibid., p. 535; and *Meyer v. Nebraska*, p. 402.

42. *Stanley v. Georgia*, 394 U.S. 557 (1964).

43. *Paris Adult Theater v. Slaton*, 413 U.S. 49 (1973).

44. Compare *Ravin v. State*, 537 P. 2nd 494 (Alaska 1975) (State constitutional right of privacy protects the use of marijuana in the home) and *People v. Sinclair*, supra note 18, at 896 (Kanvanagh, J., concurring: The Michigan statute criminalizing possession of marijuana "violates the Federal and State constitutions in that it is an impermissible intrusion on the fundamental rights to liberty and the pursuit of happiness, and is an unwarranted interference with the right to possess and use private property. Big Brother cannot in the name of *public* health, dictate to anyone what he can eat or drink or smoke in the *privacy* of his own home") (emphasis in original), with *Commonwealth v. Leis*, 355 Mass. 189, (1969) (No right to smoke marijuana exists under federal or state constitutions); *Borras v. State*, 229 So. 2nd 244 (1969) (Use of marijuana in home is not protected by First Amendment or right of privacy); *People v. Aquilar*, 257 Cal. App. 2nd 597 (1968) ("no constitutionally protected right to indulge in the use of euphoric drugs"); *State v. Kanter*, 493 P. 2nd 306 (1972), cert. denied 409 U.S. 948 (1972) (conviction for possession of marijuana upheld, with two dissenting justices who would have found the criminalization of private possession of marijuana violative of due process, and one concurring justice indicated that he would have joined that position if the issue had not been conceded at trial). See also *Scott v. United States*, 395 F. 2nd 619 (1968), suggesting that laws regulating personal use of marijuana would bear close scrutiny for due process violation on a more complete record; *Louisiana Affiliate of Norml v. Guste*, 380 F. Supp. 404 (E.D. La. 1974), claim of constitutional protection for use and possession of marijuana on privacy grounds does not present a substantial federal question requiring convocation of three-judge court.

45. Bentham, *Principles of Morals and Legislation*.

46. See E. O. Wright, *The Politics of Punishment: A Critical Analysis of Prisons in America* (New York: Harper and Row, 1973).

47. C. Brown, *Manchild in the Promised Land* (New York: Signet, 1965).

48. N. Morris, *The Future of Imprisonment* (Chicago: University of Chicago Press, 1974), p. 62.

49. *Gitlow v. New York*, 268 U.S. 652 (1925).

50. *Whitney v. California*, 274 U.S. 357 (1927).

51. *Brandenburg v. Ohio*, 395 U.S. 444 (1969).

52. *U.S. v. Obrien*, 391 U.S. 367 (1968).

53. Thomas Hobbes, *Leviathan* (New York: E. P. Dutton and Co., 1950), pp. 266-360.

54. E. Feari, *Criminal Sociology* (New York: Agathon Press, 1967), p. 19.

55. F. A. Anen, *The Decline of the Rehabilitative Ideal* (New Haven, Conn.: Yale University Press, 1981), p. 2.

56. See J. E. McTaggart, ''Hegel's Theory of Punishment,'' *International Journal of Ethics* 6 (1896), 482.

57. Ibid., pp. 486-487.

58. A. C. Ewing, *The Morality of Punishment* (Oxford: Clarendon Press, 1962), p. 97.

59. McTaggart, ''Hegel's Theory of Punishment,'' pp. 493-494.

60. Ibid., p. 496.

61. Ibid., p. 498.

62. R. Martinson, ''What Works? Questions and Answers About Prison Reform,'' *Public Interest* (Spring 1974), pp. 22-54.

63. Norval Morris, *The Future of Imprisonment* (Chicago: University of Chicago Press, 1974), p. 16.

64. D. J. Rothman, ''Of Prisons, Asylums and Other Decaying Institutions,'' *Public Interest* (Winter 1972), p. 13.

65. J. Mitford, *Kind and Usual Punishment: The Prison Business* (New York: Vintage Books, 1973), pp. 87-103.

66. W. Gaylin, *Partial Justice: A Study of Bias in Sentencing* (New York: Vintage Books, 1974).

67. See, e.g., N. N. Kittrie, *The Right to be Different: Deviance Enforced Therapy* (Baltimore, Md.: Penguin Books, 1971).

68. An excellent summary of such arguments is provided by F. T. Cullen and K. E. Gilbert in *Reaffirming Rehabilitation* (Cincinnati, Ohio: Anderson Publishing Co., 1982), Ch. 7, and what follows is a comment on their formulation of the arguments in favor of rehabilitation.

69. Ibid., p. 247.

70. Ibid., p. 253.

71. Ibid., p. 255.

72. Ibid., p. 257.

73. Ibid., p. 260.

74. Ibid.

75. For an in-depth look at the attacks from both sides, see Ibid., Ch. 4.

76. Ibid., p. 261.

77. Ibid., p. 263.

78. Ibid., p. 263.

4

Restitution as an Absolutely Just Form of Punishment

One thing that we have been arguing is that the present criminal justice system divides up the social benefits and burdens of crime in a discriminatory manner. Another thing that we have argued is that by comparison with other forms of punishment, restitution can do a better job of redressing the present imbalance, an imbalance that is reinforced day by day and hour by hour as our courts dole out their punishments for crime. But this only partly solves our problem. In the beginning we set ourselves to the task of developing and justifying an approach that is not just comparatively good (i.e., good from time to time), but both consistently good and flexible enough to countenance rapid social change as we try again and again to make our society a better place to live. Consequently, we must argue that restitution is good in some absolute sense; we must have another shot at its justification.

One might think that the problem we are going to have in arguing that restitution is "just" in some absolute sense will be to find a criterion of justice that will satisfy everyone. However, this is not, in fact, the problem; it is simply impossible. We could not settle on any particular criterion of justice without oppressing some among our many diverse and overlapping classes, races, religions, ethnic, philosophical, economic, social, and political groups. Instead, our problem is to find a method of punishing that can gain the allegiance of all these groups by meeting all of their criteria for justice simultaneously. So, first we must lay out those criteria, and then we must show exactly how restitution meets their requirements.

Each different criterion will, of course, suggest a different set of priorities in law enforcement. Thus, we must also become involved in the concrete dimension of justifying restitution in some absolute sense: We must show how restitution either meets these priorities or establishes a set of priorities each school of thought can readily accept. So after we have asked what sort of criteria different groups stress as the proper ones for a just distribution of the benefits and burdens of crime, we must ask what is the proper set of priorities for a system meeting all those requirements simultaneously.

THE PREVALENT CRITERIA

One plan that has often been proposed is to allow each person that share of the benefits and burdens that he or she merits by dint of either hard work or some peculiar and productive talent. In the area of criminal justice this generally reduces to "fitting the punishment to the crime." Since we no longer consciously punish people for simply being evil, they must first do something that is contrary to law. Thus we punish according to the heinousness of the act; we give them what they deserve. The ethical problems with this are legion, and they have just been explicated in great detail. Still, as we have pointed out, merit has a utilitarian dimension that we have argued restitution meets. It is this dimension, concerned with furthering human welfare and avoiding its opposite, that we will argue is "just" according to the criterion of merit.

Many consider this discussion of merit to be quite beside the point. This criterion, after all, puts people above God. Simply, there are given ethical distributionary systems; their basic precepts have been given by God and worked out in detail through reason or revelation. These provide the only really proper criterion for an absolutely just way of dealing with crime and the criminal. Because our cultural heritage is Judeo-Christian, we will take a look at the compatibility of restitution with each of these theories of absolute justice.

On the other hand, some people think that merit does not give too much attention to people but too little. They think that the absolute good is the full and complete development and satisfaction of the individual and that all of our distributionary devices, including the criminal justice system, ought to be set up to facilitate the maximum development of uniquely human capabilities. Merit may be a fine short-term or tactical goal, but the strategy is to enable people to make the best of themselves. This is the secular philosophical tradition in American ethical thought.

Another plan appeals to those who share the sympathies of secular humanists but are not quite so optimistic as they. Instead of striving for the overall development of human potential, they would be content to dispose of social benefits and burdens equally. Now, everyone understands that this does not mean that everybody is to get exactly the same quantity of burdens and benefits, even if we could somehow devise a way of comparing the quality of each benefit and burden. Instead, treating everyone equally means treating no one only as a means to someone else's welfare but also as an end in themselves. Of course, we have a tendency to convolute this principle. Thus, for their own good (or so we reason) we unencumber women of the right to be drafted and encumber men of that burden that they might all individually be free. This principle of equality is always taking such interesting twists (e.g., presently we are trying to unencumber blacks of being bussed to white schools and whites of being bussed to black schools so that everyone will have a better education, the modern form of "separate but equal"), but what we want to point out is that this principle is really the generic form of another idea, that of distributing benefits according to need and burdens according to who can best support them. So we will treat both equality and need together as one criterion in our analysis of how restitution is just in some absolute sense.

What we restitutionists say is that all of these criteria have value and are necessary to any full understanding of "justice." Our society's concept of justice is intricate enough to recognize that always stressing any one of these to the exclusion of the others is probably unjust. Only through the simultaneous and balanced pursuit of each might we obtain some optimum among them and approximate as a society what we mean by "justice." This is particularly so in our rapidly changing pluralistic society, with its racial, religious, ethnic, and class diversity. It is even more true given the conflicting life-styles and value orientations constantly developing within the diverse American subcultures themselves. But what is more important is that in the area of criminal justice all these criteria appear to converge on the concept, practices, and priorities of restitution, and this argues very strongly that restitution is what we ought to be doing. Therefore, we are going to take each of these critera one after another and examine them until we see exactly how they converge on restitution and what priorities this suggests.

Now, you might ask, why not measure retribution, deterrence, and rehabilitation against all these standards as well? Then we might better choose among them and restitution. Well, in fact we already have. In Chapter 3 we set forth what the literature offers as the best arguments for and against retribution, deterrence, and rehabilitation. Those arguments were either derived from the ethical systems just mentioned (e.g., "promoting human welfare and avoiding its opposite" is one form of the secular philosophical ethic), or were different forms of the arguments from merit, equality, and need (e.g., "desert" is a form of the "merit" argument, and "self-determination" is a form of the equality and need argument). In that chapter we were trying to show the comparative advantage of restitution by showing how it precludes the negative criticisms of these other approaches and simultaneously accomplishes the same or more good. Thus, we were interested in the particular form the best negative and positive arguments took. Here, we are measuring restitution in an absolute sense and so must employ the core, fundamental, or ultimate criteria from which the other negative and positive criticisms are derived.

We are, of course, biased in this regard; restitution is our favorite plan. So we want to leave no stone unturned in arguing its justification. However, some of you may already be convinced of the superiority of a restitutionary approach and consider what immediately follows as an interesting but unnecessary detail; if restitution is comparatively the best, then that is sufficient. If that is the case you might just skip to the "Priorities" section of this chapter before going on to the question of implementation.

MERIT AND RESTITUTION

We are interested now in whether free and rational people, organized into groups concerned with furthering their own interests, would accept restitution as a just distribution of the benefits and burdens of the criminal justice system. Moreover, we are interested in this question given that some mix of our ethical systems and our concepts of merit, equality, and need are considered fundamental to the idea of justice. Since the answer to this question is likely to be biased according to the history, social position, and expectations of the different groups and individuals in our society, it seems that we must ask this question in the way suggested by John Rawls as he considered the abstract definition of a just society in the secular ethical tradition.[1] In *A Theory of Justice*, Rawls argues that the acceptance must be such as groups and individuals would make under a "veil of ignorance," that is, without knowing social positions, abilities, roles, social and economic resources, or personal situation in relation to the criminal justice system. Rawls's method is to develop from this hypothetical situation principles of justice according to the theory of social contract (particularly as formulated by Immanuel Kant). Because it will facilitate analysis and help make explicit the convergence of ethical thinking in the criminal justice area, we will adopt both this starting point and this method.

How compatible, then, is restitution with the principle of a "just" or "balanced" distribution according to merit? We must begin by examining our ways of justifying the reward of merit in order to see how we might behave under Rawls's veil of ignorance. When we speak in terms of rewarding merit, we usually speak of three types of merit: moral merit, industry, and talent. Now all three are usually justified both in terms of utility and in terms of intrinsic worth. Regarding industry, for example, we often seek to promote and preserve certain forms of industry while discouraging others. This idea is generally justified on grounds of utility, though it may be effectively justified simply as a desirable state of affairs to have people doing one set of things rather than another. One might argue, for example, that promoting cooperative human interaction (as a more desirable way for people to live) justifies policies decreasing competition even though competition might increase overall utility. Similarly, rewarding those whose talents are no fault of their own is usually justified on grounds of promoting those talents for socially desirable ends. But when it is practically feasible, we also seek to promote less useful talents, justifying this as an aid to the "fulfillment" of the "whole individual." It makes for a generally happier person (a generally nicer state of affairs even if not the most practical or efficient state of affairs in terms of overall increases in utility) if one can develop his or her talents to the fullest possible extent. Finally, the rewarding of morally virtuous action is usually justified only by considerations of utility. Virtuous actions tend to be useful while vicious actions tend to be harmful. But beyond this, virtue is sometimes considered its own reward, valuable in itself to the integrity and dignity of the individual and consequently definitive of a valuable social order.

Assuming a Rawlsian "veil of ignorance," then, it seems quite plausible that individual members of society would opt for a restitutionary system of criminal justice in light of the principles of justice according to merit just outlined. People in such a situation are ignorant of their social status, wealth, and power and might as easily be criminals as victims. They might realize that the extent of harm produced by any criminal act would vary at the minimum with the position and background of the victim. They might also realize that in highly interdependent societies there is little victims can do to protect themselves against feeling the impact of certain types of crime, and that the difficulties in detecting offenders (particularly in the area of white-collar crime), combined with the magnitude of the payoffs from certain criminal acts, is sufficient to tempt any basically decent person whose talents and industry should neither be lost to society nor severely diminished in their expression. Given all this, fairness might then seem to indicate that the rewards of talent, industry, and moral virtue be protected, preserved, and if necessary restored to victims, while criminals remain an integral part of the productive processes of society. Furthermore, since any increased benefits criminals realize from their offenses could not be justified as a redistribution of social goods redounding to everyone's benefit, fairness might also seem to require that the offender compensate or restore the distribution he or she has upset. Finally, under the veil of ignorance citizens might recognize that different value systems, priorities, and moral codes would exist simultaneously in their society. They might recognize, in other words, the need for value-neutral arbiters and mutual accommodation in the decision-making and law-enforcing processes. As we argued earlier, restitution is an effective guarantor of both these ends, as it seeks neither the imposition of a single moral code nor the promotion of certain interests to the exclusion of others. It looks primarily, if not exclusively, at the objective damage done in light of all the interests involved and not in light of any preferred moral standard (that is to say, "damage" is derived in terms of the various interests involved rather than in terms of a single all-encompassing standard; what constitutes an interest must, of course, be defined in as value-neutral a way as humanly possible, and we will attempt to do this in the chapters on implementation).

It seems, then, that considerations of justice based on the idea of merit are fairly compatible with punishment as restitution. We now turn to considerations of justice based on the principles of Christian ethics.

RESTITUTION AND CHRISTIAN ETHICS

Broadly speaking, Christian ethics is fundamentally concerned with (1) protecting and enhancing the individual (spiritually first, but also intellectually and even economically), and (2) protecting and enhancing the community as an integral mutual support system. This is, of course, another form of the idea that social action can only be justified to the extent that it enhances human welfare and avoids its opposite, while distributing the burdens and benefits of social life (and action) equitably. Early Roman Catholic views (based on the writing of Augustine) did hold that Christians should (1) mostly ignore the mundane, (2) set natural law above positive law, and (3) create an ecclesiastical legal order apart from the political order. Further, they maintained that salvation through the proper ethical life was only possible within special Christian communities and orders. The Protestant Reformation, however, rejected both this legal structure and much of its separation of positive and natural law. It also maintained that membership in a special community or institution was not necessary for personal salvation. More recent Catholic thought on this issue has also been critical of the Church's early stance.[2] More importantly, though, even the early stance seems to give at least equal weight to both the needs of the individual and the interests of the community. This integration of the concerns of both individual and community as a single fabric was developed by Aquinas and finds modern expression in the writings of Jacques Maritain.[3]

Let us now consider the compatibility of each of these fundamental concerns with the idea of punishment as restitution. There are three contemporary Christian schools of thought on ethical behavior and how the individual might best enhance his or her own development and the development of others: (1) the "rule ethics" school, or the school of deontological ethics, (2) the "consequentialist" school, and (3) the "situationalist" school. The "rule ethics" school has its historical roots in the Mosaic code and in the Christian legal-moral tradition of Augustine. Stress is laid upon the following of rules established to avoid *intrinsically* wrong behavior, and there is something of a disregard for the quality of an actor's intentions. Ethics in this school is covenant centered. As God is committed to persons, so they "ought" to commit themselves to each other and follow the rules for ethical action. Consequentialism, on the other hand, looks not at the act itself but at the relationship between an actor's intentions and the foreseeable consequences of an intended act. What one "ought" to do is determined by an estimate of the consequences of intended acts and how they tend to promote a balance of good over evil. Finally, situationalism embraces a "principled relativism"[4] in deciding what ought to be done in a given instance. Situationalism recognizes the importance or necessity of principles, maxims, or general rules for illuminating the decision-making process. But it also recognizes the insufficiency of any general rule or set of rules for decision making given the multiformity of circumstances requiring action. There must be a technique of fitting the rule to the situation, and for the situationalist this technique must involve an intertwining of love and prudence.

What is most interesting for our purposes here is that regardless of the school, the fundamental concept in Christian ethics is the idea that individuals must "Love thy neighbor as thyself" (Matthew 23:37-40) and in doing so respond to his or her needs. As Paul Ramsey writes for the "rule ethics" school, for example, "Christian ethics is a deontological ethics," and therefore, "neighbor love is not good, it is obligatory."[5] Clearly to Ramsey, the love commandment is the basic rule or principle of Christian morality. "God requires total concern with neighbor need."[6] Similarly, Joseph Fletcher (the father of "situation ethics") writes that the "ultimate norm for Christian decision-making is love: nothing else."[7] Further, "it is love that is due our neighbors— *only* love. Owe no man anything except to love. Love is justice, justice is love."[8] How very similar this is to Ramsey's "Everything is lawful, *absolutely everything* is permitted which love permits, everything without a single exception" and "*absolutely everything* is commanded which love requires, absolutely everything without the slightest exception or softening." Similarly, C. Curran, in wrestling with the problem of linking natural law ethics to Christian norms, writes that "the distinctly Christian aspect found in the Scriptures [is] agape or koinonia."[9]

Concern for "love as the primary ethical principle among Christians often takes the form of a special concern for the poor and weak. The 1972 General Conference of the United Methodist Church stated it succinctly when it said in its *Statement of Social Principles* that "in order to provide basic needs such as food, clothing, shelter, education, health care, and other necessities, ways must be found to share more equitably the wealth of the world."[10]

This concept of love also expresses itself in the ideas that law serves people rather than rules, and that forgiveness and mercy are preferable to condemnation and retribution. Regarding the rule of law, the New Testament says "before faith came we were kept under the law, shut up unto faith which would afterward be revealed. Wherefore the law was our schoolmaster to bring us unto Christ that we might be justified by faith. But after that faith is come we are no longer under a schoolmaster'' (Galatians 3:23-25). Thus law is not the primary concern. Rather, we ought to focus on Christ-like ''forgiveness.'' The primacy of forgiveness over law is probably best illustrated by the story of Christ's directive to an adulteress to ''go and sin no more'' (John 8:11). In context, this was said in response to the Pharisee's question: ''Now Moses in the law commanded us that such should be stoned: but what sayest thou?'' (John 8:9). Similarly, we find through the New Testament variations on the basic theme ''If you forgive men their trespasses, your heavenly Father will also forgive you. But if you forgive not their trespasses, neither will your Father forgive your trespasses'' (Matthew 6:14-15).

Finally, it should be noted that although the idea of retribution is exalted by some Christian writers,[11] many more express sentiments similar to those of H. Schrey, H. H. Walz, and W. A. Waterhouse in *The Biblical Doctrine of Justice and Law*: ''Christians' love for each individual, even the sinner and the enemy, can humanize the impersonality of law.''[12] Jacques Ellug, for example, writes: ''Neither exaltation of power nor the search for vengeance will ever serve any human situation.''[13] Similarly, Paul Ramsey writes:

Christian love which alone of all ethical viewpoints discovers the neighbor because it alone begins with neighborly love and not with discriminating between worthy and unworthy people according to the qualities they possess. Justice does not depend upon a person's stake in the community, the very fact that, although an alien, or a forgotten man, he comes in effect to belong or still belong to the communtiy, this depends on ''justice being done.''[14]

In summary, we can say that the primary and fundamental Christian norm is love of one another on an individual level. This love is defined in terms of protecting the poor and weak, forgiving violators of the law, ''serving'' the individual human situation (even the situation of a transgressor or enemy) so as to promote human dignity and growth, promoting an equitable distribution of wealth, and treating others as we would treat ourselves.

Interestingly, this set of norms defining Christian love looks very much like the norms Rawls derives in the secular philosophical tradition as principles for a just society accepted by rational persons under a ''veil of ignorance'':

First Principle

Each person is to have an equal right to the most extensive total system of equal basic liberties compatible with a similar system of liberty for all.

Second Principle

Social and economic inequalities are to be arranged so that they are both:

1. to the greatest benefit of the least advantages, consistent with the just savings principle, and
2. attached to office or positions open to all under conditions of fair equality of opportunity.[15]

Both principles, of course, are derived under the veil of ignorance and are concerned with treating others as we would treat ourselves. Beyond this, however, arranging social inequalities to the benefit of everyone bespeaks a concern for both the poor and weak and for serving the individual in his or her particular situation. Securing offices and positions as open to everyone promotes human dignity and growth, and the first principle evinces a concern for an equitable distribution of the goods of society so as not to burden overly any individual's freedom. Indeed, Rawls's principles can be seen as directing the way to the ethical goals of Christianity. His principles, in other words, are one way of formulating for political action the Christian idea of love.

Earlier, we argued the necessity for assuming a Rawlsian "veil of ignorance" as a device for explaining the relationship between punishment as restitution and the distribution of social benefits and burdens on the basis of merit. We can now argue that Christian ethics and punishment as restitution are compatible, since the Rawlsian principles argued above are but a statement of Christian ethics in practice. That is, since punishment as restitution is compatible with Rawls's principles for a just society (i.e., punishment as restitution is derivable from the "veil of ignorance" and Rawls's two principles), and since those principles are a statement of Christian ethics in practice, punishment as restitution is compatible with Christian ethics.

Moreover, we begin to see how the Christian ethical tradition, our ideas of justice according to merit, and the secular ethical tradition (à la Rawls) converge in this area. Substantively, all three ethical systems require that in any situation we do the best possible for all affected individuals. Ignoring vitally affected individuals is a violation of all three major ethical traditions as we have just described them. Most certainly, the immediate victim of crime is profoundly affected, and a system of criminal justice leaving the victim unaddressed needs a reorientation to make it compatible with our principle of equality, the Christian ethical tradition, and secular ethical concerns. But in addition, both the victim's family and the offender's family are affected, and the offender also has significant interests that deserve consideration. These interests, along with the forgiveness and nurturing of transgressors and enemies, a concern for the weak, and the idea that law should serve all affected parties, all argue for a restitutionary system of punishment according to each of these ethical traditions. As argued in the preceding chapter, restitutionary approaches most adequately address all of these interests. Moreover, it places criminal law in the position of a social institution serving the weak, forgiving transgressors, and continuing to nurture everyone involved. The positive effects reported earlier of a restitutionary process on the relationship between a criminal and a victim is only the beginning of the nurturing process.

Given that the Christian ethical idea of enhancing and protecting the individual through the concept of love is quite compatible with both punishment as restitution and the other ethical systems discussed so far, what of the Christian idea of protecting and enhancing the community? In the Gospel of John, Christ is reported as praying for his disciples "that they may be one, even as we are one," and again "that they may all be one; even as thou, Father, art in me, and I in thee, that they also may be in us" (John 17:11,21). Though at first this community was sought in sects and orders, more modern writers argue that the scope of the community must expand. J. Sellers writes, for example: "The gathering of men into commonness under God, must take a radically new form in today's pluralistic world."[16] He argues for a coalition of human purpose despite individual presuppositions and variations. A similar stress of community on a worldwide scale was demonstrated at the 1972 General Conference of the United Methodist Church.[17]

This concern for community often takes two forms. First, there is the idea of "judge not, that you be not judged" (Matthew 7:1). This warning against self-righteousness is meant to put no individual above or against another, leaving God the only judge and thereby relieving the social strain that might naturally follow people judging each other. This idea certainly converges with both those of justice according to merit and those of the secular ethical tradition that were united under the "veil of ignorance." Remember that people under this veil "judge not" both because they are ignorant or their own position in the social structure (i.e., they might be faced with crime as a most rational choice), and because they realize the diversity of moral codes and priorities they might have to live under (i.e., what some might consider a crime might be a moral duty to others, like the Mormons and polygamy in nineteenth-century America).

Concern for community also takes the form of a recognition of community responsibility for both individual violations of the law and individual virtue. Many Christian philosophers and theologians argue, for example, that the concept of "original sin" signifies a network of responsibility and influence relating past generations and contemporaries. Hostilities, fears, biases, and assumptions are both passed on from generation to generation and elicited in others by our own failure to control them in ourselves.

Continuing along this line, when victims are left effectively without remedy,[18] resentment and frustration are probably inevitable. Irrational angers, hatreds, and demands for retribution are the natural concomitants of this frustration and resentment and may be sublimated and redirected far from their source. Expanding circles of social tension resulting in this way are destructive of community. Restitution is likely to preclude much of this resentment and frustration.

Generally, punishment as restitution is most effectively directed at reestablishing the unity and order of a community broken by the criminal act. First, it helps overcome the distance between socioeconomic classes, races, and sexes enhanced by law enforcement as presently practiced. Two attitudes are fostered by the present practices. First, there is little understanding or identification between those usually victimized or committing crimes (predominantly the poor and minorities) and those responsible for making laws, establishing penalties, and enforcing laws. Second, present practices foster the idea that victims are responsible in some way for the crimes they experience.

Crime in America is not widely understood in structural terms (i.e., as the result of "structured in" needs, opportunities, and costs of both victims and criminals). The present system focuses almost exclusively

on the individual (lack of education, poor socialization, etc.). Consequently, the idea that the victim is somehow individually responsible
follows naturally. Restitution helps stress the idea that there are social
dimensions to the criminal act. As Arthur Goldberg suggested, for
example, "since society had failed to protect the person who is victimized, society should assume responsibility for making him whole."[19]
More strongly, it is arguable that certain crimes are "encouraged" by
the present set of legal priorities and socially established needs, opportunities, and costs. Much literature has recently argued, for example,
that the attitudes of courts, police, and attorneys both toward women
who have been raped and toward accused rapists, reduce the potential
costs of rape while increasing the opportunities.[20] These attitudes work
as disincentives to report crime for fear of police and prosecutor questioning, embarrassment, harassment, and possible danger from the accused (likely to be released on bail for some time awaiting trial).
Simultaneously, social values, theories, and assumptions foster at least
the inclination to rape.[21] A good-faith restitutionary approach might
provide an incentive to report such crimes, offsetting the disincentive
just mentioned. Not only might the victim look forward to some compensation, but a good-faith inquiry into the damages done could help
dispel many myths about rape and encourage an in-depth look at the
personal, social, political, and economic consequences of this widespread and largely unreported crime.

A second way that punishment as restitution helps reestablish the
unity and order of a community has to do with the rapidly increasing
complexity of our society. As society changes, the legitimacy of its
legal norms opens to challenge. Interest groups and individuals having
special interests or attachments to established norms or situations often
seek both to have them reaffirmed through law and to control the threatening behavior of others.[22] Similarly, many laws reflect the morality of
times and situations long past (socially if not chronologically) and are
inconsistent with the knowledge, technology, and norms of modern
society. The criminal law thus becomes a political battleground.[23] Old
laws, or new ones reaffirming old values, become symbols of dominance
for those supporting them and symbols of condemnation for those challenging them.[24] Should those seeking reaffirmation be successful, dissenting groups begin widespread "patterned evasions" of the law."[25]
This state of affairs is in itself destructive of community, and in addition
leads to practices by law enforcers that further strain social unity and

order. A restitutionary approach, however, could alleviate many of these problems.

To begin with, many of the crimes we are talking about are "victimless" (gambling, prostitution, homosexuality, etc.). Consequently, there are rarely complaining witnesses, and the social danger of such acts is at best indirect and distantly related to the offense. Police are, therefore, reduced to using informers, eavesdropping, engaging in questionable searches, propounding false arrests, harassing, and entrapment. Similarly, judges and attorneys often reflect community ambivalence toward these crimes. In the face of often severe penal sanctions, many attorneys informally negotiate for reduced charges or penalties and seek informal "diversionary" patterns for handling offenders. Judges often go along with these bargains and diversions, using their own discretionary sentencing power to facilitate the process. Additionally, selective enforcement of these laws, for political or other reasons, may develop. In the face of this behavior and because of significant social feeling that the moralistic laws themselves are unjust, disrespect for the law and the legal process is greatly encouraged. With this disrespect come increasing "patterned evasions" of law and the resulting social disunity and disorder the law and its process are intended to counteract.[26]

Restitution, of course, addresses itself directly to the core of this complex problem. Courts enforcing a restitutionary approach more easily act as arbiters or balancers of interest among competing social groups. The severity of a sentence depends most directly on demonstrable harm caused, and this issue itself can be litigated among the parties (at a minimum: state, criminal, and victim). The approach helps preclude the effective use of process for political ends since good faith enquiry concerning damages would, in such cases, usually result in little (if any) sanction being applied.

The use by governments of "inchoate crimes" such as conspiracy to bring charges against political dissenters presents another set of problems. In such cases (like the trial of the "Chicago Eight"), it is questionable whether the government ever really intends to win such a suit. The tactic of bringing such charges may be directed at (1) harassing the dissenters, (2) casting aspersions on dissenters (to many, the mere fact that charges are brought indicates some wrongdoing), or (3) baiting the dissenters into further acts which are punishable (e.g., contempt of court, interstate flight to avoid prosecution, etc.). This is different from, for example, selectively prosecuting and convicting a political dissenter of "fornication" (intercourse with one to whom you are not married). Restitutionary systems do not address the former problem as directly as the latter. Nevertheless, inchoate crimes as a general category would become fairly obsolescent under a restitutionary system, as they are by definition crimes that have not yet produced damages.

Similarly, the use of law to exalt certain moral values over others would be greatly reduced for the same reasons. Plea bargaining, peculiar uses of discretionary powers, and diversionary tactics would be less attractive. A great deal of the time, effort, and money presently expended on this sort of crime (at the expense of more serious crimes) could easily decrease. Repetitive cycles of arrest in cases of, for example, prostitution, public alcoholism (nationwide, one out of every three arrests yearly is on charges of public intoxication), and vagrancy could easily be eliminated altogether. The idea here is not necessarily to condone such behavior nor to deny the social problems it produces. The idea is that if certain behavior is genuinely considered not evil or destructive by significant numbers or groups of people, the law should not be an effective tool for others to express conflicting sentiments. On the other hand, if there is some demonstrable social harm, methods with fewer adverse social costs should be found to deal with the problem. Restitutionary systems have a self-checking device (honest inquiry into damages done by a particular act), helping to keep criminal law within effective limits so as not to alienate groups or individuals in society.

Overall, then, we might say that punishment as restitution does not conflict with Christian ethical concerns for the protection and enhancement of both the individual and the community. In fact, much of what has been said here argues that punishment as restitution strongly reinforces Christian ethical concerns. Moreover, we have pointed out places where Christian ethics, secular ethics, and ideas of punishment according to merit begin to converge on the question of a proper approach to criminal justice. We now need to be sure, however, that all of this holds in the Jewish ethical tradition as well.

RESTITUTION AND JEWISH ETHICS

Two fundamental ideas of restitution are quite explicit and consistent throughout the Jewish ethical tradition and converge with the Christian tradition, the secular tradition, and the idea of justice according to merit. These are: (1) that an offender ought to be reintegrated with society, and (2) that the community bears some responsibility for individual transgressions. As was the situation with Christianity, not only is punishment as restitution not in violation of Jewish ethics, but it seems, on examination, a reaffirmation thereof.

But you might say: "Surely the Bible clearly says 'an eye for an eye and a tooth for a tooth'; certainly this is retributionary." Well, while there is no modern theory of punishment that cannot, in some form or another, be traced back to biblical passages, it is grossly unfair to say that the principle of *lex talionis* (which has often been quoted as the basis for punishment) is a principle of the Jewish ethical tradition. "One who kills a beast must pay for it, life for life" (Leviticus 24:18); "As he did, so must be done to him" (Leviticus 24:19); and "Whenever someone harms a person, thus must be done to him" (Leviticus 24:20)— are all famous passages which seem to call for rectification through retribution. Yet, there is in Jewish history no instance of the law of retaliation ever having been carried out literally, eye for eye, tooth for tooth.[27] In the passage in the Mishnah (M. B. Kamma, viii., I) where such cases are handled, and in the discussion of that passage in the Gemara, there is no hint that the old savage law had ever been enforced. There is instead the opinion that no one could ever have been so cruel and so brutal as to take the written commandment literally.

You might argue that even if early Jewish communities did not practice what they preached, that only serves to demonstrate that their practice did not live up to their ethical ideals; *lex talionis* was written and that's what they thought they should be doing if only the flesh were as willing as the spirit. But we must remember that even our own statutory law requires something more than its mere statement to be meaningful and applicable to specific events and changing times. Thus we have common-law interpretations of the written law, constitutional interpretations by the Supreme Court, law review exegeses, and opinions by the attorneys general (state and federal). This is because the written word can only be properly understood within a given historical and cultural framework. This framework is constantly changing, and so must our understanding of the written law. In the same way, besides the canonical scriptures themselves, oral traditions, explanations, instructions on how to keep the law, and exegeses of scripture were needed to make the law relevant and applicable to the everyday working of early Jewish communities.

In the case of *lex talionis*, a literal understanding of the written command became obsolete at a very early time. The order of savage retaliation was abolished and the law of *lex talionis* and retribution was interpreted by the rabbis in terms of a monetary restitution to victims for damages suffered. For example, in the words of Rabbi Saadia (Gaon: Egypt and Babylonia: 882-942), "If a person strikes the eye of his fellow, and a third of the vision is lost, how is it possible that he be struck with the same injury, without greater or lesser (damage)? Perhaps he will become completely blind, or the burn or wound or bruise will be more severe. Reason cannot tolerate this."[28] This is the problem of commensurability we have wrestled with before. Here is the interpretation of "an eye for an eye": It should have been "his eye for his eye, if he does not pay its compensation." Hence, the phrase "life for life" was read as a technical term (a legal fiction) being equivalent to fair compensation; it became a demand that adequate and equitable compensation be paid the victim after due and judicial appraisement of the injury inflicted was made.[29] At a very early time, then, the biblical command "an eye for an eye" had become a mere expression of the law of equality—a restoration of the *status quo ante*, which is a central characteristic of restitution.

What is important to our discussion is that the movement by the rabbis from a literal interpretation of punishment as a concept of retribution to the idea of restitution and compensatory damages demonstrated an advance to an ethically higher meaning of the written text, a meaning that repudiated peremptorily the idea that retribution constitutes the reason of the law or a motive of action and points instead to a restitutionary approach.

In addition to those phrases so often wrongly interpreted as divine support for the *lex talionis*, Leviticus explicitly forbids taking vengeance or holding a grudge: "No doubt there are crimes which cry out for vengeance, but even these are to be avenged only by God" (Leviticus 19:17-18). This proscription of vengeful punishments not only supported the early dismissal of retributionary understandings, but it also reinforced the two other themes of restitutionary punishment: those of community responsibility for transgressions and the reintegration of the offender and society.

First, consider the idea of community responsibility for violations of the law. Jewish ethical writings presuppose the idea of a close interpersonal responsibility for others, which begins in the family and extends to all people.[30] This sense of community responsibility and oneness has at its roots (among other things) the historical idea of community atonement for certain transgressions of its members (as in the case where a murderer is not known and the whole community is held responsible for the crime perpetrated by one of its members).[31] The exhortation, "Ye shall be holy" (Leviticus 22:26) sums up the whole end and aims of the laws. The people whom a holy god has chosen and covenanted with for his own must, like him, be holy, and hence a community responsibility existed for the acts and welfare of its members. Through the covenant between God and Israel, the community takes upon itself responsibility for what is done in it. All Israel is part of one community, one body, and all are responsible for the acts of each. A continuing example of this oneness can be seen in the Hebrew prayers of confession which are spoken by the congregation in the plural: "Our God and God of our fathers . . . we are righteous and have not sinned. But we have sinned. We have committed iniquity, caused unrighteousness . . ."[32] They have sinned and they have not sinned; this stresses both the identity of individual and community and the identity of individual and community responsibility.

Now consider the idea of reintegrating offenders and society. The rationale for reintegrating offenders into the community began with the presumption of innocence and strict rules of evidence found in Deuteronomy. The idea was to avoid easy or frivolous stigmatizations of individuals that would set them apart from the community. Even after they were stigmatized by conviction, however, offenders were still considered part of the community,[33] and everything was done to reintegrate community and offender and reestablish the mutual responsibilities violated by the offending act. The strongest indication that transgressors never left the community and that the community's responsibility for them never ended is found in Leviticus 19:18: "Ye shall not take vengeance, nor bear any grudge against the sons of your own people." The prohibition of the grudge is an important element of the Jewish approach not only to punishment but to the relationship of the offender to the rest of the community—the idea is both that respect for the offender continues regardless of his or her criminal conduct, and that he or she continues to hold a place in the community.

Thus it might be said that regarding even the most persistent recidivist, the Jewish tradition holds that "no man is beyond human concern. No man is so bad that the community may be resolved of responsibility."[34] No person is merely a criminal, and if the state treats him or her as a criminal and nothing else, it makes a mistake and commits an injustice. The ancient Hebrews regarded injustice as a disturbance of the equilibrium in human relations. Justice included the reintegration of returning offenders to equal status in the community—an understanding that full restitution has been made by the offender to the victim. Clearly two themes are central to the restitutionary argument we are presenting, are explicit in the Jewish ethical tradition, and converge with central themes of the Christian and "merit" traditions. The ideas of community responsibility and reintegration are cornerstones of our own justification of restitution, the Christian ethical tradition, and ideas of justice according to merit. Nothing is clearer than the specifications of the Mishnah (the foundation principles of the Talmud): "A man who injures another becomes liable to him—on five counts: for damages, for pain, for healing, for loss of time, and for indignity."[35]

Of course, we have also dealt (though cursorily) with the secular ethical tradition by way of Rawls, and it seems that the ideas of community responsibility and reintegration are points of convergence there, too. But we need a more detailed analysis to be sure of this.

RESTITUTION AND AMERICAN SECULAR ETHICS

The central theme of most writings on American secular ethics is the full and complete development and satisfaction of the individual. Brand Blanchard writes: "The good, in the sense of the ethical end, is the most comprehensible possible fulfillment and satisfaction of impulse-desire."[36] John Dewey and James Tufts take a similar tack,[37] as do Peter Bertocci and M. Millard: "The criterion of value . . . is experimental, growing coherence within the total life in self and others and all the factors relevant to the creation of value experience."[38] The message is clear that we must value ourselves and our desires, others and their desires, and work both to meet these desires and to foster the growth necessary to perceive and fulfill these needs and desires.

Toward this end, "certain basic rights must be distributed equally and . . . they must be consonant with the dignity of human personality."[39] Moreover, "an action is just if, and only if, it is prescribed exclusively by regard for the rights of all whom it affects substantially."[40] Paul Weiss points out similar ideas in Hobbes, Kant, Mill, Aquinas, and Hillel.[41] In addition, the full growth and fulfillment of the individual requires "the obligation to respect every person's freedom. . . . Persons and only persons are ends in themselves.''[42] Similarly, Frankena writes: ''[Society] must remember, that morality is made to minister to the good lives of individuals and not to interfere with them any more than is necessary.''[43] In summary, through the use and guarantee of freedom and equality the full growth and fulfillment of the individual is to be sought.

Interestingly, freedom and equality (and hence fulfillment) are not sought only negatively (through the absence of external constraints or former inequalities). Instead, there is a positive dimension, an obligation to seek positively the well-being of all. John Dewey, for example, says, ''Ours is the responsibility of conserving, transmitting, rectifying, and expanding the heritage of values we have received that those who come after us may receive it more solid and secure, more widely accessible and more generously shared than we have received it.''[44] Paul Freund argues in a similar vein that concepts of justice must move beyond considering the individual. True social justice, he argues, is ''artificial and unsatisfactory to consider individual justice apart from the interests of larger social groups.''[45] Finally, Bertocci and Millard argue ''love'' should be the ''style of life'' in our society. ''Love is the total orientation of a person's thinking, feeling, and willing insofar as his controlling commitment is the ideal growth of personality in himself and in all other persons.''[46] We find, in brief, the same stress on community responsibility that we have found in the Christian, Jewish, and merit traditions.

Our present criminal justice system commonly focuses narrowly on the individual defendant alone. But the secular philosophical tradition (like the Christian, Jewish, and merit traditions) in America clearly argues that we need to take positive action not only regarding the accused but regarding everyone affected both by the criminal act (e.g., the victim) and by the impact of the criminal process (e.g., accused's family). Both groups certainly have had at least their relative freedoms reduced by the criminal act and its aftermath. Consequently, their potentials for fulfillment and satisfaction must be proportionately reduced. Under each of the ethical traditions discussed so far, actions by the criminal justice system in disregard of these two groups are necessarily unjust. More strongly, a failure to take positive steps to ensure the well-being of these groups is a denial of both society's ethical traditions and our concept of distributionary justice that argues for a broadening of our ideas of the legally relevant in the criminal justice system. The idea is "to take more complete and intelligent account of the social facts upon which law must proceed and to which it is to be applied."[47]

EQUALITY, NEED, AND RESTITUTION

The final plan, distributing benefits and burdens equally or according to need, has already been shown to converge with the American secular tradition in the area of criminal justice. Equality is Rawls's first principle, for example, and need is really embodied in his second. In addition, equality is one condition secular philosophers hold necessary to a full flowering of the individual. We need only then make explicit how equality and need converge with the Christian, Jewish, and merit traditions to secure our argument that restitution meets each of their terms.

As we pointed out initially, equality and need are really different forms of the argument that people ought always to be treated not only as means but also as ends. This principle embodies both the idea that the community ought to be equally concerned with the welfare of offenders and the welfare of victims, and the idea that the community might bear some responsibility for crime should it adopt policies that enhance some people at the expense of others (e.g., increasing unemployment to bring down inflation thereby increasing the buying power of those left employed). These ideas, of course, are fundamental principles in the Christian, Jewish, and merit traditions.[48]

An objection might be offered at this point that we have previously criticized both the retribution approach and the deterrence approach on the grounds of commensurability. That is, we have argued that these approaches are unjustified partially because we cannot, for example, work out how much punishment is equal to a given amount of evil. You might ask: "How can you expect to measure things out equally and how are you going to determine how much everyone needs?" "Needs," after all, are as subjective and abstract as "deserts," and by a simple extension we can see that "equality" is of the same nature. "Merit" suffers a similar fate, of course, because as we argued before, you can't really measure out what any person deserves. So there you are; why bother with these criteria at all? Why not simply dismiss them as abstractions and altogether avoid the problem of demonstrating restitution's compatibility with them?

Well, we cannot dismiss these criteria that easily because regardless of the commensurability problem, we all seem to value certain types of interpersonal behavior we call "seeking equality" or "treating people equally" or "ensuring equal protection." These behaviors are consistent patterns in our day-to-day living and have meaning and value for us. What we are trying to do, of course, is to justify restitution as consistent with these patterns or forms of our life. This, after all, was one of the things we originally argued any acceptable approach must do.

Punishing through retribution or deterrence, on the other hand, is something special we do. All of us do not engage in it, and those of us who do, do not do so all the time. Moreover, we do not value such behaviors for themselves. At most, we hope they make things safe for behaviors we do value for themselves. Consequently, retribution and deterrence must be justified in a different way than the seeking of equality or the fulfillment of need. Approximating deterrence, for example, is no good; approximating equality is much better. And working for closer and closer approximations of fulfilling people's needs seems more sensible than working for closer and closer approximations of vengeance. In brief, the commensurability problem is not nearly so bothersome when it comes of equality and need as when retribution and deterrence are at issue.

PRESENT PRIORITIES AND THE ETHICAL CRITERIA

We have now surveyed the prevalent ethical criteria and found them to converge on the idea of restitution as a just form of punishment in some absolute sense. In order to go on and determine what our priorities in criminal justice ought to be given this convergence, we must first understand what those priorities actually are at the present time. We must understand exactly how bad things are in light of our criteria before we can decide whether it is worth the time to change them.

Presently, first priorities in law enforcement generally run to what are broadly referred to as "street crimes." These include murder, assault, burglary, vandalism, and robbery. A close second in priority are "vice crimes": prostitution, homosexuality, gambling, pornography, and drug offenses. A distant third (often so distant as not to be in the running when it comes to allocating resources) is a large category of offenses referred to euphemistically as "white-collar crimes," including "corporate crimes."

These white-collar and corporate crimes fall into four broad categories: (1) various forms of fraud and embezzlement, (2) bribes and kickbacks, (3) tax evasion, and (4) business violation (price fixing, collusive bidding, trust formations, etc.).[49] Certainly there is nothing inherently necessary to social organization about this particular order of priorities. In fact, it can be forcefully argued that the greatest economic and social threats to the stability and effectiveness of our entire social system obtain from white-collar and corporate crimes and few, if any, from crimes of vice.[50] Furthermore, the impact of street crimes on the total economic stability of American society has been effectively reduced through insurance and cost spreading among the populace at large. More importantly, the average street crime simply does not dent the total economic structure upon which our social and political system is dependent. By way of illustration:

the average bankrobber steals several thousand dollars; computer felons, however, steal more than $400,000 on the average. Some frauds have cost the public as much as $2 billion. With the advent of the cashless society . . . the traditional felon may actually be a dying species.[51]

We believe that the distribution of benefits and burdens under this scheme of priorities is not according to principles of merit, need, or equality. Certainly those forms of behavior we ought rationally to consider most detrimental to our existing order, and therefore most in need of discouragement, are not discouraged under this set of priorities. There seems, in fact, to be nearly an inverse relationship between desert (merit) and punishment. Furthermore, a disproportionate amount of the burden for pursuing proscribed behavior falls on the "less equal" and more needy. Due to the sophisticated nature of the ordinary white-collar and corporate crime (computer fraud, bank fraud, trust formation, price fixing, political bribes and kickbacks, security frauds, insurance frauds, tax frauds, etc.), offenders are usually of higher socioeconomic backgrounds than perpetrators of street crimes, can afford effective legal representation, and can take advantage of every legal means for obtaining favored treatment from the courts.[52] We will now make this argument in some detail.

To begin with, white-collar and corporate crime constitute an economic and social threat of such scope and dimension as to test the social fabric much more severely than does "street crime." In strictly economic terms, more white-collar crime is committed than street crime

Table 1

The Economic Cost of Crime (1967)

	Annual Economic Cost (in millions of dollars)
White-Collar Crime	
Embezzlement	$ 200
Fraud	1,350
Tax Fraud	100
Forgery	80
Crimes of the Poor	
Robbery	27
Burglary	251
Auto Theft	140
Larceny, $50 and over	190

Source: Based on data in the President's Commission on Law Enforcement and the Administration of Justice, Task Force Report, *Crime and Its Impact*, 44–49.

(see Table 1). It is actually impossible to get even very gross statistics on the number of white-collar crimes committed each year, not only because many go undetected, but also because most federal and state agencies dealing with these crimes do not investigate publicly. They dispose of their cases administratively, often in closed sessions or at the discretion of investigating officers. Nevertheless, a minimum of 800 categories of consumer fraud alone have been identified,[53] significantly more than the standard categories of street crimes employed in most criminal codes. More importantly, many of the same economic effects that many saw as "dissolving the bonds of the social order" and necessitating a constitutional convention in 1787 to restructure our political and legal system can be identified with white-collar and corporate crime in the modern setting.

First of all, capital is handicapped in seeking profitable outlets by a decreased security of investments. Security related offenses like churning (involving short-term buying and selling by brokers), stock manipulation, boiler-room operations (hard-sell tactics inducing the uninformed to invest in speculative enterprises), and ponzi schemes (paying dividends to early investors out of income from later investors and then absconding with increased later investments made on strength of original returns), tend to weaken public confidence in investment markets, chill investor enthusiasm, and saddle investors with unacceptable losses. Bankruptcy fraud (including forming a company with a name similar to an established firm to induce investment, forming a new company with plush accoutrements and placing increasingly large orders which are converted into cash rather than production after establishing credit, and seeking quick profits by trading on the established credit of a firm though that firm is financially unsound at present) have similar effects as do insurance frauds and computer frauds.

Secondly, many forms of white-collar and corporate crime tend to decrease the value of public securities by indirectly straining a public authority's ability to pay interests on its debts. Thus, fraud in both government contracts and government programs drives the costs associated with those programs to a point where monies otherwise slated to repay debts must be transferred to keep the programs running. Among such frauds are (1) shoddy work in need of continual repair, (2) non-existent services, and (3) "ghost" consultants. Bribes, kickbacks, and other political frauds have a similar and reinforcing effect.

Finally, consumer-related frauds, antitrust practices, restraint of trade practices, and environmental offenses impose severe strains on individual monetary resources. It is estimated that twenty billion dollars annually are lost by consumers to auto repair frauds, medical frauds, and home repair frauds.[54] Antitrust and restraint of trade practices have their effect primarily in higher prices, estimated to amount to a minimum of twenty billion dollars annually and to strain severely the military budget.[55] As far as environmental offenses are concerned:

For the last century, we have abused and polluted our environment as no other society before us. The water, land, and air that we daily use has been poisoned and contaminated and, perhaps in some cases, lost for centuries. The cost has been enormous, not only financially but also in terms of ill health and even death. Criminologists have long neglected to study or include within their scope of interest offenses against the environment. For too long, we have studied only the interaction between individuals and have neglected that between the individual and his environment. In the last analysis, it is this wider scope of activity that may determine if our civilization survives or falls. Crimes against the environment merit concern and study.[56]

All of this argues rather strongly for a reorganization of criminal priorities to address white-collar and corporate crimes much more seriously than at present and to give traditional "street crimes" a much less exclusive focus. They certainly deserve such a restructuring of priorities. However, even if we could not say that white-collar and corporate crimes merited a higher priority than street crimes for economic and utilitarian reasons, a reorganization of priorities would still be called for because the present set of priorities is unjust from the standpoint of equality and need.

Remember that we are taking equality and need together for purposes of analysis because it seems to us that the distribution of social burdens and benefits according to need is fundamentally but one manifestation of the view of justice as equality, and that justice as equality is fundamentally an argument for the treatment of individuals as ends in themselves. Remember also that under the scheme of priorities outlined above, a disproportionate amount of the burden for pursuing proscribed behaviors falls on the "less equal" and more needy. Two reasons were given for this: (1) the present system of priorities allocates resources (money, available officers, time) to street crimes and vice crimes first, leaving less to concentrate on corporate crime, and (2) the present set of priorities encourages the idea that white-collar and corporate criminals are somehow less invidious than other criminals. Additionally, remember that it is common business practice to cover up much of the corporate crime in order to avoid public embarrassment and the loss of public trust. Finally, due to the sophisticated nature of the ordinary corporate crime (trust formation, price fixing, political bribes, tax frauds, etc.), the offenders are usually of higher socioeconomic backgrounds than perpetrators of street crimes, can afford legal representation, and can take advantage of every legal means for obtaining favored treatment from the courts.

The effects that the inequality fostered by this set of priorities has on the "bonds of our social order" are readily apparent. First, by allocating resources in the manner indicated, the present system fosters a situation in which the threats to our social order from corporate crime (detailed earlier) can proceed with very little hindrance. Corporate criminals are thus "more equal" than other criminals. They bear both a smaller amount of risk in their criminal activity and a smaller amount of punishment if caught. Concomitantly, the payoff or reward for the crime is greater if they go undetected.

Second, the differential treatment of corporate criminals tends to increase feelings of alienation in those socioeconomic classes whose crimes (street crimes) are dealt with more severely by comparison. This in turn increases feelings of class antagonism, arguably leading to more crime out of a growing feeling of repression. The other side of this coin, of course, is that "in traditional societies those lowest in the social order have more often expressed their feelings by a sense of fatalism than by active resentment."[57] Thus an apathetic approach to life and society develops among certain socioeconomic groups. In either case (apathy or antagonism), the bonds of society are strained.

Third, given the situation described so far, the present set of priorities decreases respect for law in both the upper and lower classes. This, in turn, encourages both a disrespect for individual rights and a disregard for those interpersonal duties and responsibilities the law embodies and enforces. Of course, there are other social institutions (church, family, etc.) that may encourage a continued respect for such rights and duties. But the law is an overarching institution (as opposed to individual churches, religions, and families) acting on a society-wide basis. Its role cannot be completely compensated for by other institutions. It cannot seriously be argued, then, that our present priorities embody the principles of justice according to merit, equality, or need. Restructuring priorities as described above and enforcing that structure through restitution, however, could go a long way toward redistributing benefits and burdens in a more equitable fashion according to the needs of those portions of the public most seriously affected by the shift of some costs of production to the public (white-collar and corporate crimes) as well as street crimes.

The adoption of such a policy would certainly enhance the prospects for successfully institutionalizing punishment as restitution. Criminals in this area more often have the ability or potential ability to make restitution than do criminals involved in street crimes. Moreover, they will often be more disposed to do so in order to continue their business as usual. Additionally, they are a potential source of fines that might be accumulated into a fund directed at compensating victims of street crimes immediately, so as to allow courts to develop and employ restitutionary forms in the cases of those financially unable to make restitution (more will be said on this later).

Finally, such a restructuring of priorities would more honestly recognize the principles of justice as merit, equality, and need. Because of the priorities discussed so far, "the poor, the young, and very old (especially if poor), and disadvantaged minority group members receive a disproportionately large share of the sanctions and a correspondingly small share of the benefits allocated by the legal process in comparison to other individuals in society.''[58] Equally important is the fact that the majority of economically comfortable, middle-aged, educated, and cultured people of our society receive a disproportionate share of the burdens of both the economic development and the production of goods and services in this country, and they are effectively unable to seek redress through the courts. Though the law sometimes recognizes, through regulatory statutes and commissions, the essential injustice of shifting major portions of the cost of production (in terms of pollution and the various forms of fraud already discussed) to the general public, the present structure of priorities shapes enforcement mechanisms in such a way as to leave the victims of most white-collar and corporate crimes effectively remediless.[59]

Do the present priorities fare any better under the Christian, Jewish, or secular ethical traditions than they have under the criteria of merit, equality, and need? Not really. If we consider the points on which these three traditions converge, we can see that the present priorities do not meet their concerns.

Briefly, the two points of convergence for these three traditions were (1) the protection and enhancement of each individual, and (2) the enhancement of the community as an integrated mutual support system. These two points are central purposes that societies ought to have according to our ethical traditions, and these two points are clearly violated by our present priorities. First, a community is anything but enhanced under our present priorities as our discussion of merit, equality, and need has just demonstrated. The present priorities work more to provide certain groups and individuals with economic, political, and social advantages and to distribute to others a disproportionate share of the burden of social living. In this sense present priorities foster a class society, not a community.

As far as the individual is concerned, under our present priorities no one is enhanced, and many suffer even if they appear to gain in some relative sense from the present situation. Individual victims are helpless before the present system. Their concerns are shunted aside; at most they are used as witnesses to make the state's case and then left to fend for themselves regardless of their physical, emotional, or psychological state. Offenders are brutalized by present prison conditions, taught docility and how to play the prison game in the name of rehabilitation, and further socialized into a criminal way of life. The biases, prejudices, and uncritical philosophies of judges are allowed free play in sentencing, and even those individuals whose interests are supposedly secured by the present priorities suffer from both increased crime rates and either a developing apathy or a developing hostility toward them because of their property and protected position.

All in all, the present priorities leave everyone pretty miserable, hoping either that there will be less crime at some unspecified time in the future or that some immediate impulse for vengeance will be gratified. What we need is a different set of priorities and a different model of criminal justice than we have now, and as we have argued, restitution provides such an alternative model and set of priorities meeting all the necessary requirements.

THE PRIORITIES OF THE RESTITUTIONARY APPROACH

The first thing we have to settle is what we want most, and according to our ethical criteria that is, first, to encourage the full development of each person's uniquely human capacities (including giving them what they deserve, treating them equally, and seeing to their needs), and second, to encourage community development as a mutual support system. On the individual level, then, first priority ought to go to making the victims whole again; they are usually the ones whose personal development, needs, and deserts are most directly and intensely affected by a criminal act. Second priority ought to go to others injured by the act, with a "scope of the risk limitation like that found in tort law." It is a quite uniform policy of our civil courts that where a defendant's negligence consists of his or her violating a statute, there should be no liability for consequences which no reasonable person would expect to follow, or which were surprising in light of ordinary experience. Third priority should go to reintegrating offenders into the community, both so that they may be allowed to continue to develop personally and so that the community is not robbed of their talents and contributions. Of course, everyone understands that there may be individual offenders too dangerous to put back into the community. Our fourth priority ought therefore to be the making of prisons a humane and economically productive place for such offenders to spend their time.

On the community level, first priorities in terms of allocating money, time, and effort ought to go to the detection and prosecution of white-collar and corporate crime. This is the greatest economic and social threat to our community. Second priority should go to street crimes, and a distant third priority (if we must bother with them at all) to vice crimes. Under this new set of priorities there would be less suffering for victims, less brutalization of offenders, less gratification of the immediate impulse to vengeance, and less inequality among classes in the distribution of the burdens and benefits of crime, but there would be more justice according to our ethical criteria, a more economically and socially productive penal system, and more real security to everyone in our society (e.g., even if you are a victim, your damage is repaired).

HOW THINGS GOT THIS WAY AND WHY THINGS HAVEN'T ALREADY CHANGED

If our present system is really so bad, and if we have a satisfactory alternative ready to hand, how did we ever come up with the present scheme of priorities, and why do so many people still defend it?

Historically, this scheme of priorities can be traced to at least three factors: (1) the evolution of ritual purgations, (2) the development of hierarchical social systems, and (3) the desire for peace within economically developing communities. As mentioned before, the practice of sacrificing offenders or ousting them from the community as means of making restitution to offended deities was an early form of social punishment. However:

Immolation and excommunication of the offender are undoubtedly the most effective means, but they are not the only means of placating an irate god. The transgression may be of a venial character, and expiatory rites are then sufficient to rehabilitate the wrongdoer in the eye of the deity. The idea of substitution suggests at an early date, and the scapegoat takes his place on the altar of sacrifice. The goodwill of the god may be recovered by liberal offerings, or lustration may be restored to, to wash away the impurity of guilt. We thus arrive at the distinction between wrongs which rouse the divine wrath to such a point that nothing but the blood of the culprit or his removal from the community can avert a calamity, and wrongs which may otherwise be atoned for.... It is not always the gravity of the offense that makes the difference.[60]

Ritual purgation is in the nature of a penal substitute resorted to where the infliction of punishment is either impractical or inexpedient.[61]

Though the objective rationale for the recognition of ceremonial practices has faded (i.e., in America we seldom placate irate gods anymore), the pattern of thought it engendered has struck roots. It has been both impractical and inexpedient in many ways to punish white-collar crime seriously. As mentioned before, the crimes and the criminals are both sophisticated, and this makes detection very difficult. Moreover, those involved are often in positions of influence or control and can effectively thwart investigation. Finally, during the last few decades business and professional malfeasance has been often overlooked because of the explosive economic growth our society has experienced—a growth that seemed to benefit everyone and was to some extent perceived as facilitated by certain fast and loose practices. During the 1960s, for example, commercial bribery involving American firms overseas was justified by the companies involved as a necessary "cost of doing business abroad."[62] Thus, the combination of (1) low visibility, (2) ambiguity as to exactly how "wrong" such activities are, and (3) the difficulties involved in detecting and prosecuting such offenses, has led to the imposition of ritual purgations and ceremonial punishments for those offenders who are in fact uncovered.

Besides the pattern of ritual purgations carried over from religion into the secular and economic sphere, there is the pattern of thought growing out of European philosophy as to what should be considered deviant behavior. As A. Bequai explains:

With the fall of Rome, Europe entered what was later called the Dark Ages. A system of feudalism evolved, and the state came to be viewed as the personal manor of the ruling family (the monarch). Numerous dynasties emerged and declined, for example, the Carolingians, Normans, Plantagenets, Burgundians, Hapsburgs, Bourbons, and Hohenzollerns, to name a few. These families, at one time or another, ruled and controlled Europe.

Although each dynasty had its own peculiar views and ideologies, they all had one thing in common: the state was their domain; treason to the state was treason against them. As Louis XIV would note, "I am the state." Because of this attitude, the monarchs and their underlings saw themselves as being above the law. Since the state was theirs to be used as they pleased, they saw nothing wrong with their actions[63] . . . well, after World War I, the upper classes in many countries in Europe and throughout the world viewed themselves as being above the law. Thus the modern law enforcement apparatus that began to take shape in the nineteenth century addressed itself to the poorer, more visible criminal element. The upper classes viewed themselves as being above the laws of the state; in many instances, their control of the prosecutorial and judicial machinery ensured them de facto immunity from prosecution. The evolving police forces concentrated their thrust in the area of traditional offenses commited by the lower classes.[64]

Thus hierarchical social systems historically had two profound effects. First, they instilled the prejudice that the higher people are in the socioeconomic structure, the less likely are their actions to be truly iniquitous. Secondly, they tended to shape developing institutions in such a way that they were most effective in addressing the sorts of crimes most often committed by those of lower sociocultural status.

A final trend working historically to establish and maintain our present criminal priorities was the desire for peace within economically developing communities. As mentioned earlier, public authority did not normally intervene between contending parties on its own initiative until it became possible or necessary to do so in order to secure certain of its own ends or interests. Many of these interests were, of course, fiscal, and this often led to a protective attitude toward economic institutions and practices and a desire to secure and encourage practices enhancing quick economic development. Historically this protective attitude has directed itself primarily against immediate, sometimes violent, threats most likely to come from lower socioeconomic classes. In America the protective dynamic can most clearly be seen during the period between the Articles of Confederation and the adoption of the present Constitution. During this period there was a well-documented dichotomy of interest between economic groups in America.[65] Small farmers, hired laborers, small businesspeople, artisans, and mechanics were basically satisfied with governmental management under the articles. The distribution of political power under the articles effectively allowed them to lighten the burden of their debts and keep prices down by proscribing interstate and international tariffs. On the other hand, public and private creditors, shipowners, merchants, and the professional occupations most dependent on this group (lawyers, accountants, newspaper editors, etc.) experienced severe economic disaster threatening their very existence. State efforts to bolster the economic security of those in commerce and finance were either turned back by the popular legislatures or forcefully resisted by the populace. It was this latter development that led most directly to a constitutional convention. After an armed revolt in Massachussetts, where farmers violently opposed state efforts to confiscate property for failure to pay debts and taxes (Shay's Rebellion), a number of popular leaders (including George Washington) became convinced that "the bonds of the social order were dissolving." The result was a new foundational document which some have argued is a blatant codification of class interest.[66]

Whether or not you accept an economic interpretation of the Constitution, the historical existence of such a dichotomy of interest is well documented. In concert with the shaping of criminal institutions to address lower-class crimes and the ritual cleansing of those involved in sophisticated (i.e., upper-class) crimes, the social utility of which are ambiguous, this final trend can be seen to have a significant (if not determinative) impact on shaping our present criminal priorities.

The continuation of these priorities today undoubtedly arises from the fact that the values, beliefs, rituals, and institutional practices these trends have established work systematically and consistently through our courts of law, schools, communications media, and religious organizations to shape people's perceptions, understandings, preferences, biases, and beliefs in such a way as both to benefit certain persons and groups over others and to gain acceptance of this inequality by leading most to believe either that there is no workable alternative, or that the way things are is natural and right (i.e., divinely ordained or inherent in the rational order of things).

Even if some manage to resist this onslaught of social forces, they might themselves be the victims of crime or close to someone else who is. They therefore experience firsthand the degradation, lost sense of security, fear, and anger that understandably follows. They may wish to strike back, once and decisively, to regain their equanimity. In most, this feeling is of short duration and is soon replaced by a more rational and humane approach to recouping their losses and reestablishing their security. But in many it remains, and they derive a certain gratification from seeing criminals brutalized by our penal system. But as we have come to know, the inevitable result of this littleness of mind is the recidivism of most offenders, a burgeoning crime rate, and the victimization of more and more innocent citizens. The new victims are usually someone else about whom we seldom hear, and if we do, it often makes our vengeful self-indulgence seem justified.

Another thing that makes us cling to present priorities is that occasionally someone is actually deterred or rehabilitated. We read of "The Birdman of Alcatraz," or this or that pusher who is now into drug counseling, or we hear of many who are "born again" in their prison cells and giving testimony on television. This happens just often enough to keep most of our hopes up that sooner or later we might just get things right using the old schemes. Forgotten are the thousands who are dehumanized day to day as we glory in the one who has met our expectations.

CONCLUSION

We who have come around to restitution think that most people have too much natural good sense to be forever blinded by our institutions or satisfied with the one success in thousands of tries. We are also in possession of an alternative whose purpose, priorities, and justification should by this time be clear. More strongly, you should now be equipped with a fairly complete answer to the question why we should abandon all the other justifications and proposed central goals of punishment and adopt restitution instead. Now we must address the question of methods for obtaining these purposes and implementing these priorities. We must provide you with a fairly complete idea of how to implement a restitutionary criminal justice system concretely and practically, so that those who might properly demand constructive plans and practical routines will not be disappointed.

NOTES

1. J. Rawls, *A Theory of Justice* (Cambridge, Mass.: Harvard University Press, 1971), pp. 17-22.

2. See for example, C. E. Curran, *Contemporary Problems in Moral Theology* (Notre Dame, Ind.: Fides Publishers, 1970), especially pp. 225-226.

3. J. Maritain, *Science and Wisdom* (New York: Charles Scribner's Sons, 1940); also by the same author, *The Rights of Man and Natural Law* (New York: Charles Scribner's Sons, 1943).

4. This term is taken from J. Fletcher, *Situation Ethics* (Philadelphia: Westminster Press, 1966), p. 31.

5. P. Ramsey, *Deeds and Rules in Christian Ethics* (New York: Charles Scribner's Sons, 1967), p. 15.

6. Ibid.

7. J. Fletcher, *Moral Responsibility: Situation Ethics at Work* (Philadelphia: Westminster Press, 1967), p. 15.

8. Fletcher, *Situation Ethics*, p. 17.

9. Curran, *Problems in Moral Theology*, pp. 228-229.

10. *The Book of Discipline of the United Methodist Church 1972*, (Nashville, Tenn.: The United Methodist Publishing House, 1973), pp. 95-96.

11. See for example, E. Brunner, *Justice and the Social Order* (New York: Harper and Brothers, 1945), p. 223; A. Dewolff, "From Retribution to Prevention and Social Restoration," *The Jurist* 33 (Winter 1973), 25-48.

12. H. Schrey, H. H. Walz, and W. A. Waterhouse, *The Biblical Doctrine of Justice and Law* (London: SCM Press, 1955), p. 195.

13. J. Ellug, *Violence: Reflections From a Christian Perspective* (New York: Seabury Press, 1969), p. 174.

14. Ramsey, *Rules in Christian Ethics*, pp. 15-16.

15. Rawls, *A Theory of Justice*. p. 302.

16. J. Sellers, *Theological Ethics* (New York: Macmillan, 1966), pp. 133-134.

17. *The Book of Discipline of the United Methodist Church 1972*, p. 95.

18. Though our present system does provide civil remedies for crime, from the victim's point of view they are more form than substance. Often criminals are "judgment proof," and the expense and delay involved in pursuing civil remedies are more often than not beyond the average citizen.

19. A. Goldberg, "Equality and Governmental Actions," *New York University Law Review* 39 (1964), 205.

20. See, for example, S. Griffin, "Rape: The All American Crime," in *Issues in Feminism*, S. Ruth (ed.) (Boston: Houghton Mifflin Co., 1980), p. 300.

21. See, for example, Kate Millett, "Theory of Sexual Politics," in *Issues in Feminism*, S. Ruth (ed.) p. 524. See also S. Griffin, "Rape: The All American Crime."

22. See, for example, H. S. Becker, *Outsiders: Studies in the Sociology of Deviance* (New York: Free Press, 1963), esp. Chs. 7 and 8.

23. See A. T. Turk, *Criminality and Legal Order* (Chicago: Rand McNally, 1969), pp. 47-48; J. H. Skolnick, *The Politics of Protest* (New York: Simon and Schuster, 1969), pp. 323-324; I. Horowitz and M. Liebowitz, "Social Deviance and Political Marginality: Toward a Redefinition of the Relationship Between Sociology and Politics," *Social Problems* 15 (Winter 1968), pp. 280-296.

24. See J. R. Gusfield, *Symbolic Crusade* (Urbana, Ill.: University of Illinois Press, 1963).

25. R. M. Williams, *American Society* (New York: Knopf, 1970), p. 421.

26. For more in-depth discussions of these problems and this dynamic, see H. L. Packer, *The Limits of Criminal Sanction* (Stanford, Calif.: Stanford University Press, 1968); E. M. Schur, *Our Criminal Society* (Englewood Cliffs, N.J.: Prentice-Hall, 1969), and his *Crimes Without Victims* (Englewood Cliffs, N.J.: Prentice-Hall, 1965).

27. See, e.g., J. H. Hertz (ed.), *The Pentateuch and Haf Torahs* (New York: Metzudah Publishing Co., 1941).

28. I. J. Kazis in Manachem Kellner (ed.), *Contemporary Jewish Ethics* (New York: Sanhedrin Press, 1978), pp. 309-327.

29. Hertz, *The Pentateuch*.

30. Jacob Neusner, *The Way of Torah* (North Scituate, Mass.: Duxbury Press, 1979).

31. See Hertz, *The Pentateuch*; also, *Encyclopedia Judaica* (New York: Macmillan Publishing Co., 1971), vol. 13, p. 1386.

32. Neusner, *Way of Torah*, pp. 62-63.

33. Erwin Rosenthal (ed.), *Judaism and Christianity* (London: The Sheldon Press, 1938).

34. See H. Cohn, *Jewish Law in Ancient and Modern Israel* (New York: KTAV Publishing House, 1971), p. 75.

35. *Bava Kama* 5:4.

36. B. Blanchard, *Reason and Goodness* (New York: Macmillan Co., 1961), p. 311.

37. J. Dewey and J. H. Tufts, *Ethics* (New York: Henry Holt and Co., 1910), p. 414.

38. P. Bertocci and M. Millard, *Personality and the Good* (New York: David McKay, 1963), p. 316.

39. Alan Geruvita in R. B. Brandt (ed.), *Social Justice* (Englewood Cliffs, N.J.: Prentice-Hall, 1962), pp. 125-126.

40. W. Frankena, *Ethics* (Englewood Cliffs, N.J.: Prentice-Hall, 1963), p. 44.

41. P. Weiss, *Man's Freedom* (Carbondale, Ill.: Southern Illinois University Press, 1950), pp. 138, 298-308, and 314.

42. G. Viastos, in Brandt (ed.), *Social Justice*, p. 48.

43. Frankena, *Ethics*, p. 98.

44. J. Dewey, *A Common Faith* (New Haven, Conn.: Yale University Press, 1934), p. 87.

45. Brandt (ed.), *Social Justice*, p. 102.

46. Bertocci, *Personality and the Good*, p. 403.

47. A. Pound, *Jurisprudence* (St. Paul, Minn.: West Publishing, 1959), I, 350.

48. Of course, it may be argued that bringing down inflation might eventually increase employment by producing more demand. But this is really beside the point. Some must suffer unemployment that others might directly benefit. Those who suffer are used as means only. Perhaps they will be reemployed at some later date, but only if certain others have benefited first and then deign to reinvest their benefits in ways that put those people already used as means back in a position they originally held.

49. This classificatory scheme is taken from W. N. Seymour, *Why Justice Fails* (New York: William Morrow Co., 1973), pp. 71-73.

50. See E. H. Sutherland, "White Collar Criminality," in *White Collar Crime*, G. Geis and R. Neier (eds.) (New York: The Free Press, 1977); A. Bequai, *White Collar Crimes: A 20th Century Crisis* (Lexington, Mass.: Lexington Books, 1976).

51. Bequai, *White Collar Crime*, p. 79.

52. Interestingly enough, even the slightest forms of legal advantage seem to produce significant differences in the final outcome of the total process. One fascinating example is the apparent effect of pretrial detention (as opposed to freedom under bail) on the outcome of cases. As reported in J. Eisenstein, *Politics and the Legal Process* (New York: Harper and Row, 1973), pp. 238-242: "Nearly every study of bail practices has found that jailed defendants are more likely to be convicted than defendants out on bail." This effect was found to hold even when investigators controlled for the nature of the crime and first-offender status. This benefit, however, is not distributed equally among defendants. In general, freedom prior to trial depends upon the defendant's ability to convince a bondsman that he is a good financial risk. In effect, then, the benefits of a pretrial release are shifted to the less needy and the burden to the more needy.

53. Chamber of Commerce of the United States, *White Collar Crime* (Washington, D.C.: Chamber of Commerce of the United States, 1974).

54. Ibid.

55. Bequai, *White Collar Crime*, p. 93.

56. Ibid., p. 119.

57. F. Parilin, *Class Inequality and Political Order* (New York: Praeger, 1971), p. 60.

58. Eisenstein, *Politics and the Legal Process*, p. 323. Eisenstein does a fair job of documenting this claim throughout parts IV and V of his book. For single case examples, Seymour, *Why Justice Fails*, is good, and for a combination of overly general statistics and overly specific examples, Bequai, *White Collar Crime*, is interesting.

59. In fact many enforcement agencies positively discourage complaint of the white-collar variety and may even take reprisal against persistent victims. Seymour, *Why Justice Fails*, reports many individual cases where complaints about requested bribes resulted in "teams of inspectors" swarming all over every public aspect of a complainant's life. See especially Ch. 11, "The Individual, Government and the Courts."

60. H. Oppenheimer, *The Rationale of Punishment* (Montclair, N.J.: Patterson-Smith, 1975), p. 148.

61. Ibid., p. 149.

62. Bequai, *White Collar Crime*, p. 3.

63. Ibid., p. 6.

64. Ibid.

65. See any of the following. A. McLaughlin, *The Confederation and the Constitution* (New York: Collier Paperbacks, 1962); C. A. Beard, *An Economic Interpretation of the Constitution of the United States* (New York: The Free Press, 1941); M. Jensen, *The Articles of Confederation* (Madison, Wisc.: University of Wisconsin Press, 1940); R. A. Watson, *Promise and Performance of American Democracy* (New York: Wiley, 1978).

66. For a rather good discussions on the whole C. A. Beard question, see: A. H. Kelly and W. A. Harbison, *The American Constitution: Its Origin and Development* (New York: Norton, 1976); C. Rossiter, *Seedtime of the Republic* (New York: Harcourt, Brace, 1953); R. E. Brown, *Charles Beard and the Constitution* (New York: Norton, 1956); F. McDonald, *We the People: The Economic Origins of the Constitution* (Chicago: University of Chicago Press, 1958).

PART II
IMPLEMENTING RESTITUTION

Introduction:
The Restitutionary Model

By now you should know exactly what restitution is, why we are advocating it, and how it meets the common objections to punishment raised by deterrence, retribution, and rehabilitation. We can now settle down to an examination of restitution in practice. To begin with, restitution requires changes both in the way our courts behave in doling out punishments, and in the way our penal system behaves in supervising the punishment. Thus, we must provide individual models of both. Before doing so, however, we would like to summarize briefly the central elements of a restitutionary model from which both the model court and the model penal system must derive if they are to remain true to restitutionary goals.

First, for punishment to be "just," it must be individualized, not just in terms of the offender but in terms of the entire context and impact of the criminal act. It must fit not only the criminal or the crime, but the social and individual needs created by the offense. At the same time it cannot be indeterminate. Criminals must know exactly what is required of them to put right what they set askew, and the rest of us must know exactly what we're getting in recompense for our injury.

Second, the principle of damage done and not that of moral turpitude or individualized treatment or deterrence should regulate the sentence an offender receives. We must do this to the best of our human ability, understanding that monetary awards will often be a poor recompense. The question of what damage was done must have recourse to proof by victims first, but the interests indirectly affected should also be considered (within a "scope of the risk" limitation as already explained).

Third, the nature and duration of sentences should depend upon both what offenders are capable of doing to earn the money they owe and how long it actually takes them to do so. Nothing like "determinate sentencing" or "flat" sentences or legislatively fixed ranges of sentences is *apropos*. Judicial discretion in sentencing will be regulated by a good-faith inquiry into the damage done. Judges should be required to set down the rationale and basis for their particular awards as part of the trial record, and appeals should be allowed on the basis of that record.

Fourth, prison sentences should be the exception and not the rule. The deprivation of liberty should be a last resort. Perhaps they should be restricted to those guilty of repeated violent offenses or those we have some other honest reason to believe are dangerous to the person of others. The duration of the prison term should be limited to that time necessary to earn sufficient funds to repay both the damage done and the cost of the prison stay.

Fifth, prisons should be a place from which restitution can be made. Prison environments must evolve toward performing some industrial, agricultural, or professional function for society, and income should come from selling some product or service to a community. No suffering or coercion beyond the loss of liberty or being made to work can be legitimate under these circumstances. Offenders should have the maximum number of constitutional rights enjoyed by the general population and consistent with a prison environment (i.e., living, eating, sleeping, and taking amusement together in a mass whose individuals are required to remain together in a restricted area). Sanctions necessary to keep order should be applied only after the principles of due process have been observed.

And, finally, most restitution should involve supervision outside the prison and within the community. This is the way most consistent with the goals of the restitutionary approach as taken from Christian, Jewish, and secular ethics and from our understanding of justice according to merit, equality, and need. Along this line, voluntary rehabilitation programs should continue, but, of course, they should have no influence on the duration of an offender's sentence. Nor should they affect how long an offender continues to make restitution in a prison setting. We must remember that sending an offender to prison is reserved for the very dangerous. The decision to imprison, therefore, should not be conditional or subject to subsequent conditions. Nor should the promise of freedom be available as a tool to manipulate the behavior of criminals in a prison setting. This leads, as we have seen, to much abuse by prison officials and diverts attention from the primary purpose of a restitutionary prison environment.

Much of this is very vague from a practical point of view. How can we figure out exactly whose interests or needs were so damaged by a criminal act as to deserve recompense? How exactly do we determine the damage done and translate that into money? What if a victim needs recompense immediately and will suffer irremediable damages if he or she must wait for an offender's payment to trickle in once the offender is sentenced? Exactly what is a "productive prison environment"? How can we see to it that offenders make restitution while in the community? These are the very practical questions that we can effectively address now that we know what we should be doing. In addition to these concerns you will find other matters constantly on the minds of people anxious about leaving our present way of doing things behind. You will constantly be asked, for example, what about murderers? What about people who simply refuse to make restitution? What about class differences in earning power; won't that unfairly affect the length of sentences? Can't the rich just buy their way out? How do you punish a corporation as opposed to an individual? And why should the government provide jobs for criminals while the rest of us must fend for ourselves? So, after we address the very practical questions on the nature of restitutionary courts, how they will determine who gets restitution, and how you set up a restitutionary penal system, we will take each of these last questions in turn and try to satisfy those who think restitution will turn our world upside down and upset all our institutions.

5

The Model Restitutionary Court

Our restitutionary courts differ from traditional criminal courts in two very important respects: First, they allow for different defenses at the trial stage; second, the sentences they dole out are vastly different. Beyond this, the restitutionary model is actually quite similar to that of today's courts. Existing crimes would not change but would remain the same. That is, the definitional exercises for establishing what is to be called a crime would remain a societal effort exercised through legislatures. Nor would restitutionary courts change in any fundamental way the criminal process prior to the sentencing stage. The burden of proof would remain what it is and where it is. The rules of evidence, the Exclusionary Rule, the right against self-incrimination, and all other due process guarantees would remain in place. Those values which speak to efficiency in the repression of criminal conduct (e.g., rapid apprehension and trial of criminal offenders) would certainly retain a lofty place in the system, as would guarantees against cruel and unusual punishment and the rights to appeals.

But during the two stages the restitutionary court clearly sets itself apart and becomes established as a significant alternative to existing criminal courts. There, the restitutionary approach becomes a viable moral response to the contemporary crisis existing in our criminal justice system, a crisis of crowded prisons, recidivism caused by increasing alienation from society, and the socialization of offenders into a criminal life-style.

First, let us take a look at sentencing. For the most part, traditional criminal courts do not concern themselves directly with the issue of how their sentences immediately distribute to the people involved the benefits and burdens of the particular criminal act they are judging. Rather, courts to a great extent address themselves only to the broad and speculative effects their sentencing may have (such as "protecting society," "setting an example," or seeing that "justice" is served). Fairness toward the accused is defined in terms of applying a ready-made balance of social interests (rules and policies) to evaluate his or her behavior. Consequently, the criminal courts have a very restricted role in defining or affecting the public welfare. To the extent a criminal case might do so at all, it would be through an appeal to higher courts on the grounds that government officials acted in a socially undesirable way. Most appeals, however, focus on the accuracy, efficiency, or fairness of the finding with regard to the accused and not the specific social interests affected by either the crime or the lower court's ruling (except, again, in the broadest social terms such as general deterrence). It is specifically at this point that the restitutionary model differs dramatically from that of traditional criminal courts. While the values of accuracy, efficiency, and fairness still count heavily, the final focus of the court at the sentencing stage (where the full impact of substantive justice comes into being) is broadened to include an interest in the particular social context of the case before it, specifically the interests of victims and their families, the interests of society, and the interests of the families of convicted offenders. In this way criminal courts seek to affect public welfare directly and immediately by seeing to the welfare of those involved in the specific context before them.

In reaching this substantive end, restitutionary courts will necessarily be open to new and creative defenses; defendants, for example, might claim that certain factors in the context of their situation mitigate the damages done or even entitle them to some damages as well. We will provide specific examples of how this might work in just a minute. Suffice it to say now that the sentencing stage will become, in effect, a total consideration of all interests involved in a particular context in order to decide exactly what the proper distribution of benefits and burdens should be according to the ethical criteria and priorities we have already described. Thus, under our model, a restitutionary court will be "impact oriented" in a way unfamiliar to the traditional criminal court. But we must remember that under this scheme justice as we understand it can only be done if criminal courts act as truly neutral arbiters. How they can be truly neutral is what we must discuss next, and it depends upon how they (1) go about the business of adjusting interests, (2) specify the range of interests legally adjustable, and (3) pursue and facilitate "public policy," while at the same time doing justice to the particular individuals involved in particular criminal cases.

ADJUSTING INTERESTS

There are three things that courts might reasonably do to "adjust interests." First, they might simply explicate, reinforce, and validate preexisting balances or accommodations of interests already worked out through other social, economic, or political mechanisms. This way of doing things comports best with the classical view of courts in which they simply apply established rules (already worked out relationships among interests) to specific fact situations. Second, courts might become engaged in the practice of striking an acceptable balance in situations where both harmony and balance are absent and recognizable interests are in conflict. This view comports best with the view of courts as policy-making and facilitating bodies. Finally, the "adjustment of interests" might involve the task of identifying interests that the parties do not explicitly bring to their attention (and perhaps do not even realize are involved), and drawing them into some balance or harmony with the interests at contest in the trial. This is most consistent with the view of courts as "activists." Activist courts would differ in degree from courts as policy makers or facilitators in that they might initiate interests into the contest of interests, rather than merely adjusting interests presented to them by contending parties or revealed to them as preexisting in the larger social context.[1]

Ideally, of course, courts should do all three. It would be hoped that courts might facilitate policy with enough sensitivity to accommodate (1) established interests, (2) overt contending interests, and (3) unrecognized but nevertheless real interests likely to surface sooner or later in some troublesome manner if left unheeded. But "activist" approaches threaten both overreach and speculation in concrete situations with little that can be done practically by way of safeguard. For this reason, we are suggesting that the role of restitutionary courts as neutral arbiters is one of "adjusting interests" in the first and second senses outlined above. What distinguishes courts from legislatures and administrative agencies is that this adjusting is done on a situation-by-situation basis with attention being paid to the specific needs of the individuals affected.

What distinguishes criminal courts from civil courts is the intense interest the state has in seeing a proper balance struck. As we have said before, the interests involved are too weighty to be left to private bargaining.

Our criminal law already both embodies certain established interests and enforces a particular balance among them, and the violation of those interests constitutes a "crime." But interests not presently thrown into the balance include those of the victims, their immediate families, and the immediate families of offenders. These interests are recognizable and often pressed, but not usually accommodated in courts acting as agents of retribution, deterrence, or reformation. These will be the most pressing concerns of our restitutionary court at the sentencing stage.

DETERMINING THE RANGE OF INTERESTS TO BE CONSIDERED

Given that the purpose of courts during the trial is to accommodate and adjust established and contending interests as just delineated, we still don't know which established and contending interests should be cognizable at law. Roscoe Pound defines an interest to be given legal recognition as "A demand or desire which human being either individually or in groups seek to satisfy, of which, therefore, the ordering of human relations in civilized society must take into account."[2] The idea, in short, seems to be that any point pressed upon a court must be considered a valid interest to accommodate if at all possible. Probably this is the only sensible way to proceed in accommodation, as all interests (social, political, economic, and individual) are so mutually intertwined from their origins to their consequences that the selection of any set of interests on the basis of any particular classification scheme must arbitrarily frustrate numerous equally valid interests and claims. Interests might be grouped, for example, according to how they arise, or what problems they create, or how they have traditionally been handled. The truth is that there are no sufficient conditions for identifying a legal interest. Those that are recognized may have cross-cutting similarities or "family resemblances," but their recognition depends not so much on these similarities as on what the court perceives as its purpose or function.

To fulfill their purpose as both neutral arbiters of restitutionary needs and policy facilitators, restitutionary criminal courts must engage in a continuing process of interest definition and redefinition using the following criteria for guidelines:

1. Which interests are seriously being pressed as needs or strong desires of truly interested or affected individuals or groups?
2. Are there effective legal tools (concepts, principles, or procedures) available for expansion, construction, or other manipulation in recognizing an interest and providing a remedy?
3. Are there any practical (economic, political, social, or even physical) limitations on effectively carrying out the recognition of these interests?
4. To what extent will the recognition and satisfaction of any interest meet with opposition from other significant political, economic, or social interests?

The important point is that "legal interests" must be "built up" on a context-by-context basis rather than defined through a set of abstract conditions used as a yardstick to measure competing claims. Under the restitutionary model, the court will approach each case with the explicit understanding that subject to the limitations just mentioned, no particular interests or sets of interests are inherently superior, and that all are deserving of consideration by the simple fact that they are seriously pressed upon the court: "Any desire . . . makes itself valid by the fact that it exists at all . . . *the essence of good is simply to satisfy demand* . . . must not the guiding principle for ethical philosophy be to satisfy at all times *as many demands as we can.*"[3]

All of this is not to deny that there may be some very important "interests" frustrated by both the legal order and society itself because of some fundamental assumptions about the way things are ("paradigms," "world views," or "cognitive templates"). Insofar as the values and value priorities derived from these very deep orientations are reflected in the legal and social orders, it may be difficult for other "interests" even to reach awareness. The idea of a right to welfare payments, for example, was hardly cognizable in America, even to those who might have such a right, prior to the last half of this century. For such an interest to become cognizable, changes in fundamental ideas about the nature and function of government and the relationship of government to private wealth (e.g., Keynes as opposed to Adam Smith) were necessary. Additionally, ideas of "property," "liberty," "wealth," "entitlement," and "equal protection" had to be reformulated and made consistent with each other and other concepts and values.[4] Prior to these changes, an interest might be at most felt but not capable of articulation. For our purposes, however, such felt but not articulate interests are thought to be beyond the competency of courts to reify and balance with more expressible interests. Once interests are articulated, however, it is our position that it is the court's responsibility to try to provide them a proper hearing; procedures for the adequate expression of those interests must be provided. Such interests should not remain unconsidered only because legal procedures and definitions have structured them out.

There is, however, a significant problem in recognizing all articulated demands. A tension cannot help but develop between openness and integrity. There is a very real possibility that as courts open themselves up to more and more claims, and flexibly adapt their rules and procedures, an unguided adaptation to events and pressures will result. At the extreme, a rampant instrumentalism and opportunism could develop. Courts might then lose their capacity to command obedience and moderate the use of power (political, economic, social, or even physical).

A very obvious example of this in the criminal law is the practice of plea bargaining. Through plea bargaining courts opened themselves to considerations of interests in addition to those of the social interests in crime control and justice. The interests balanced in that practice include those of the prosecutor (his or her conviction rate), the defense attorney (his or her ability to ''represent'' the client effectively), the court system (efficient disposition of cases), and arguably the public (an offender does get *some* punishment).[5]

The usual justification for plea bargaining, of course, is that without plea bargaining the heavy caseloads that our courts must bear would make any efficient handling of cases impossible.[6] Consequently, it is argued, many trials would be delayed extensively and convictions would drop (due both to the difficulty of preserving evidence—e.g., witnesses' memories, etc.—and the loss of a potent tool for inducing guilty pleas from those against whom the evidence is of questionable sufficiency).

The problem as we see it is not that interests are being balanced (or even that some of those interests are individual rather than social interests) but that the interests central to the purpose of criminal courts are subordinated to what should be more peripheral concerns. The argument from necessity holds this inevitable. But there are a number of studies indicating that caseload is unrelated to the frequency of plea bargaining.[7] Instead, these studies indicate that plea bargaining is a function of (1) "the belief that (specific) disputes settled (immediately) through negotiations and/or pleas of guilty provide mutually advantageous benefits for all involved parties,"[8] (2) the belief that it is in the long-term interest of prosecutors, defense counsel, and judges to work together as a team,[9] and (3) the fact that everyone in the criminal system from judges to janitors is "interested in getting through the calendar as quickly as possible so that they can leave the courtroom for the day. If the calendar is completed by noon, many of them can leave and go home. For others the incentive is not to go home but to get back to an office and other work.[10]

By taking the opportunity to use individual defendants to everyone's advantage, however (i.e., by opening itself to the consideration of all these interests), courts have lessened respect for the criminal law among the public, professionals, and criminals alike.[11] Consider, for example, some of the undesirable side effects that have been identified so far. First, the weaker the evidence against an individual offender, the greater the pressure to plead guilty.[12] Second, blatantly illegal acts by officials are often "covered up" by offering attractive bargains to defendants whose rights were violated.[13] Finally, legal guilt is determined more by an adversarial examination of the case's merits.[14] Each of these strikes at certain fundamental ideas of justice and fairness most of us understand as basic to our legal order. Clearly the integrity of the legal system and the courts is lessened by this practice.

On the other hand, court integrity might also be lessened should it refuse to take certain interests into consideration, that is, should it be too exclusive in what it considers and tries to adjust. Consider, for example, the trial of Dennis Banks and Russell Means, two leaders of the American Indian Movement who engineered the takeover at Wounded Knee. Both were charged with burglary, assault on FBI agents, obstructing federal officials, unlawful possession of firearms, and conspiracy. The assistant U.S. attorney prosecuting the case successfully sought to limit consideration to these acts alone. That is, he sought to secure only the public interest in private property, the authority of federal agents, the public peace, and the orderly processing of disputes. As he said:

I don't care and it doesn't make any difference if conditions on the Pine Ridge Reservation are good or bad. Conditions everywhere should be improved....
I don't care if the 1868 treaty was violated or was not violated by the United

States. In our society we have methods and means of redress. Primarily there are two. There is the courts, and there is the ballot box ... if people in their vigor can inflict violence, then a system of democracy cannot exist, it is anarchy.[15]

However, it was the honest perception of the American Indian Movement that they had been effectively cut off from normal means of seeking redress. Treaty commitments had been violated by the federal government, local government was hostile, the Bureau of Indian Affairs had been unresponsive, and even the Tribal Council was dominated by those whose interests were tied to the federal government. In short, Russell and Banks argued that the interests of most Indians were simply unrepresented in and by the existing political structure. In effect, they had been structured into technically criminal acts if they were to have their interests addressed at all. Consequently, the courts, a coequal branch of government, were now being asked to act. To continue ignoring the foundations and motivations of the Indian behavior at Wounded Knee would, in effect, balance and adjust nothing. Nor would it facilitate the smooth and efficient pursuit of public policy. For many, the court's integrity would necessarily be lessened by its failure to engage the interests that were then overtly contending.

Courts, then, are faced with a dilemma regarding the recognition of interests. Both recognition of too many or too few, and recognition of the wrong kinds, can lead to a breakdown in court integrity. The solution perhaps lies in a firm grasp of court purpose. A clear idea of purpose can set standards and orient courts in difficult and complex cases. Purpose thus allows for both openness and integrity. Given purpose, established interests, their priorities, and their balances can be criticized. Courts are thus open to change. On the other hand, interests tangential to the purposes of courts can be put into perspective. Regarding plea bargaining, for example, it is convincing to argue that it is not within the scope of a court's purpose to make prosecutors or defense counsel look good. What's left is legitimate interests in punishing criminals. Balancing these two, we see that the point of purpose of institutional efficiency is to further the ability of courts to punish criminals effectively and protect society. Neither efficiency for efficiency's sake nor efficiency as a primary goal can, consequently, be justified.

By defining punishment in restitutionary terms, of course, we specify a purpose. Courts are, as far as humanly possible, to make whole those who are injured by a criminal act. Restitutionary criminal justice is, as previously pointed out, result oriented and not indifferent to the social and individual impacts of its rulings. Plea bargaining as presently practiced does not address itself to this purpose. Similarly, were we to ask who was harmed by the acts of the Indians at Wounded Knee, we can argue persuasively that while the federal government and its agents did realize some loss, the acts of the governmental agents in attempting to deny the Indians their only recourse in gaining a hearing for their interests also caused damage. Moreover, the damage caused by federal agents was arguably more serious than that caused by the Indians. The activities of federal agents in such situations can be understood to threaten some very important democratic values.

Let us take a closer look at this for a moment because it makes clear what sorts of new defenses are available in some kinds of criminal trials under a restitutionary approach that is more open to considering overtly contending interests. Now, the Indians at Wounded Knee were of course engaged in civil disobedience. Civil disobedience is an act addressed to those holding political power which is guided by the idea and directed at the purpose of preserving the Constitution and our political institutions from what is understood to be a threat from those holding positions of authority in those institutions and under that Constitution.[16] As Rawls indicates:

Civil disobedience ... is one of the stabilizing devices of a constitutional system, although by definition an illegal one ... by resisting injustice within the limits of fidelity to law, it serves to inhibit departures from justice and to correct them when they occur.[17]

Seen in this light, police action against those engaged in civil disobedience does damage not only to the rights and interests of protestors but to the constitutional system itself.

This argument of course makes certain important assumptions. It makes the assumption, first of all, that the acts of civil disobedience are honestly sought, appropriate objects of civil disobedience, and that this is clear or should be clear to police and public officials: "If one views such disobedience as a political act addressed to the justice of the community, then it seems reasonable ... to limit it to instances of substantial and clear injustice."[18] Secondly, it assumes that normal legal means of redress have failed and all reasonable options have been exhausted. Finally, the argument assumes that the civil disobedience does not threaten the ultimate integrity of the state, that is, that disobedience will not lead to a breakdown of legitimate authority (though it may affect those in authority) and the ability of political institutions to respond to and deal with the situation, hopefully to everyone's benefit.

Given these constraints, however, it does seem that civil disobedience is a legitimate and perhaps necessary form of political participation, the denial of which should constitute a redressable injury. This, then, is one kind of novel defense opened to offenders by a restitutionary approach. In the case of the Indians at Wounded Knee, each of these constraints was apparently met. The court's failure to take this into account arguably removed it from the role of neutral arbiter and placed it squarely on the side of one wrongdoer over another. Not only did the court fail to accommodate all directly involved interests, but it can hardly be said to have contributed to the smooth functioning of society. The result of such a decision necessarily increases animosity and feelings of alienation. As one witness at the trial of Banks and Means put it, "I would say that this was not the beginning of a war between the United States Government and the Indians. We've been at war with the Government all our lives."[19] This attitude clearly stemmed from the frustrations with local, federal, and state officials that the Indians experienced in trying to have their interests accommodated and which eventually led to their lawbreaking. Thus the time was ripe and the situation appropriate for court action to mitigate this frustration and establish (or work toward establishing) a workable balance of interests among the various levels of government involved and the Indians. Had the court kept these purposes clearly in mind, such failures might well have been avoided.

Many criminal courts do, in fact, keep these purposes clearly in mind, and we have several well-publicized instances of this. The Daniel Ellsburg "Pentagon Papers" trial was an excellent example. Ellsburg's activity in leaking classified documents on Vietnam may well have caused damage to the war effort. The behavior of government officials in attempting to discredit Ellsburg publicly, however, damaged not only Ellsburg's reputation but the constitutional foundation of our government. Moreover, it contributed to a growing disrespect for the executive branch. Finding that the government had in fact engineered and executed a burglary of Ellsburg's psychiatrist's office in an attempt to procure damaging information to be made public, the court dismissed the government's case.[20]

In balancing the interests involved the court placed itself in the role of neutral arbiter between the claims of Ellsburg that he did the morally correct thing and the claims of government that he did not. This was a clear case of two conflicting needs (the people's need to know about how their government is conducting a war and the government's need for some reasonable degree of secrecy in the conduct of war), neither of which we can reject out of hand or prioritize out of context. But thrown into this balance was the fact that the government, in pursuit of its needs, threatened the ultimate justification of the war effort; the preservation of a certain way of life guaranteeing individual rights and freedom was threatened. Condoning such action would necessarily have disrupted the functioning of such a society and would possibly have contributed to a change in its nature. Understanding its purpose of balancing and prioritizing such claims in specific context, and working to preserve the proper functioning of society according to the principles of individual rights, the Ellsburg court was guided in a highly complex situation to what we can recognize as an equitable resolution of the case.

RESTITUTIONARY COURTS AND PUBLIC POLICY

The model of the restitutionary court we have outlined so far is essentially that of a day-to-day arbiter among interests promoting the smooth functioning of society and the pursuit of public policy. However, "public policy," "law," and "individual interests" are often understood as three distinct and often contradictory things. Argument usually centers around the extent to which courts are bound to follow "settled rules of public policy" and neither act creatively nor legislate interstitially. Additionally there are controversies over whether public policy should preclude the operation of certain laws in particular cases and the extent to which it must prevail over the interests and desires of individual members of a society in various situations. Roscoe Pound argues, for example, that public policy concerning the general security of the social group, its institutions, its corporate mentality, and the conservation of its social resources must all take precedence over public policies addressing social interests in individual life.[21] Individual interests, to gain recognition and effect, must be expressed in terms of one of the public interests just mentioned, about which there is either a settled public policy courts follow, or an attempt by the court to harmonize and adjust overlapping and conflicting claims and demands.[22] Though Pound speaks of courts as arbiters, "public policies" and "individual interests" are quite distinct. Similarly, critics of the Warren Court have argued that subordinating doctrine to the achievement of desired individual outcomes demonstrates an "interest-voting" philosophy casting doubt on whether there is or can be any substance to the distinction between law and politics.[23] Thus, for many, there is law, individual interest-voting (politics), and public policy, each distinct and each in potential conflict with the others.

Consider, however, what we mean when we talk about "following (or obeying) a rule of law" and "following (or obeying) a settled rule of public policy." If we deal with this question conceptually rather than empirically, "what we call 'obeying a rule' is not something that it would be possible for only *one* man to do, and do it only in his life ... it is not possible that there should have been only one occasion on which someone obeyed a rule."[24] Following (or obeying) a rule is a custom, practice, or institution. It presupposes a society. If customs, practices, and institutions disappear, so do "rules" and "following (or obeying) rules." "How does it come about that this arrow *points*? Doesn't it seem to carry in it something besides itself? ... The arrow points only in the application that a living being makes of it."[25]

This can perhaps be more easily seen if we consider what we mean when we say that a court has followed a rule of law (or public policy) even though no rule was formally written prior to the case at hand. "Knowing a rule" does not necessarily involve beginning with a particular formulation of how to act in our heads. When we count, for example, we usually do not begin by saying "all right, the rule is: n, $n + 1, n + 2 \ldots$ " rather we just go "one, two, three." The formal rule may never occur to us. There may be no point (no need) to formalize the practice in a statement about how to proceed. Yet, don't we "know a rule" (know how to count) by knowing how to proceed? When a judge says "we have done *this* in this case, and *this* in another case, and then *this* in a third, hence we should do *this* now because there is the following rule," it does not mean the rule is only just being created. The judge, rather, is reminding us of our practice and in so doing pointing to actions (practices) that are the rule. If, for example, there is only one instance of a practice (one precedent case) to look at, that practice is the rule. The single case "points" (as does the arrow) according to the use made of it by the judge. If, on the other hand, we can find no case (no practice) on the specific issue at hand, we look to our principles (e.g., as laid out in the Constitution) and our social, political, and economic policies to remind us of how we practice generally. These provide a general model or general paradigm for practice in the instant case. Policy and rules of law, then, are fundamentally not two separate things; they are formulations of human social practices.

Again, consider what courts do in deciding which cases are precedents (which cases are "the same" as the one at hand) and thereby "follow the rule of law" or "the settled rules of public policy." It seems that courts do not really mean that there is one essential thing common to them all. There is not really a single set of necessary and sufficient conditions to any set of cases justifying the use of the term "the same." But the cases do *resemble* one another. Rather than necessary and sufficient conditions, "family resemblances" among fact situations and issues (complicated networks of similarities, overlapping and criss-crossing) allow us to call them "the same."[26] How to choose and understand what fact situations and issues count as "the same" is largely a matter of socialization into the paradigms and practice of the legal profession. Written rules of procedure, constitutions (i.e., due process ideas), model precedents (e.g., law school texts), and actual practice in the profession all serve to orient and put limits upon what it is reasonable to distinguish and what can be called "the same." The appeals process can be seen as a method of adjusting the distinctions and similarities drawn in lower courts to an authoritative understanding of the paradigm (a kind of ongoing socialization process providing for resocialization as the paradigm changes). To "follow the rule of law," then, requires all of this complicated social practice, as does determining whether an instant case is "the same" as those usually directed by "settled rule of public policy" that must be adhered to by the courts.

We might say, consequently, that what we mean when we talk about public policy and law being in conflict is that different practices (i.e., different ways of acting) that are supported by different interests are in conflict. Recognizing public policy, according to this understanding, is not something different from accommodating interests. Simply, it is an understanding that certain interests cannot be ignored and that they may necessarily take precedence or be weighted more heavily in the adjustment process.

Much of the argument in favor of a restitutionary approach as so far presented is to the effect that (1) other approaches presently tend to obstruct the realization of publicly announced values and interests, and (2) those values and interests should be more heavily weighted in the criminal justice system in order to seek a more equitable distribution of the benefits and burdens of crime in our society. Seen in this manner there is no conflict between a restitutionary court's role as accommodator and its role as facilitator of public policy. When traditional interests are involved and no new interests muddy the water, courts weigh those interests in context and determine which are predominant according to our past practice, principles, and the particular context in which their conflict arose (thereby facilitating public policy in specific instances). When interests are not settled (the case is unprecedented either in that most of the interests seeking accommodation are new or in that a new interest is challenging a traditional one for priority), there is a basic conflict of interests to be adjusted and the court must act in its role of accommodator.

It should be noted, however, that public policy precedents are no different from any other sort of prior interest adjustment. They must be open to a continuing process of redefinition and reapplication. Extending or evoking public policy in novel situations or curbing it through redefinition so that its scope of application is narrowed are both parts of the conflict and compromise of interests lying behind all practices in the law.

We are now in a position to summarize what it means to be and behave as a restitutionary court of criminal justice. First, restitutionary courts are experimental, accommodating, and facilitative. Their adjustments of overtly contending interests or reinforcement of existing balances are impact oriented experiments meant to be tested again and again in our dynamic, pluralistic society. Inevitably, adjustments made one time must ultimately fail or become irrelevant to new concerns requiring their own adjustments and accommodations.

Secondly, restitutionary courts consider all articulated demands as proper objects of accommodation to the extent that they are seriously pressed, can be accommodated in a practical sense, and are not overwhelmed by considerations of other equally important or more important demands.

Finally, restitutionary courts recognize public policy, law, and individual needs as requiring accommodation and facilitation, and not necessarily involving any conflict in their mutual pursuit. To function as a neutral arbiter, then, courts must function according to these understandings. This is generally how restitutionary courts function equitably.

Of course all of this is still very vague and we now need to give some examples and specify exactly how certain specific types of interests might be balanced and accommodated by the neutral arbiter we have just described. But before taking this up in the next chapter, there is a final difference that we would like to suggest between the present notion of a criminal court and our notion of a restitutionary court. The present notion in criminal law is that an adversary approach best provides for both accuracy and fairness, though certainly not for efficiency. In fact, many studies show that the adversary approach is to a great extent avoided in lower criminal courts for this reason.[27] Our problem is that there are studies indicating that certain rules and procedures of adversary courts discourage wrongdoers from making restitution.

First, relevant legal rules most commonly rest on some aspects of "fault."[28] The problem here is that while fault is commonly a judgment based on the "beyond a reasonable doubt" standard, it is often defined in terms only of immediate intention and overt behavior. Thus, the processes and structures (social forces, rules, and institutions) that may have produced the immediate intent and action are ignored. Consequently, defendants come to understand the situation as one of "them against me," rather than one of conflicting social interests. Second, the plea bargaining experience tends to counter the idea that a wrongdoer ought to make good the harm done, stressing a concept of finding the best balance of self-interest possible between a wrongdoer and society (the victim is not considered).[29] A less adversarial and more "problem-solving" approach (such as that suggested above concerning the American Indian Movement) would go a long way toward facilitating a restitutionary goal.

This analysis, of course, makes some assumptions about the nature of crime. Briefly, we assume that many (though not all) crimes are products of the structure of wealth, opportunity, and power in our society. Similarly, we assume that the frequency and nature of the suffering that results from criminal acts are functions of the same structure. This is not to deny that explanations are available and quite correct that place primary responsibility for the criminal act on the wrongdoer. It is only to point out that our social structure creates different problems for individuals differently placed in that structure, provides them with different sorts of opportunities for resolving those problems, and places different constraints on different people in making use of those opportunities.[30] We thus assume that much criminal behavior is not the result of innate greed, brutality, or corruption. But even if these last explanations are the case, considerable evidence suggests that wrongdoers will often exert considerable effort to make restitution if an opportunity is provided,[31] and we cannot argue too strongly that the criminal courts should take advantage of this tendency rather than discourage it.

Finally, even if a particular crime turns out to be the result of a conscious, knowing, and entirely unpressured (socially or psychologically) choice simply to do harm to another for no particular reason, it seems that this fact would simply reduce the interests of the wrongdoer that require balancing. That is, in such a case, none of the concerns that we argued should be balanced in cases like that of the American Indian Movement would be present, and the courts would need to consider only those rights and interests of a wrongdoer that are constitutionally guaranteed.

Now we are not suggesting that criminals should not have the very best of personal counsel looking out for their best interests, nor that the public should have anything less than a vigorous prosecution. We are only suggesting that the very best interests of both society and the offender will probably be better served if criminal justice is not played like a zero-sum game. Both our ethical beliefs and our ideas of merit, equality, and need require something more of us. They require that we seek a benifit-maximizing result, and this is better sought through a problem-solving approach than an adversarial approach.

Of course, a problem-solving, benefit-maximizing court is not necessary to a restitutionary approach; it would probably just work better both practically and ethically. If such a court is just too deviationist for us, restitution will work quite well as part of an adversarial proceeding modified only to the extent that prosecuting attorneys must represent the interests of victims and their families as well as the public in seeking damage awards. Optimally, however, we would like to see courts get beyond the idea that the right thing to do can only be found through some sort of fight. We would like to see an intelligent inquiry into all of the evidence (not just that chosen by attacking and defending partisans), and all of the interests (not just those most likely to prevail in a head-on clash), and all of the context of a suit (not just those elements of a context predetermined by precedent to be relevant), in order to grasp the truth better about a crime and the person committing it, and so to ascertain better exactly what needs to be done in setting things right again.

CONCLUSION

We have now come down to specifying exactly whose interests in what sorts of things deserve to be thrown into the balance of our neutral arbiter and considered for restitution, and the following chapter will go into this in some detail. But let us summarize the points we have made in this chapter about the nature of our restitutionary court:

1. It should be "problem solving" rather than adversarial in method; it should try to solve the problems born of the crime by sentencing individuals to make monetary recompense to those they have injured;

2. In keeping with this problem-solving approach, courts should act as neutral arbiters among conflicting value systems; they should address the damage done by an act and not its intrinsic evil, or its possible deterrent effect, or the rehabilitation of offenders;

3. In keeping with its role of neutral arbiter, all seriously pressed demands of any involved individual or group should be given a hearing as an interest possibly damaged by the criminal act and deserving of monetary recompense.

4. Finally, as neutral arbiter it must consider the possibility that the offender may have been forced into the crime (and so mitigate damages) or might have had *damage done to his or her rights by the ways and means officials used in enforcing the law (and so possibly collect damages).*

Now, we might suggest that this last point could offer an altogether better approach to the problem we face as law enforcement officials trample on individual rights while ferreting out crime and the criminal. Offenders might better be awarded damages for the violation of their rights, and the evidence against them might better be admitted as part of the problem-solving exercise, than to have that evidence excluded. Excluding the evidence and setting an offender free clearly solves none of the problems created by the initial crime even though it is some recompense to the criminal (as we argued earlier) for the crime committed by the law enforcement officials. But we digress. It is time now to get down to brass tacks on who gets exactly what, when, and how under a restitutionary approach.

NOTES

1. The terms "order," "balance," and "harmony" are, of course, used somewhat loosely here. They are meant to refer to those considerations of a proper or balanced distribution of human welfare as defined in Chapter 3 (and to whatever approximation to these ideals we can produce through the accommodation process).

2. R. Pound, *Social Control Through Law* (Hamden, Conn.: Anchor Books, 1965), p. 87.

3. Ibid, p. 102.

4. For two classic articles in this area see C. A. Reich, "The New Property," *Yale Law Journal* 73:733 (1964), and "Individual Rights and Social Welfare," *Yale Law Journal* 74:1245 (1965).

5. A. S. Blumberg, "The Practice of Law as Confidence Game," in *Before the Law*, J. Bonsignore et al. (eds.) (Boston: Houghton Mifflin, 1974), pp. 191-194.

6. See, for example, J. Eisenstein, *Politics and the Legal Process* (New York: Harper and Row, 1973), p. 11.

7. See M. Heumann, "Plea Bargaining Systems and Plea Bargaining Styles: Alternate Patterns of Case Resolution in Criminal Courts," in *American Court Systems*, Samuel Goldman (ed.) (San Francisco: W. H. Freeman, 1978), pp. 105-110; and M. M. Feely, "The Effects of Heavy Caseload," in Goldman (ed.), *American Court Systems*, pp. 110-118.

8. Feely, "The Effects of Heavy Caseloads," p. 117.

9. Eisenstein, *Politics and the Legal Process*, pp. 101-110.

10. Feely, "The Effects of Heavy Caseloads," p. 116.

11. See W. N. Seymour, *Why Justice Fails* (New York: William Morrow Company, 1973), pp. 87-88; and J. Mill, "I Have Nothing to Do with Justice," in *Life Magazine*, March 2, 1972.

12. See A. W. Alschuler, "The Prosecutor's Role in Plea Bargaining," *University of Chicago Law Review* 36:62 (1968).

13. See A. Rosett, "The Negotiated Guilty Pleas," *The Annals of the American Academy of Political Science* 374 (1967), 74.

14. See D. J. Newman, "Pleading Guilty for Considerations: A Study of Bargain Justice," *Journal of Criminal Law, Criminology and Police Sciences* 46 (1956), 790.

15. *U.S. v. Dennis Banks and Russell Means*, 116 Fed. 2d 1128 (1973).

16. See, for example, J. Rawls, *A Theory of Justice* (Cambridge, Mass.: Harvard University Press, 1971), p. 383.

17. Ibid.

18. Ibid., p. 372.

19. Transcript, *U.S. v. Banks and Means*, 116 Fed. 2d 1190 (1973).

20. *U.S. v. Ellsburg*, 97 S. Ct. 1225 (1977).

21. R. Pound, *Criminal Justice in America* (New York: DaCapo Press, 1975), pp. 6-9.

22. Ibid., p. 9.

23. R. Bork, "The Supreme Court Needs a New Philosophy," *Fortune*, December 1968, p. 138.

24. L. Wittgenstein *Philosophical Investigations* (New York: Macmillan, 1968), section 199.

25. Ibid., section 454.

26. Ibid., section 462.

27. See J. Eisenstein, *Politics and the Legal Process* (New York: Harper and Row, 1973), pp. 99-119.

28. R. I. Rabin, "Some Thoughts on Tort Law from a Sociopolitical Perspective," *Wisconsin Law Review* 51-65 (1969).

29. See L. M. Friedman, *Law and the Behavioral Sciences* (Indianapolis, Ind.: Bobbs-Merrill, 1969).

30. See, for example, E. O. Wright, *The Politics of Punishment* (New York: Harper and Row, 1973), pp. 3-21.

31. See Eric Bersheid, "When Does a Harmdoer Compensate a Victim," *Journal of Personality and Social Psychology* 6 (1967), 435-441; T. C. Brock, "Debriefing and Susceptibility to Subsequent Experimental Manipulations," *Journal of Experimental Social Psychology* 2 (1966), 314-323; Allan Gross, "Some Effects of Guilt on Compliance," *Journal of Personality and Social Psychology* 2 (1969), 232-239; James Freedman, "Compliance Without Pressure: The Effect of Guilt," *Journal of Personality and Social Psychology* 7 (1967), 117-124.

6

Who Should Make How Much Restitution To Whom

Given the way we do things in our society, the effects of any single act ripple on indefinitely; problems start many times in places very far removed from the people who experience their effects. Economists are fond of pointing out that it requires the labor of thousands of individuals to produce a single pencil, and should someone in one of the companies involved in the intricate web of pencil production embezzle some funds, then all of us must pay more for our pencils, though we may have no idea that a crime has even been committed (in effect and without ever knowing it, we subsidize the crime and make restitution to the company). But we cannot make restitution to everyone who buys a pencil. It is simply not cost effective to find each injured party and mail him or her a penny. Restitution might better be made directly to the company, which can then repay consumers by lowering their pencil prices or not raising them in the first place.

Unfortunately, all of our problems about who should get restitution and who should make restitution are not quite so simple. Suppose, for example, the criminal act involved is not the act of a single individual but the culmination of a series of acts or decisions (none of which are criminal in themselves) made by a number of individuals over a period of time. This is often the case when corporations pollute. It often requires an extensive and sophisticated investigation to determine exactly how certain forms of pollution occurred, let alone which people were involved (e.g., is the fault for radiation leaks with designers, builders, or users of nuclear reactors? And who in the design or manufacturing or using processes should bear the blame?). Usually, the findings result in suggested changes in manufacturing processes, or changes in waste disposal systems, or changes in industry standards for testing the effects of their production. Since we cannot clamp the blame on any particular individual, we blame the system, and we try to restructure the system so that the people functioning within it cannot contribute to the problem as they have done in the past.

But who is to make restitution? Everyone in the process? This might certainly be an incentive for people to "blow the whistle" on the dangerous practices of their company. But it puts everyone between a rock and a hard place—a catch-22. If they don't report the practice they may be found criminally liable. If they do report the practice, they may lose their jobs, and employers and fellow workers alike have a thousand ways of making life at work unbearable that no court could isolate even if it ordered that whistle blowers could not be fired. Besides, the return from such practice to most people in the process is miniscule. At best they may get increased wages if the practice shifts enough costs to the public to increase the general profit of the corporation; even then it is more likely that the profits will simply increase the return to investors.

In the same way, who is to get restitution for an act like pollution? Some forms of pollution clearly damage immediately adjacent properties, but the effects also ramify throughout the entire ecosystem. Thousands of people end up paying for the manufacture of goods not through increased prices but through a decrease in the quality of their lives. Can we give recompense to these individuals? Can we even find out who they are? Assuming we can determine who is to pay, can we determine to whom the payment should be made?

So, we have some problems, and the ones mentioned are not unique. Who's hurt by "morals offenses"? And who pays for the violation of an offender's rights if, say, prison conditions are found to be "cruel and unusual"? We could go further, but things would only become more burdensome. The fact is that in the abstract things are usually more overwhelming than in practice. We can both elaborate the most intricate of logically possible problems and create the most convoluted of theoretical problems for ourselves by trying to fit particular cases into predetermined categories of who should get how much from whom, but most of the intricacies resolve themselves if we keep our purposes clearly in mind and consider each case on its own actual, concrete merits. This is exactly what we are trying to empower restitutionary courts to do, and the most they will need if so empowered is a general orientation or a general idea of the sorts of things we all feel deserve recompense. They can then decide specific claims by analogy or "family resemblance" to these socially accepted instances of deserved restitution.

Perhaps the simplest way to organize our discussion of what our society generally considers deserving of recompense is to divide the interests involved into three categories: (1) public interests, (2) victim interests, and (3) the interests of wrongdoers. This about covers the field, and now we need specific examples of the kinds of things we should make restitution for and the kinds of people who should do it.

PUBLIC INTERESTS

Perhaps the most highly touted public interest is that in the security (internal and external), integrity, and efficiency of our political institutions. This is the primary interest of the criminal law as presently practiced. It includes keeping the public peace, punishing treason, forbidding nepotism in public office, proscribing the use of public authority for private ends, defrauding the public or its political institutions, and a host of interpersonal dishonest dealings that threaten our political stability should they become widespread. Under our restitutionary approach, restitution for damage done to these interests would be due the public in the person of its political institutions. Payments could be made directly to the public treasury. Instead of money leaving the treasury to support criminals, it would enter the treasury from the labor of criminals to provide paved, lighted, and policed streets and help pay for public utilities.

Another type of interest that presently finds itself under the rubric of "public interest" is the so-called public interest in the general morals. Of course, insofar as this phrase suggests that there are minimal fundamental interests requiring balancing, absent which there would be no point in trying to have a society at all, there is no problem from a restitutionary point of view. "Such rules overlap with basic moral principles vetoing murder, violence and theft; and so we can add to the factual statement that all legal systems in fact coincide with morality at such vital points, the statement that this is, in this sense, necessarily so."[1] Beyond those minimal interests, however, quite well covered by the general public interest in internal security, "The purposes people have for living in society are too conflicting and varying to make possible much extension of the argument that some fuller overlap of legal and moral standards is necessary."[2]

The problem is that a "concern for the general morals" seems quickly to become an attempt to define and delimit sexual practices and relationships (e.g., laws against homosexuality, prostitution, polygamy, "unnatural acts," etc.). Similarly, there is a tendency to try to control individual states of consciousness (e.g., laws prohibiting the use of certain drugs, laws against public drunkenness, laws against selling "obscene" material, etc.). Finally, "concern for the general morals" is often a way of trying to take decisions out of the hands of private citizens and placing them in the hands of governmental institutions regardless of how directly, intimately, and uniquely the individual is affected (e.g., the abortion issue).

In general, a "concern for the general morals" quite often becomes a way of legally denying privacy to certain individuals and thereby intruding into very sensitive and personal areas of individual self-definition and self-determination. In enforcing some concept of public morality beyond the minimum mentioned above, courts cease being neutral arbiters balancing interests in a complex society. Consequently, the responsibleness making them a unique political institution decreases, and the integrity of the courts is ultimately diminished.

We should mention, however, that we might go on being just as obtrusive into individual practices as we are at present and still have restitutionary courts. The most violence we would do would be to the fundamental philosophy of criminal justice from which a restitutionary approach most naturally flows. We could still pursue a restitutionary course in practice while sticking to our old philosophies about enforcing "the public interest in the general morals." We would simply have a theory/practice gap of greater or lesser proportions depending upon how zealously we pursued the enforcement of a public morality.

Now, a theory/practice gap is not a novel approach in criminal justice, but it is not the most productive approach either. If we must have a public morality it seems the public should receive the maximum profit we can possibly derive from it. And if we can't have restitution through the courts because we want our theory and practice to be consistent, there is another way we might get it. An enormous proportion of the offenses that our courts, prisons, and police are entangled with, for example, involve illicit drug trafficking. This trafficking is extremely profitable for two reasons. First, its illegality strains demand and increases price (oddly, then, the more successful we are at limiting the trafficking, the more successful are the traffickers in making a profit). Second, the traffickers take all the money and leave the general public to pay for all the mischief created by users and addicts. Our present criminal justice system, then, helps to redistribute income in a very peculiar fashion: from the law-abiding to the lawbreaker. The solution, of course, is for government to regulate drug traffic, not prohibit it. That way, the profits the public derives from the sale of drugs to addicts and users can be used to compensate for the mischief they cause. It is a form of restitution worked out through the executive branch and its administrative agencies rather than the courts. We mention this here only to demonstrate the versatility of a restitutionary approach and how its extension to other branches of government might relieve the courts of much that is now burdensome. It is a slight digression but we believe a profitable one. We can eliminate our theory/practice gap, control drug traffic, and make a profit all at the same time.

A final set of public interests that would be included in the balancing process under a restitutionary approach does not figure prominently at all in present approaches to criminal justice. These are the public interests in what becomes of both the families of wrongdoers and the wrongdoers themselves after their release from the criminal justice system. Immediate problems revolve about the likelihood that both will end up on the welfare rolls, or that other family members will resort to crime to solve financial problems occasioned by the imprisonment of the offender. There is also the loss to society of a certain amount of productive capacity when offenders lose their jobs and cannot find employment upon release. Finally, there is the problem of encouraging recidivism. Simply releasing a wrongdoer into the same situation that resulted in the original crime is likely to reproduce the experience to society's detriment.

Consequently, these concerns ought to be weighed in the balance when deciding the form and amount of restitution. A certain percentage of a wrongdoer's income might be set aside to support the family and perhaps even to train the wrongdoer for employment after release. Under appropriate circumstances some might even be allocated to welfare agencies taking care of such families or providing such training. Regarding recidivists (as opposed to professional criminals), the problem is often that they cannot make a satisfactory life for themselves outside the regimented structure of prison. Under a restitutionary system recidivists would be productive during their sentences and might develop the requisite habits for better adapting to their freedom. In fact, many might never be reimprisoned, and potential recidivists might never experience prison in the first place. Assuming that the crimes they commit are not overly grave (along the lines of a professional criminal), they may be assigned to a nonprison environment (as we discuss in Chapter 7) to fulfill their restitutionary assignments, thus never having an opportunity to become dependent in the first place. Additionally, an extra fine (up to some maximum) might be placed on recidivists and directed to a restitutionary fund, which will be discussed in more detail later.

VICTIM INTERESTS

The point of repaying the victim is simple. Without law there is no secure liberty. Our present criminal justice system has, in effect, no law relevant to victims; it leaves them as they are, ignoring their plight in its zeal to punish, deter, and rehabilitate. Restitutionary systems provide victim-focused law and therefore address the issue of securing liberty for those whose ability to pursue their social options has been damaged by a criminal act.

Broadly, victims of crimes have interests in their property and in their person. Interests in their person include (1) interests in physical integrity (e.g., immunity from physical impact: assault and battery, rape, murder, manslaughter), (2) interests in physical and mental freedom (e.g., immunity from physical and mental coercion: extortion by physically threatening either the victim or a third party the victim wishes to protect as in kidnapping, false imprisonment), (3) interests in their emotional state, good name, and privacy concerning any "weaknesses" they might have (i.e., immunity from any anxiety, humiliation, embarrassment or invasion of privacy not ordinarily expected in the day-to-day commerce of society), and (4) interests in their general physical and mental health (e.g., immunity from reasonably preventable health hazards resulting from pollution or from being used as an object in experimentation). Any given crime might include a trespass on any or all of these interests. Of course victims, like all members of society, have personal interests in the general peace and order, the general safety, and the efficient functioning of the economic and political systems as well. But these interests are collectively looked after by the government as a whole. Damage to these interests is, in this sense, done to the public as a whole and falls under the public interests described above.

Victims of crime should be awarded restitution for the violation of each of these interests and any reasonable collateral medical, surgical, nursing, and hospital expenses. Similarly, in cases of murder or manslaughter, direct injury is experienced by the victim's family through loss of a member. This family should, therefore, be allowed restitution both for the loss itself and for collateral losses such as funeral expenses, expected monetary contributions to the family by the lost member, the family's grief and emotional distress, and any medical expenses they might pay or the victim's estate might lose (e.g., in case of non-instantaneous death).

Property interests of victims include (1) earnings and earning capacity, (2) interests in any depreciation of property value caused by the crime, (3) any loss of use of the property or repairs necessary to make it useful, and (4) any nonpecuniary (sentimental) value the property might have. As in the case of damage to the person, reasonable collateral expenses should be included in the restitution.

This is all straightforward enough. The problem comes in trying to decide exactly who is actually a victim. Remember, in keeping with their roles as neutral arbiters restitutionary courts cannot reject any claim of damaged interests out of hand. This raises problems of both how small and how remote an injury might be before it does not deserve recompense.

Now, the purpose of criminal law as we defined it in our introduction is to preserve and secure the stable functioning of society against threats so direct, fundamental, or dangerous that their control cannot be left to the vagaries of private power. As far as individual victims are concerned, then, we are talking about making restitution to those whose fundamental personal interests are directly threatened in a dangerous manner. Moreover, these threats to the individual must be of such a nature that if left unchecked by the power of the state, they would produce such widespread damage that the state itself would ultimately suffer. Nothing less must be expected to mobilize the coercive power of our state against the individual. Consequently, trifling damages or damage to one's "aesthetic sensibilities" usually would not be given restitution, and indeed, behavior resulting in such damages would not be criminal. This, of course, implies that many misdemeanors should be shifted out of the criminal law jurisdiction and into the jurisdiction of administrative law.

Traffic control, for example, could be shifted to an administrative agency, which could perform all the functions police now perform. Many resources of the police could thereby be released to concentrate on felonies, particularly in the white-collar and corporate crime area.

What is required, then, is that for each case, the judge must decide what sorts of interests are arguably within the zone of interests the law intends to protect when it defines certain behaviors as criminal. This definition of a zone is, of course, subject to the court's power to protect other interests in accordance with the needs of justice. It is very possible that an individual might be injured as a very natural and direct result of criminal behavior but in a way unforeseen by the legislature. So we must add to our ''zone'' test the caveat that any person fundamentally and directly harmed by a criminal act might possibly be deserving of restitution as well; once again, their claims cannot be rejected out of hand. But, this zone test should be the central thrust simply because we would like to limit exercises of the state's coercive power against the individual to the narrowest possible circumstances. And while we would like to see courts free to fashion just restitutionary rewards, there is always the problem of overreach should the courts become too free-wheeling. Beyond a reasonably established zone there should be a rebuttable presumption that harm is neither so direct nor so dangerous that restitution is needed to set things right again. A very heavy burden to show otherwise should be on those outside the zone.

INTERESTS OF OFFENDERS

The interests of offenders that would immediately seem to require balancing are (1) due process guarantees, (2) perhaps rehabilitation, (3) the problem, if any, that originally disposed the offender to the crime, and (4) certain collateral interests such as families or jobs. Most of the due process guarantees do not concern us here, since arrest, trial, and appeal (except for the additional defenses mentioned before) would be exactly the same procedures as they are now. The guarantee against cruel and unusual punishment would still be of concern, though hopefully of much less concern. In addition, the wrongdoer's interest in his or her family and work is an interest shared to a very great extent by the public and has been addressed under that topic. Consequently, we will focus on the second and third listed interests of the wrongdoer.

As argued earlier in Part I, punishment as restitution is compatible with a rehabilitation approach to criminal justice only if we understand that rehabilitation cannot be coerced. It is easy to deny the effects of education, vocational training, individual or group therapy, or any kind of training or treatment program if there is no desire or need for change. Consequently, this interest need not be thrown into the balance in every case. Nevertheless, in determining what kind of work the individual ought to do to make restitution, where he or she should work and with whom, some consideration ought to be given to whether rehabilitation is needed, desired, and likely to be effective.

Perhaps the most important interests of the wrongdoer that a restitutionary approach allows us to address are those that tend to "structure in" crimes. As we argued before in different contexts, certain types of crime, certain levels of crime (crime rates), and certain patterns of crime can be traced to policy choices. They are often unintended consequences of economic and political programs.[3] Examples that are often cited demonstrate (1) how deliberate government manipulation of the economy often results in unemployment and a consequent increase in crime rates, (2) how failure to enforce strictly the laws against driving while intoxicated increase traffic fatalities, and (3) how property laws, capitalist systems of finance, and consumer-oriented economics present certain classes of people with problems and options that make criminal behavior the lesser of many evils.[4]

For purposes of restitution, our primary concern in this area is that of civil disobedience. The reason for this is that this is the only situation in which we might recognize that a wrongdoer has lost something of value. Arguably, of course, many heroin addicts who commit crimes to support their habit have been "structured into" the crime by the prevailing socioeconomic structure. But it seems that the solution here lies in rehabilitation where desired and other forms of social support where possible. Cases such as these are "hard cases" for which no entirely satisfactory resolution seems possible. A restitutionary approach, however, at least takes care of the public and victim interests and might address those of the wrongdoer (through rehabilitation) in appropriate cases.

On a broader level, of course, the solution to the problems of "structured in" crimes lies in political change, and it is here that civil disobedience is so important. Civil disobedience, as the final act when nothing else is working to have honest interests and needs addressed, is evidence that certain rights and opportunities have been effectively denied. Something has been taken away for which restitution is deserved.

This argument assumes, of course, that those denied an honest consideration of their needs and interests are politically conscious, organized, mutually supportive, and concerned enough to have sufficient feelings of personal efficacy to pursue their claims. Clearly, this will often not be the case. But just as clearly, this puts these problems beyond the competency of criminal courts. These are, then, in the last analysis, problems for the educational system, religious and social welfare sectors of society, and the social consciences of those involved in the political and legal system. A doctor who defrauds the Medicare system, for example, should perhaps be given a more rigorous restitutionary task than someone stealing by fraud in order to eat. Not only might our society be more greatly threatened by the first act than the second (as argued above), but one can perceive a certain socially imposed necessity in the second act that is clearly not present in the first. In such cases it would not seem inequitable to require the doctor to make good on the public interests he or she has violated, while requiring the other wrongdoer to make good only the victim's loss.

By now you should be fairly well oriented concerning who should get restitution for what sort of injury. It is time to pass over to the question of who should make restitution. Normally, this task would be placed on the person who actually committed the act that directly caused the damage. But the criminal law as it now stands both extends culpability for acts to people who aided the crime or the criminal and recognizes some acts as crimes which are inchoate (i.e., nothing or relatively little has happened toward the completion of a criminal act as in conspiracy, solicitation, attempt). How do these fair under a restitutionary approach? Also, criminal law usually requires an appropriate *mens rea* (though there are strict liability statutes in some places, for example, in serving alcohol to minors), and we have been promoting the idea that corporate crimes deserve more attention than street crimes. But how do we ascribe intent to a corporation, and who deserves to pay for corporate criminal acts? These are the questions we will wrestle with for the remainder of this chapter beginning with the problem of how to treat those aiding the criminal and taking the others in their turn.

ACCESSORIES

Actually, there is no problem with accessories before the fact. If they take active part in furthering and encouraging a crime, they have contributed to the damages caused and should be made to contribute to the restitution in a proportionate amount. As this suggests, the restitutionary approach would not hold all accessories before the fact equally culpable with the perpetrator. Accessories have committed a different criminal act than the person they aided and encouraged, and this requires a separate inquiry into exactly how much damage they provided. People who actually take part in the crime or cooperate to such an extent that the crime would be impossible without them are no longer accessories but perpetrators in their own right.

The present criminal law treats all accessories before the fact as principals regardless of whether they actually did some act furthering the crime or simply stood around cheering the perpetrator on. This impulse is understandable. It is rather like the parent who, irked by the general rebelliousness of his or her children, spanks them all on general principle. As in the family, so in society. This sort of thing usually insures either more rebelliousness or a general fecklessness and apathy as well as a disrespect for an authority that is so lacking in discrimination.

Accessories after the fact are not treated as principals at the present time. For restitutionary purposes they should, like accessories before the fact, be treated as having committed separate crimes against the public. But, unlike accessories before the fact, they may have committed no offense resulting in damages to the victim of the principal crime unless their assistance resulted in the perpetrator's escaping. In that case they may have done damage to the victim's interest in obtaining restitution and should be held liable for the damages themselves.

INCHOATE CRIMINALS

Of course, conspiracy is our most peculiar crime. We punish two or more people for having evil thoughts together, though each alone, with exactly the same thoughts, is guilty of nothing. Certainly it is no more dangerous for two people together to want to kill another than it is for one person to have such designs. And clearly it is more dangerous for five independent people to have designs on the same bank than it is for five people working in concert to pull off a single robbery. Also, since charges of conspiracy are easy to bring and a *prima facie* case easy to make out (though in the last analysis conspiracy is very difficult to prove beyond a reasonable doubt), it has become a favorite tool of state and federal governments in their struggle with political dissidents. Even if dissidents don't end up in jail, they are tied up in court for the longest time and their cause discredited in the eyes of many (unfortunately, many in our society still equate the bringing of charges with actual perfidy and assume that those charged are guilty of something approximating the crime for which they are arrested).

Restitution rids us of this complex of peculiarities by simply and directly requiring that someone be shown to have been hurt by the conspiracy in a manner important enough to engage the entire society (through its criminal laws) in the remedy. Absent damages there is no crime.

Attempt presents a different problem. At the very least people are made to feel insecure by attempts even when they experience no personal or property damage. This could justify a restitutionary award, particularly if potential victims expend funds in ways reasonably calculated to regain a sense of security lost as a direct result of the attempt (e.g., installing special locks, security alarms, etc., in their houses following an attempted burglary). Along this line, attempt would not be merged into the crime. The trend today is to allow conviction for attempt even though the crime is not successfully completed. And given the different types of damage that attempt produces, a separate recovery should be allowed under a restitutionary approach as well.

Solicitation might be handled in a similar way. If the potential victim discovers that solicitations for a crime against his or her property or person are being made, the insecurity and subsequent precautions might justify a restitutionary award. Also, if the solicitation takes a coercive turn (i.e., the person solicited is being blackmailed or otherwise forced into committing the crime), a reward of damages might well be due the person solicited.

So, you probably now have a pretty good idea of who should make restitution so long as we are talking about crimes committed by individual real people. Mythical people (i.e., corporations) are next, and they present their own sort of problems.

CORPORATE CRIMINALS

First, as we mentioned before, it is very difficult to talk about "intent" for the type of corporate behavior we are now discussing. The corporate personality is a myth created for purposes of the civil law (entering contracts, being sued, etc.). So, criminal law ideas of *mens rea* are difficult to apply, both because of this myth and because many corporate crimes result from the complex interlocking behaviors of many individuals or groups within a corporation. Guilt, in short, is difficult to assign. For this same reason, it is difficult, if not pointless and impossible, to employ effectively any of the traditional sanctions for lawbreaking except fines. Second, ordinary criminal procedure is generally inappropriate in case of corporate crime both because of the complex statistical and economic issues likely to be raised in this area, and because of the lack of the social concern for such behavior as compared to the concern about "street crimes." Finally, from a utilitarian point of view, certain types of "corporate crime" might, under appropriate circumstances, be justifiable in terms of the overall social good they produce. That is, while under ordinary circumstances they might damage individuals and the public, specific contexts might work to turn them to a greater public benefit. It is recognized by law, for example, that some acts in restraint of free competition and the open market are necessary to maintain any competition at all. There are, in brief, times and circumstances where competition can be destructive and corporate practices that keep this from occurring might, therefore, be justifiable. More generally, there is a delicate balance to be struck between the equally desirable social interests in freedom and competition on the one hand and a sound economic system on the other. This is not the kind of intricate dealing that the criminal process with its adversarial approach is designed to accomplish.

However, criminal jurisdiction is most desirable in this area regardless of the obstacles. First, it is clear that there is a "public threat" from corporations justifying criminal law jurisdiction. The scale of corporate enterprise in our society is so great that its products and services touch every aspect of our social, political, and economic life. For this reason, both what is produced by corporations and the way it is produced have a significant impact on the fulfillment and frustration of individual human needs, interests, and desires, as well as the general well-being of the society. Furthermore, control of corporations is generally in the hands of a small number of individuals against whom there are, at present, few checks or balances (other than government regulations and their legal enforcement) to ensure that the power at their disposal is used responsibly. Finally, what constitutes "responsible use" of corporate power is not well defined in our present system. For whom are corporate directors trustees? Shareholders? Workers? The general public? The beneficiaries of their goods or services? Or are they more broadly responsible for something like "social progress"? Both because there is such widespread social dependence on a relatively small number of large corporations (e.g., in the fields of energy, communications, medicines, etc.) controlled by a limited number of persons against whom only government provides a meaningful check, and because corporate crime presents a threat to the overall society as a result, there is a need for the criminal law to have jurisdiction. Indeed, it must have jurisdiction if we are to approximate anything like the "greatest good for the greatest number."

So here we are: We need criminal jurisdiction, but the approach of our criminal justice system is inappropriate to this need. Certainly we need a new approach, and it should be no surprise that we think restitution fits neatly. Simply put, in situations where the law is violated and interests are harmed as a result of corporate activities that cannot be traced to any single individual, restitution must be made by the corporation as a whole according to the interest-balancing, problem-solving model of restitutionary courts we have already outlined. As we have said before, the corporate person is a legal fiction created for the purposes of civil law. In the final analysis, therefore, a corporation is the capital invested by stockholders and the activities of executives and workers (at all levels) putting that capital to work in different ways. Since, by definition, neither executives nor workers can be held responsible for the type of harm we are now considering, courts must look for satisfaction toward the capital of a corporation. This, of course, means that in the end it is the stockholders who are held responsible for making restitution.

This seems a reasonable place to locate responsibility because, even though they took no action themselves, activities by those acting on behalf of stockholders have the ultimate purpose of benefiting stockholders. Since it is activity ultimately toward their benefit, it is reasonable to hold them ultimately responsible for the costs of such activities.

Restitution, then, becomes a cost of doing business, an externality for which corporations are held responsible. This is also quite in keeping with the strong and growing tendency in tort law to allocate the more or less inevitable loss to be charged against a complex and technologically dangerous civilization to the parties best able to bear the cost.

Now that we understand why corporations should make restitution and who in a corporation should be held responsible for the damages, we must finally address the question of who should receive the damages being paid out. For reasons that echo both our first discussion of why white-collar and corporate crime are more dangerous to our society than are street crimes, and our just-concluded discussion of why corporations should be held criminally liable for many of their acts, it is clear that society is one victim of corporate criminality. Restitution must be made to the general revenue, from which so much of the costs of corporate crime is presently taken.

Beyond the right of society (in the person of its political institutions) to recover for corporate crimes, we must keep in mind what was said about interests and interest balancing in the previous chapter. Any group or individual who feels some interest has been damaged should have a right to make a claim for restitution, and the court must sort out exactly the best way of dividing up the recovery. We would like to suggest some guidelines for sorting out proper from improper recoveries, however, keeping in mind all the while that the context of each case should ultimately control who receives what.

Our basic idea differs only slightly from the simple proposition that someone who is hurt by a corporate crime should be given restitution; injury in fact (economic or otherwise) should be the only basis of recovery, just as it is when individuals commit a crime. So much is generally understood and reasonably clear in its general thrust, but it is uncertain around the edges. For example, we must once again be concerned with how small or how remote an injury should get restitution. And our answers here must be different because the nature of corporate crime is different; corporate crimes like pollution, for example, drift far from their source and sometimes increase in effect in direct proportion to the distance. (The damage caused by chemical and nuclear pollution, for example, compounds itself as it travels through our ecosystem. Moreover, even small exposures accumulate over time to produce life-endangering consequences.) So where do we draw the line?

Unlike the situation where a crime is committed by an individual, some trifling individual damages should clearly be allowed restitution when they are so widespread that they add up to a great amount of damage. So, for example, if some corporation makes criminally fraudulent claims for its product which justify its charging five dollars more to each customer, and if the district attorney discovers the fraud and brings charges, it does seem that each of, say, 100,000 purchasers should be allowed to recover if only to insure that the corporation does not benefit from its criminal activity.

Similarly, if damages are small but the crime also involves the violation of some principle we hold dear, we might want to allow for something like punitive damages. So, for example, if a corporation, through some criminal method, managed to learn the lowest bid on a public project and then underbid it, even if the public benefited from getting the public work at a cheaper price, we might want to award punitive damages as restitution to the public just because the corporation acted unethically.

Finally, there should be nothing like the zone test we previously suggested for allowing recovery when the damage is done by an individual. This is just because of the scale and duration of the harm corporations can do as opposed to individuals (e.g., illegal chemical and nuclear waste dumps) and because of the powerlessness of individual victims even to recognize corporations as the source of many problems. At present the power of government is the only effective check against the power of corporations, and that power needs to be extended as corporate power and influence expand. It is not at all like the situation where the whole panoply of government power is exercised against the individual.

HOW MUCH RESTITUTION?

We cannot say beforehand how much any victim should receive; we would have an endless list mirroring the infinite nuances of the human situation. But we can suggest the sorts of concerns that might go into formulating a just restitution, keeping in mind that there are, indeed, injuries for which no amount of restitution is commensurate. We do the best we can, and it is often little enough.

Our first step is to keep in mind our purposes in having criminals make restitution. Our primary purpose, of course, is to restore or indemnify victims for all losses suffered and gains prevented because of criminal acts while forcing criminals to disgorge the fruits of their wrongdoing. Our secondary purpose is to reap what benefits we can in terms of deterrence and rehabilitation (keeping in mind that justifiable retribution is restitutionary in character as we demonstrated earlier). Our purposes thus suggest the following "working hypothesis" for determining the amount of a restitutionary award:

1. The amount of a restitutionary recovery should be equal to the victim's loss or the offender's gain, whichever is greater.

2. Doubts as to the victim's loss or offender's gain should be resolved in favor of the victim.

3. Punitive recovery should be allowed if and only if there is concrete evidence that it will have a deterrent or rehabilitative effect on either the wrongdoer or others who might be about to commit the act or are (as with corporations) already engaging in activities likely to result in criminal responsibility.

4. If it is at all possible and appropriate, victims should have returned to them any personal property with sentimental value or unique properties. If the property can be traced to another who is an innocent possessor, offenders should make restitution to that person as well.

CONCLUSION

In summary our argument has been:

1. That the following people should make restitution:
    (a) Accessories before the fact (but they should not be treated as principals to the central crime but as having committed a separate offense);
    (b) Accessories after the fact whose aid resulted in the criminal's escape;
    (c) Conspirators, attemptors, and solicitors whose conspiracy, attempt, or solicitation caused damage in and of itself;
    (d) The principle individual actor whose criminal behavior caused injury in fact and,
    (e) Corporations (from the profits of their stockholders) for offenses that result from the concerted effort of many individuals in the "normal" pursuit of business.
2. That the following people should get restitution:
    (a) The public for injury to the public peace, public security, or quality of public life including:
        (1) violent acts against people or property
        (2) treason

     (3) nepotism

     (4) defrauding the public and its institutions

     (5) using public authority for private ends

     (6) but not for offenses against "the general morals"

  (b) People within the zone of interests reasonably intended to be protected by the criminal code, unless the offender is a corporation in which case no zone limitation is appropriate;

  (c) Others whose fundamental interests are directly and extensively harmed as a result of the offense when the demands of justice so require; and

  (d) Offenders, for any wrong done them in the course of the investigation or prosecution of the case against them, or in the carrying out of their sentence (with special attention to those guilty of civil disobedience); and,

3. That the amount of restitution should depend upon both the injury to the victim and the benefit to the wrongdoer while keeping an eye on possible rehabilitative and deterrent effects.

Now we are ready to outline our model penal system, which is calculated to effect all of our goals in the most justified manner.

NOTES

1. H.L.A. Hart, "Positivism and the Separation of Law and Morals," *Harvard Law Review* 71:593 (1958).

2. Ibid., p. 410.

3. See E. Wright, *The Politics of Punishment* (New York: Harper and Row), Ch. 1.

4. Ibid.

7

Enforcing Restitution: The Penal Model

Today it is a commonplace to confess that our penal system is altogether detestable. It sends often naïve first offenders through a mindless and brutalizing routine, so that they come out of the other end ignorant, angry, and unable to engage in the simplest social intercourse that has not been arranged for them by their jailers. It crowds people into prison cells to a point that is "cruel and unusual," leaving inmates at the mercy of one another and reducing many to a condition of abject helplessness in the face of the most terrible abuse. And then it turns everybody loose, ignoring both them and us (for that is what it has become) and expecting us to be happy and them to be good. It is a peculiar thing, this modern penal system, with its astonishing spread of brutality, ignorance, and hatred, boasting all the time of how enlightened it has become and how educated are its personnel.

Can you have any more patience with such a system? Those of us who advocate restitution have none. In the place of massive gray concrete tombs, underground societies, early release for malleable behavior, and the inevitable recidivism of it all, we are proposing a simple three-component system consisting of (1) small in-prison programs that are production oriented, (2) residential in-community programs, and (3) nonresidential in-community programs. In-prison programs will be primarily for offenders who, because of the nature of their crime, their tendency to recidivism, their psychological characteristics, or their addiction to alcohol and drugs, evince a need of constant supervision. The residential in-community programs would have jurisdiction over where offenders would live and spend their leisure time after working at jobs available in the community, while the nonresidential in-community programs would allow the offender to live at home under supervision similar to that provided for parolees.

Some people may be much more amiable and tolerant than we and tell us that in fact things are not quite as bleak as we make out. There happen to be, after all, halfway houses, rehabilitation programs, and an army of social workers, psychologists, and psychoanalysts all working toward the reintegration of offenders into our community. There are also criminologists, political scientists, criminal psychologists, and just ordinary citizens working tirelessly to ameliorate the in-prison conditions that are so dehumanizing. Everyone at every point in the system is now more educated and more aware, and it is certainly better than the mental and physical torture and general human neglect characteristic of the system it replaced and that still operates in many countries.

To all this consolation we can only add that while the present penal system richly deserves the very worst that has been said of it, it was in its origin thoroughly well intentioned. Nevertheless, we must point out that most of these just-mentioned virtues operate not as part of the present system but either in spite of it or because the present system creates the very problems they address. So, while there may be oceans of goodwill flooding our system, our system is not the right way to go, and we must remember that doing things the wrong way is often worse than doing the wrong things altogether. Finding the right way is what restitution is all about, and making it work will require much alert observation, sound reasoning, and dedicated conscientiousness. It will also require money properly spent on proper programs, and that is now our topic.

THE PROGRAMS AND HOW TO FINANCE THEM

The most bothersome problem facing us in establishing in-prison restitutionary programs is a classic one: finding the capital to invest in the development of production-oriented prison facilities. We should be very direct about this: We plan to raise capital in the classic capitalist tradition, by turning prisons into businesses and financing them both through tax-free municipal and state bonds and through the offering of stock to the general public. Similarly, for the residential in-community programs we propose that houses be purchased or built with the government securing the mortgage and the prisoners paying it off in the form of rent. If despite the incentives of tax-free returns on investment and government-secured loans, sufficient financing can still not be found, then it will be necessary for the government to front the money until an ongoing business is established in prison, and the prisoners in in-community programs begin earning returns. While this initial outlay could be substantial in some cases, it would be a one-time cost as compared to the continuing expenditures for prison maintenance which presently cost our nation as a whole over four billion dollars annually exclusive of new prison construction.

Where prison facilities are to be constructed or turned into factories or service centers, extensive research will of course be required to ascertain the feasibility of producing any particular product or providing any particular service, and a study of the economic impact such a facility would make on the immediate community will have to be made. This sort of research is a prerequisite aimed at avoiding competition with existing businesses in the community. Insofar as possible, participants in the residential and nonresidential in-community programs will earn their income from private-sector employers in local factories, businesses, service centers, and professional buildings, underscoring the important goal of societal reconciliation for the offender and avoiding the problem of competition with private producers.

Another way of avoiding competition with private producers and local business would be to target production to those fields where traditional private capital investment doesn't work. To begin with, there are many necessary things that private people won't invest in because you cannot make everyone who benefits pay. Roads are a good example. Everyone benefits from the general commerce carried by our roads even if he or she never sets foot or tire on them. And having a toll booth spring up on each road to make at least those on them pay (and pass it on to the rest of us, of course) would so impede the flow of commerce and increase its cost that it is better to scotch the whole idea. So convict labor might be used for the building and maintenance of public highways, and convict engineers might even have a hand in planning and designing them. This is necessary work that private capital cannot do and so the state must step in anyway. We might as well turn it to the most productive use possible, and adopting it for restitutional ends certainly helps to make this possible. (Some of you are of course wondering what happens to state highway commissions and the private citizens they now employ. Well, they would be phased out as we presently know them and replaced with programs oriented toward restitution. We will save the justification of this for the next chapter.) Work such as this might employ not only those in in-prison programs but those in both resident and nonresident in-community programs as well.

There are also things that need doing that you can charge everyone for and that make a profit but which take a very long time to do and so involve some risk. Private capital tends to shy away here as well. Public utilities are a good example. Constructing, putting into operation, and maintaining power plants and sewerage treatment plants is very expensive on a continuing basis. Moreover, much of the work is liable to damage and destruction (consider dams built for hydroelectric plants and accidents with nuclear reactors), and it is impossible to raise rates for these services beyond a certain point without sending individual consumers over to a competitor. The initial outlay is large, and the return slow and uncertain; this is not a prime investment opportunity for private capital. So the state must do it again, and again there is an opportunity to use prison populations and those in both residential and nonresidential in-community programs in everything from the ground breaking to the administration and maintenance of these utilities.

Finally there are certain markets where domestic investment once was dominant but where it has now slowed to a drizzle because it is more profitable to invest abroad. The clothing industry is a good example here. The costs of production at home, including labor costs, have become very high relative to what they are in certain underdeveloped countries. So much investment capital has left the United States and gone, for example, to Taiwan (except for investment in fashionable clothing, which caters to a market where price is not a prime factor). Our government could establish in-prison clothing factories that could well make up for this lost private capital. Remember, government factories need make no profit to be successful components in a restitutionary program. They merely need to cover their costs, including the income of prisoners working at the assembly line. When profit is not a concern, price can be kept down and a lost domestic labor market recaptured.

All of these seem to be very desirable arrangements for all concerned and only begin to indicate the potential that might be exploited by restitutionary programs. We, of course, are neither economists nor administrators and not so good at coming up with the possibilities as they, and there are many technical and logistical problems that will require some ingenuity to resolve. But we are pointed here in the right direction, and no system can work by itself. Any program requires the concentrated effort of people who want to make it work because they are convinced that it is the right thing to do. Having made the argument that restitution is the right way, the most we can do is sketch how it might begin and leave the growth of our idea to those more expert than we.

We are convinced, however, that in time, the residential and nonresidential in-community programs will become the major components of the restitutionary approach in the criminal justice system. Not only will the offenders be engaged in making restitution to victims, society, and others with a definable interest, but they will become an important factor in the growth of the community's economy. Community acceptance and participation in these programs can be encouraged in several positive ways. These include: (1) tax-break incentives to facilities that sign up with the program, (2) payroll subsidies for an initial trial period, (3) making available state financing at low interest rates for those facilities which expand and renovate their plants to meet the needs of the programs, (4) no-competition contracts, and (5) reinvestment by the state of any profits it realizes from investment in private facilities that start restitutionary programs.

The residential in-community programs would consist of residential centers located throughout a jurisdiction, with the exact placement depending upon a number of factors including: (1) availability of employment opportunities in the area, (2) public acceptance of such a facility, (3) availability of public transportation and similar facilities to support such an institution. A program of this sort is already operating in Georgia. There, each center is staffed with: (1) a superintendent, (2) a business manager, (3) a typist, (4) a probation/parole supervisor, (5) a counselor, (6) four counselors' aides and/or correctional officers. This core staff is supplemented by VISTA volunteers, student internees, and citizen volunteers from schools, churches, and civic organizations. The center helps residents locate and keep employment, if the state does not have its own facility, and the business manager collects the paychecks and disburses the funds for each offender according to the plan of restitution.

The nonresidential program (one of which also has been operating in Georgia since 1977) would allow offenders a degree of personal liberty and responsibility comparable to that of parolees. Offenders under this program would execute a restitution agreement developed by themselves, the district attorney, and a state restitution specialist. The plan would be submitted for court approval, and monthly progress reports would be made to the court. Monthly paychecks would be disbursed to a business manager, who would in turn distribute the funds according to the restitution agreement.

Of the two in-community programs, the residential type will require considerably more of the community than the nonresidential because of the concentration of offenders to be housed in the community. These sorts of halfway homes or centers have in many cases been the basis for public outcry, and a suitable educational program for the public will be necessary before the concept of restitution is understood and accepted. One approach would be to begin with the least threatening offenders to form the core of the population to be housed in the community. While the ultimate aim of the program would be to include those in prison, priority would lie with the newly convicted offender. Once the program is in place, functioning, and gaining community acceptance, it should begin to include prisoners already serving sentences.

THE RESTITUTION FUND

Any program can always use supplementary funding; it is a law of nature in a capitalist society. Funds are needed for experimenting and for filling in where we have bungled it badly. Anyway, there are times, as we have pointed out, when the most effective way either to make restitution or to demand that it be paid is in one lump sum. Where do we get these lumps if the wrongdoers do not have them ready to hand, and where do we put these lumps when they are ready, but there are good reasons for not giving it all to the victim at once (e.g., income tax problems: restitution includes lost salaries, wages, profits, and rents all of which are taxable)?

One way would be to establish a "Victim Restitution Trust Fund." This fund would serve as a place of deposit for any property, lump sum, or periodic payment ordered to be made by an offender to any victim. In addition, the proceeds from misdemeanor fines, discretionary fines, fines of recidivists, the "excess profits" of certain offenders, interest accrued by the fund itself, and fines for white-collar crimes could also be paid into the fund. Should "victimless crimes"—prostitution, pornography, drug abuse, etc.—be retained as one of the "public interests" to be enforced, they might also be made subject to fine rather than a jail sentence, and those fines might also be directed to the fund. In addition, profits from the sale of life stories, film rights, and so on, along with returns that do not go into maintenance from the rents collected from both those in prison and those in community residences might be directed to the fund. When the fund is initially established, the state should collapse into it any other funds previously set up to pay innocent victims of crime. An important thing to remember here is that society is included as a victim in all restitutionary schemes. Society, in the person of its political institutions, will therefore share in and be paid a determined amount of restitution from the fund for offenses committed against it. We can therefore look forward to getting back both more than we put up to get the fund started and more than it costs to keep it running.

PUNISHING CORPORATIONS

Of course, none of what we have just suggested is relevant when the crime is committed by the corporation as a whole rather than by an identifiable individual within it. In such a case there seem to be only two ways for corporation to make restitution: (1) in lump-sum payments, and (2) in continuous payments. Restitutionary remedies must be fashioned in this type of situation to insure both that victims suffer no loss and that the corporation realizes no profit from the wrongful act. It is conceivable, for example, that benefits from criminal activities that damage certain interests might in the long or short run exceed the costs of making restitution. A restitutionary award, therefore, must take this possibility into consideration. Consequently, continuing payments over some period of time over which a corporation is reasonably likely to realize benefit from any unlawful act seems appropriate in certain situations. As in the case of individual offenders, society is one victim of corporate criminal acts, and once individual victims are fully compensated, it would seem reasonable to appropriate additional payments like the ones just mentioned to the general revenue. If the benefit is realized by the corporation all at once and not over time, a lump-sum payment made by the corporation should include the total benefit it realized, anything in excess of the victims' damages going to the restitution fund. Anything in the nature of punitive damages should also go to the restitution fund.

Otherwise, whether a payment should be in a lump sum or continuous should depend upon:

1. The nature of the damage done to the victim (homicide by a corporation, for example, might call for supporting a victim's family or dependents over the course of their dependency).

2. The cash-flow situation of the corporation (we want the corporation to survive as well as the victim).

3. The court's best judgment on which might better serve such purposes as deterrence, retribution, and "rehabilitation" (i.e., the restructuring of the corporation and its practices in such a way that the complex interaction leading to crime cannot happen again).

OFFICIAL ACCOUNTABILITY

Everything we have suggested so far presumes that the right people are placed in the right programs. It wouldn't do to put demonstrable sociopaths into jobs as air traffic controllers at government airports. If we want our penal system to work well, we must structure the realities of its administrators so that it is distinctly in their interest that restitution and reintegration be effectively realized. This may be particularly difficult in the in-prison programs where prisoners might well be dangerous and the situation generally uneasy. Still there are encouragements that can be proffered.

First, we must convince administrators that restitution is not only the right way to go, but that our criminal justice system wholly supports the idea. In short, we must mobilize lawyers, judges, police, legislators and general public opinion behind restitution as a legitimate, desirable and attainable goal of our criminal justice system. This will provide the necessary milieu for holding administrators accountable for making such a system work.

Second, we ought to be something just short of ruthless in hiring and firing program administrators. Too much depends upon their getting things right to tolerate or excuse ineffective administration. If they are not equal to putting the right people in the right program and making each program work in terms of employing offenders, seeing that restitution is made, and reintegrating offenders so far as humanly possible then they must be summarily replaced. In this sense we must be more demanding than the private sector which recently (consider Chrysler Corporation and Lockheed) seems to be tolerating and even rewarding administrative ineptitude.

Finally, reasonable but firm and demanding measures of the admin istrator performance must be developed and applied to his or her work with great regularity. Administrators should be judged according to (1) their effectiveness in getting the three types of restitutionary programs established and functioning efficiently as bureaucratic entities, (2) their effectiveness in getting offenders employed, (3) their effectiveness in both managing offender incomes and training offenders to manage them themselves, and (4) their effectiveness in gaining community acceptance, meeting all the overhead, getting restitution completely paid, convincing offenders to try different rehabilitation programs, picking effective rehabilitation programs, and producing a profit that can be reinvested in the system or (if this all becomes a successful money-making proposition) contributed to the general revenue.

We understand, of course, that obstacles will present themselves, but we must take the attitude that obstacles are rarely insurmountable. The sign of a good administrator is just the ability to get where the system wants to go regardless of the obstacles. Administrations are there exactly to go over, under, around, or through obstacles, not to create them or to inform us that the situation is beyond remedy.

CONCLUSION

Our penal model, then, consists of the following elements:

1. In-prison manufacturing or service programs (when appropriate) where both labor and as much staff and administration as possible is done by offenders,
2. Residential in-community programs where offenders work at private businesses within the community or within easy commuting distance and then spend their off-work time primarily at the center, and
3. Nonresidential in-community programs where offenders are treated essentially as parolees.

This penal system should have a higher standard of performance for its administrators than the private sector presently has, failures to meet established goals should mean almost certain replacement, and it should be funded by:

1. Financing in-prison businesses through tax-free municipal or state bonds,
2. The offering of stock in in-prison business to the general public,
3. Government-secured loans from mortgage companies to pay off the costs

of acquiring in-community residential property (the mortgage to be paid off from the rents charged offenders),

4. In extreme situations, government fronting of the money that would constitute a lien on the property or business assets, and

5. A restitutionary trust fund, the principal coming from:
   (a) Lump-sum payments from corporations where this is the just form of compensation,
   (b) The proceeds from misdemeanor fines,
   (c) The proceeds of discretionary fines,
   (d) Punitive damages (usually, again, from corporations),
   (e) Fines from recidivists for doing it again (i.e., beyond their restitutionary debt),
   (f) Any "excess profits" certain offenders might realize from having committed the crime (i.e., any benefits greater than their costs including the restitution they must make),
   (g) Fines for white-collar and corporate crimes,
   (h) Fines from "victimless crimes,"
   (i) Profits offenders make from the sale of life stories, film rights, etc., and
   (j) Interest on the principal itself.

Finally, adverse economic effects might be mitigated by:

1. Feasibility studies evaluating the impact of the restitutionary program on the local economy, and

2. Targeting production and services to those areas of our economy where private capitalism doesn't work.

So now we have outlined both our model restitutionary court and our model restitutionary penal system. Still, there are some nagging questions that are always encountered in conversation with those who are convinced, as we have said, that changing our present system will topple civilization as we know it. Let us now pass over to a consideration of those objections.

8

The Final Chapter: Some Nagging Questions Answered

By now you should probably understand not only the point and purpose of restitutionary criminal justice, which is simply to pay back what is lost to those who lost it, but some ways that we might go about doing it accurately, efficiently, and fairly. Let us take all that as settled, then, and begin to discuss certain matters that cannot be omitted if only because they persistently appear in ordinary social conversation on our subject and are of grave concern to many for whom change is a certain signal of decay.

MURDERERS AND RESTITUTION

Some years ago a friend of ours mentioned in casual conversation that she had once visited an African nation where the relatives of a slain man moved in lock, stock, and barrel with the slayer. Though we have since forgotten the country, the concept still occasions animated debate. Later, doing research, we came across an account of murder in a Cheyenne Indian village[1] where, after three years in exile, the murderer returned with enough tobacco to satisfy the entire village and was readmitted to the tribe as an equal member. The slain man's family agreed on condition that the murderer be particularly nice to everyone in the village from then on. We were struck by the fact that in both cases, continents and oceans apart, murderers were both reintegrated with the community and required to make restitution for the rest of their lives.

We think that this is an eminently sensible approach, much more sophisticated, much more humane, and much more socially relevant than our own tendency to gas, hang, shoot, or electrocute. Of course, there are in our society particularly brutal murders (the Cheyenne seem to have been spared this phenomenon) and particularly nasty and aggressive murderers (the Cheyenne seem to have a lacking here as well). Certainly it would not do to treat them in exactly the same manner. But just as certainly we are inventive enough to come up with variations on this general theme that accomplish restitutionary objectives with a clear eye on the personality of the offender. In "worst case" situations it may be necessary for offenders to labor in prison factories for their entire lives, the proceeds going to both the victim's family and the general revenue. In the best cases, some time might be put in this way with the remainder done in one of the community-based programs. In either case, the barbarism stops with the murderer's act and is not emulated by our own.

OFFENDERS WHO WON'T WORK

What do we do if someone just won't make restitution? This reduces to the question of how to handle people who won't lift a finger to produce anything; once income is produced, of course, the state directs the proceeds to the proper recipients. It is difficult to imagine an offender simply sitting down and twiddling his or her thumbs indefinitely. Human beings seem incapable of such inactivity for any extended period of time. Prisoners today engage in all sorts of socially unproductive activities to fill up their time and impart a sense of personal accomplishment. Go to any major prison today and you will see them voluntarily lifting weights, running track, working in prison libraries and infirmaries, and taking on all sorts of custodial tasks just to make their jailers happy and to avoid the inevitable human decay of enforced inactivity.

So the likelihood of voluntary inactivity is small, and we can expect to face the situation only occasionally. Still, when it does happen, it cannot be allowed to continue. Decent jailers must insist on their prisoners acting decently, doing what is required of them to fulfill their obligations to victims and society, and receiving their fair share of income, opportunities for rehabilitation, and chances at reintegration. Having done everything else, we must then do the worst thing imaginable: send them to a prison, just like the ones we have today. The threat of this should be a sufficient deterrent for most prisoners should they hit upon such a plan. But if it isn't, then, they should remain there unless and until such time as they are ready to begin serving their sentence (i.e., making restitution). No time spent there, of course, should have any effect whatsoever on the requirement that restitution be fully and completely made before the state stops regulating their lives.

CLASS DIFFERENCES

Even though everyone might be working to make restitution, everyone's work is not equally valued by our society. So can't some people pay off their restitutionary debt faster than others even though they might owe the same amount? Of course, we cannot allow the particular economic position or socioeconomic background of a wrongdoer to affect substantially the making of restitution. Thus, regardless of available resources, the convicted wrongdoer should be required to work off the restitutionary debt (i.e., rich people should not be allowed to buy their way out of working it off). Moreover, all work, of whatever market value, should be paid at the same rate when directed toward restitution. This is to avoid a kind of "class bias" in the system whereby someone whose work can command a higher hourly rate on the market (say a rock singer) will not have an easier time making restitution than someone whose work is less able to demand a high rate (say a college professor). In the case of a rock singer, for example, the normal amount that he or she might make by giving a concert might be turned over to the court which would then pay him or her a particular rate (e.g., minimum wage) and direct the excess to the restitutionary fund. The singer's work is, in effect, valued in the same way as an ordinary laborer's with the "excess profit" going toward the public good. We must remember that no work has intrinsically more value than any other. It is social structure, organization, and functioning that creates a value for it. In this sense value is a policy decision, and the policy of a restitutionary approach is (1) that society, the victim, and others who might successfully press claims should be restored to the *status quo ante* by the wrongdoer, and (2) that such a process should constitute a punishment as already defined. This approach to the class problem accomplishes both objectives neatly.

SHOULD THE GOVERNMENT SEEK JOBS FOR WRONGDOERS AND WHERE NECESSARY PROVIDE THEM?

To begin with, whether the government ought to provide jobs for wrongdoers is really a question of property rights because the concept of a "property right" has traditionally been the legal device used to define the relationship between a person and any "item of wealth." This leads us naturally to think of property as a relationship between a person and a thing, but this idea does not have any meaning from either a practical or a legal point of view. Things cannot claim rights or be assigned duties; that is, they cannot bring lawsuits or be held accountable. Consequently, property is actually any complex legal relationship that we establish among individuals and groups *with respect to things.*[2] Property, then, is a way we determine status, and we deliberately differentiate among people in this way so that we can attain certain social goals. Who has what status with respect to what items is, in brief, a function of policy, and it is our policy on the status among individuals with respect to that item of wealth we call "employment" that concerns us here. Indeed one's status in relation to job opportunities and resources for employment (education, capital, etc.) may be the most fundamental "item of wealth" in our present society.

Now, it is clear that some choices must be made regarding both who gets a job when, where, and under what circumstances, and who has access to what resources either to hire others or to go into private businesses of their own. And it is equally clear that our policy on these issues must be so calculated as to attain what we consider very important social goals. Consequently, our argument that government ought to find jobs for wrongdoers in order for them to make restitution is an argument that both a significant public purpose and a significant public need justifies determining statuses in relation to job opportunities and job resources in this way. The bulk of this essay has been addressed to the argument that restitution fulfills such public purposes and meets such public needs. It constitutes, in this sense, an important part of a theory of justice in property rights as they relate to employment and employment resources. Insofar as restitution is good public policy (that is, insofar as it is consistent with and promotes a way of life we find valuable), so are the determinations of statuses regarding employment and employment resources it requires.

Now you might say "Hold on a minute." Wouldn't it be better to allow the market to make employment decisions for us? After all, how can we say *a priori* what is best? And doesn't all you've said smack of centralism and a managed economy? Well, trade in a free market cannot make these choices for us. Trade presumes an already existing theory of justice in property rights. If we are going to say, for example, that X and Y should be free to trade for A and B, we are already supposing that X and Y legitimately own A and B. Without our presupposition of legitimacy we cannot say that such exchanges ought to be protected by the state or respected by other individuals. Moreover, our government can effectively offer such protection only at the margin. When individuals in substantial numbers will not respect such exchanges, there is relatively little law enforcement officials can do. People as individuals, in other words, must provide some self-imposed limitations, or willing participation in market systems, if market economics are to work at all. The absence of a shared core of ethical values (i.e., a theory of justice in property rights), then, suggests the absence of an ethical bond among market participants and further suggests not a system of exchange but an armed police state and perhaps war. People must agree upon what constitutes a legitimate assignment of an item of wealth such as a job, and we are arguing that we as a society should consider the government's finding or providing offenders a job a legitimate activity for all the reasons we have outlined in the first half of this book (i.e., it allows us to engage in the most justified form of punishing our offenders).

Another way of arguing to the same point is to consider what is perhaps the most popular notion of "property." According to this notion, what entitles us to call something our own is the effort we make in transforming raw materials into something useful to human beings. Moreover, to incorporate our labor into an object imparts not only a right to enjoy it but a right to alienate it as well. Consequently, this notion of property is quite important to market systems. This notion is no doubt very important to the idea of a legitimate claim to something as ours. But exactly what forms of labor are regarded as imparting a legitimate claim are socially decided. Surely robbery, embezzlement, grand larceny, petty larceny, and fraud are all laborious problems. But socially we want to discourage such behavior; it is our policy to do so. So no matter how mightily robbers might exert themselves, they cannot gain property rights in the things they steal. Once again, it is not the labor itself that creates property but the willingness of large groups of people to say that the assignment of a certain status with regard to a certain item of wealth is right and good given certain policies. We must understand that certain assignments of status regarding jobs is necessary and proper as well.

As a final note on this topic we might mention that these same arguments address the questions of whether or not the government should offer things for sale in the marketplace in competition with others and whether or not the government should go into business providing items in competition with others. These questions once again deal with the assignment of property rights, and once again our social policy should be determinative. But one other thing needs to be stressed in this regard. Only the in-prison program presents these problems. The two in-community programs involve offenders working for private producers. Additionally, we have argued both that production and marketing can be so targeted as to avoid conflict with the private sector, and that this program will probably be the smallest of the three. All in all, we are convinced that with judicious planning and execution most of these problems can be overcome in practice.

THE PROBLEM OF INFLATION

Some inflation seems endemic to our capitalist system, and just as consumers buy now on credit to pay off later with cheaper dollars, so some criminals may benefit in a like manner from this tendency in our economy. Now there is no way around assessing an award in terms of the value of money at the time of the crime; we have no way of knowing what will happen to the value of money tomorrow. Our problems will then arise when there is a long period of time between the crime and the award, and when restitution is made for future losses and where payments are made in increments across time. In each case, fluctuating inflation rates, recessions, and depressions may result in underrecoveries or overrecoveries. There are, of course, three means of remedying this problem. The least burdensome administratively would be for courts to award a lump sum to victims out of our restitutionary fund established for that purpose. Restitution payments by the wrongdoer would then be made to the fund, with the trustees indexing the charges made to a wrongdoer according to the vicissitudes of the economy. The second option is to have program administrators do all this indexing on a continuing basis for each of the offenders in their particular charge.

The final method is to require victims (or the wrongdoer) to petition the court periodically for a review of the payment amounts. As to the problem of lag between the time of the criminal act and the ordering of restitution, the value at trial time should probably be substituted if the difference is substantial.

INSURANCE

Our society's insurance schemes seek to distribute losses, often without regard to personal fault, among (1) the general public (e.g., Social Security), (2) the potential beneficiaries of the insurance (e.g., private accident or health insurance), and (3) the potential beneficiaries of the activity causing the harm (e.g., workmen's compensation). For this reason insurance should not be a factor in determining the amount due in restitution, nor should a wrongdoer be allowed to make restitution using the proceeds of an insurance policy. Criminal acts are not inevitable by-products of enterprises or social living whose costs can justifiably be distributed over certain groups of society as a whole (though, as argued above, certain types of crime may be "structured in," i.e., a proclivity toward certain crimes may result from the social, political, or economic structure and the policy decisions we make). In situations where a victim has paid regularly into an insurance program, there would seem to be no problem with allowing what amounts to a "double recovery" (i.e., from both the wrongdoer and the insurance company). In cases where insurance premiums are paid by a third party, however, it might be good public policy to have the insurance proceeds paid into the restitutionary fund.

THE FREEWHEELING NATURE OF RESTITUTIONARY COURTS

How far any society will tolerate activist, open, dynamic, and progressive institutions is a pretty tough question. The quarrel between liberal and conservative approaches to government is an old one. The advantage claimed for a more staid sort of jurisprudence is that it provides us with definite rules and procedures. There is a "qualified supremacy in defined spheres of competence,"[3] courts function to "depoliticize issues that might otherwise explode,"[4] judges do not "examine basic issues of justice or public policy or even the larger social effects of his (or her) own decisions."[5] Instead, politics is subordinated to law, social control is enhanced by fixing obligations, and citizen rights and responsibilities are stabilized and laid out. Law is imposed on the unruly, and a good example of fine social living is institutionalized.

This approach is tried again and again, but its results are so stultifying that it is sooner or later recognized as an albatross and people become set against it. The greatest mischief is worked by its sacrifice of practical problem solving at the altar of legalism. "Legalism is costly, partly because of the rigidities it imposes but also because rules construed *in abstracto* are too easily substantive evasions of public policy."[6]

Of course, some problems might arise if open and activist courts become too instrumental in their decision making. This is not because it would obscure the line between law and politics (that line is permanently obscure for other reasons), but because it could compromise the integrity of courts if taken too far (of course, it can enhance the integrity of courts if taken just far enough, as we have already argued). To avoid this difficulty and still remain open and active, we would suggest that courts assume a posture that has been described as "responsible":

> To assume that posture, an institution requires the guidance of purpose. Purposes set standards for criticizing established practice, thereby opening ways to change. At the same time, taken seriously, they can control administrative discretion and thus mitigate the risk of institutional surrender. Conversely, a lack of purpose lies at the roots of both rigidity and opportunism. These maladies, in fact, involve each other and co-exist. A formalist, rule-bound institution is ill equipped to recognize what is really at stake in its conflicts with the environment. It is likely to adapt opportunistically because it lacks criteria for rational reconstruction of outmoded or inappropriate policies. Only when an institution is truly purposive can there be a combination of integrity and openness, rule and discretion. Hence, responsive law presumes that purpose can be made objective enough and authoritative enough to control adaptive rule making.[7]

The purpose of a restitutionary criminal justice system should be understood in some excruciating detail by now, and so we can confidently state that restitutionary courts can be "responsive" and not "freewheeling."

Finally, we could go on like this indefinitely, but we think we have now covered the most popular and frequently occurring objections that we have experienced. Soon you would find us restating our arguments in more and more peculiar forms to answer more and more particular questions that people with personal interests and unique concerns would find as interesting as we would find adjusting our answers to their particular jargon and approach. But that is the pastime of intellectuals and not to be confused with the very direct purpose of this book. We now know exactly what restitution is, why it is the best approach, how it can be done, and how to answer the objections to it that we are most likely to encounter. We hope that this is very nearly enough to start people working toward the changes we have suggested.

NOTES

1. K. N. Llwellyn and E. A. Hoebel, *The Cheyenne Way* (Norman, Okla.: University of Oklahoma Press, 1941), pp. 9-15.

2. See R. T. Ely, *Property Contract* (New York: Macmillan, 1914), pp. 96 and 108; R. Johns, "Point of View," *Journal of Land and Public Utility Economics* 18 (August 1942), 245-266.

3. P. Nonet and P. Selznick, *Law and Society in Transition: Toward Responsive Law* (New York: Harper Colophon Books, 1978), p. 53.

4. Ibid., p. 58.

5. Ibid.

6. Ibid., p. 64.

7. Ibid., p. 77.

Epilogue

Now we have come to our end. We have articulated our philosophy and outlined our institutions. Still, we have a last word. We have appealed in this book to your sense of justice and your sense of efficiency, to your social conscience and your economics, to your rationality, your politics and your sense of practical necessity. Our last appeal must be to your humanity. What we restitutionists are most in revolt against is the great waste of talent and human potential the present system secures, the brutalization it works upon criminals and jailers alike, and the insensitivity it encourages among judges, lawyers, and the general public. At present no one involved in, or affected by, our criminal justice system can feel like an honorable and healthy human being. We should all despair if we did not know that we could do away with our present system and replace it with a system responsive to both our hardheaded concerns and our humanity as well.

We do not believe, as we have often said, that this alternative we are offering suggests or requires any fundamental change or transformation of our culture. What we are trying to do is to recapture the fundamental values, goals, and human orientations of our culture that have been lost or forgotten in our very well-intentioned effort to deter, rehabilitate, and seek retribution. The values, goals, and orientations of restitution are rooted in our history: in our dedication to human rights, civil rights, and personal autonomy. They are rooted more generally in the union of free people into a social and political system that has serving the needs and interests of people as individual human beings at its core and as its object. An institution that is only coercive and that does nothing directly for the victims of crime or about the social damage that has already been done by crime, cannot serve these traditional values and goals.

And so we look forward to the demise of our present system not wistfully but with an eager anticipation and with a certainty that it is truer to our humanity than most anything the history of Western criminal justice has yet to offer. Of course, our restitutionary system may never develop. Most of you may be unconvinced, ambiguous, or unwilling to exert yourselves in bringing about conscious change in our criminal institutions. In that case, we will drift as we are now. Social movement is inevitable because nothing ever remains the same. And we will eventually end up with one or another system different from the one we have now and no doubt adjusted on an ad hoc basis to the immediate needs of the criminal justice system. The advantage of working for a restitutionary approach is that you will know where you are going and why you are going there, and you can take an active, conscious part in shaping things to suit the needs of people.

Bibliography

Acton, Horace B. *The Philosophy of Punishment* (New York: St. Martin's Press, 1969).

Adkins, Arthur. *Merit and Responsibility* (Oxford: Clarendon Press, 1960).

Adler, Mortimer (ed.). *Scholasticism and Politics* (New York: Macmillan Publishing Co., 1940).

Alexander, Marshall E. *Jail Administration* (Springfield, Ill.: Thomas Press, 1957).

Andenaes, James. "Does Punishment Deter Crime?" *Criminal Law Quarterly* 2 (1978).

———. "General Prevention—Illusion or Reality?" *Journal of Criminal Law, Criminology, and Police Sciences* 43 (1952).

———. "The General Preventive Effects of Punishment," *University of Pennsylvania Law Review* 22 (1966), 114.

Aquinas, St. Thomas. *Summa Theologica* (New York: Benziger Brothers, 1947).

Aristotle. *Nicomachaen Ethics*, trans. *The Works of Aristotle*, William David Ross (Oxford: Clarendon Press, 1938).

Austin, John. *Lectures on Jurisprudence* (London: J. Murray, 1921).

———. *The Province of Jurisprudence Determined* (New York: Noonday Press, 1954).

Baier, Kurt. "Is Punishment Retributive?" *Analysis* 16 (1955).

Beard, Charles A. *An Economic Interpretation of the Constitution.* (New York: Free Press, 1941).

Beccaria, Cesare. *On Crimes and Punishment* (Indianapolis, Ind.: Bobbs-Merrill Co., 1965).

Bedau, Hugo A. *The Death Penalty in America* (Chicago: Aldine Publishing Co., 1964).

Bentham, Jeremy. *An Introduction to the Principles of Morals and Legislation* (Oxford: Basil Blackwell, 1948).

Bequai, August. *White Collar Crime: A 20th Century Crisis* (Lexington, Mass.: Lexington Books, 1976).

Bertocci, Peter, and Martin Millard. *Personality and the Good* (New York: David McKay, 1963).

Bonsignore, Claude (ed.). *Before the Law* (Atlanta, Ga.: Houghton Mifflin Co., 1974).

Bosanquet, Bernard. *The Philosophical Theory of the State* (London: Macmillan Publishing Co., 1966).

Bowring, James (ed.). *The Works of Jeremy Bentham* (Edinburgh: W. Tait, 1843).

Bradley, Francis. *Ethical Studies* (London: Oxford University Press, 1927).

———. "Some Remarks on Punishment," *International Journal of Ethics* 4 (1894).

Brandt, Richard B. *Ethical Theory: The Problems of Normative and Critical Ethics* (Englewood Cliffs, N.J.: Prentice-Hall, 1954).

———. "A Utilitarian Theory of Excuses," *Philosophical Review* 78 (1969).

Brown, Robert. *Charles Beard and the Constitution* (New York: Norton, 1956).

Brunner, Eric. *Justice and the Social Order* (New York: Harper and Brothers, 1945).

Buckland, William W. *A Textbook of Roman Law from Augustus to Justinian* (Cambridge: Cambridge University Press, 1963).

Cairns, Huntington. *The Collected Dialogues of Plato* (Princeton, N.J.: Princeton University Press, 1961).

Carritt, Edgar. *Ethical and Political Thinking* (Oxford: Clarendon Press, 1947).

———. *The Theory of Morals* (London: Oxford University Press, 1952).

Chilores, Claude. "Compensation to Victims of Crime is as Old as Civilization" *New York University Law Review* 39 (1964).

Chinard, Gilbert. *The Commonplace Book of Thomas Jefferson* (New York: Arbor House, 1926).

Cohen, Irving E. "Integrating Restitution in the Probation Services," *Journal of Criminal Law, Criminology, and Police Sciences* 34 (1944).

Cohn, Haim. *Jewish Law in Ancient and Modern Israel* (New York: KTAV Publishing House, 1971).

Corwin, Ernest. *The Higher Law Background of American Constitutional Law* (Ithaca, N.Y.: Cornell University Press, 1874).

Devlin, Patrick. *The Enforcement of Morals* (London: Oxford University Press, 1959).

Dewey, John. *A Common Faith* (New Haven, Conn.: Yale University Press, 1934).

————. *Ethics* (New York: Henry Holt & Co., 1910).

Diamond, Arthur. *Primitive Law* (London: Methuen, 1971).

Durkheim, Emile. *The Division of Labor in Society* (New York: Free Press, 1965).

Dworkin, Ronald. "Lord Devlin and the Enforcement of Morals," *Yale Law Journal* 75 (1966).

————. *The Philosophy of Law* (New York: Oxford University Press, 1977).

Ebstein, William. *Great Political Thinkers* (Illinois: Dryden Press, 1969).

Edwards, Paul (ed.). *The Encyclopedia of Philosophy* (New York: Macmillan Publishing Co., 1967).

Eglash, Albert. "Creative Restitution—A Broader Meaning for an Old Term," *Journal of Criminal Law, Criminology and Police Sciences* 48 (1958).

Eisenstein, Jerome. *Politics and the Legal Process* (New York: Harper and Row, 1973).

Ellug, Jerry. *Violence: Reflections From a Christian Perspective* (New York: Seabury Press, 1969).

Ewing, Alfred C. "Armstrong on the Retributive Theory," *Mind* 72 (1963).

————. *The Morality of Punishment* (Oxford: Clarendon Press, 1962).

Feinberg, Joel. "The Expressive Function of Punishment," *The Monist* 49 (1965).

Fichte, Johann Gottlieb. *The Science of Rights* (London: Macmillan Publishing Co., 1884).

Fletcher, Joseph. *Moral Responsibility: Situation Ethics at Work* (Philadelphia: Westminster Press, 1967).

————. *Situation Ethics* (Philadelphia: Westminster Press, 1966).

Flew, Anthony. "The Justification of Punishment," *Philosophy* 29 (1954).

Flugel, J. C. *Man, Morals and Society* (London: Oxford University Press, 1955).

Freud, Sigmund. *Totem and Taboo* (New York: W. W. Norton Co., 1961).

Friedman, Lawrence. *Law and the Behavioral Sciences* (Indianapolis, Ind.: Bobbs-Merrill, 1969).

Fromm, Eric. *The Anatomy of Human Destructiveness* (New York: Holt, Rinehart and Winston, 1973).

Fry, Margery. "Justice for Victims," *Journal of Public Law* 8 (1959).

Fuller, Leon L. "The Case of the Speluncean Explorers," *Harvard Law Review* 69 (1949).

Gallie, W. B. *Philosophy and the Historical Understanding* (London: Chatto and Windus, 1964).

Garofolo, Raffaele. *Criminology* (Boston: Little, Brown and Company, 1914).

Geis, Gilbert (ed.). *White Collar Crime* (New York: Free Press, 1977).

Gerber, Rudolph J. (ed.). *Contemporary Punishment: Views, Explanations, and Justifications* (Notre Dame, Ind.: University of Notre Dame Press, 1972).

Gibbs, John P. *Crime, Punishment, and Deterrence* (New York: Elsevier Scientific Publishing Co., 1975).

Goffman, Erving. "On Cooling the Mark Out: Some Aspects of Adaptation to Failure," *Psychiatry* 15 (1952).

Goldberg, Arthur. "Equality and Governmental Action," *New York University Law Review* 39 (1964).

Goldfarb, Ronald L., and Singer, L. R. *After Conviction: A Review of the American Correctional System* (New York: Simon and Schuster, 1973).

Golding, Marshall. *The Nature of Law: Readings in Legal Philosophy* (New York: Random House, 1966).

Griffin, Susan. "Rape: The All American Crime," in S. Ruth (ed.), *Issues in Feminism* (Boston: Houghton Mifflin Co., 1980).

Grotius, Hugo. *The Law of War and Peace* (Washington, D.C.: M. W. Dunne, 1901).

Gusfield, J. R. *Symbolic Crusade* (Urbana, Ill.: University of Illinois Press, 1963).

Hamilton, Edward (ed.). *The Collected Dialogues of Plato* (Princeton, N.J.: Princeton University Press, 1967).

Harbison, Winfred. *The American Constitution: Its Origin and Development* (New York: W. W. Norton, 1976).

Hart, Henry M. "The Aims of the Criminal Law," *Law and Contemporary Problems* 23 (1958).

Hart, Herbert L. A. *Law, Liberty and Morality* (London: Oxford University Press, 1963).

————. *Punishment and Responsibility* (Oxford: Clarendon Press, 1968).

————. *Punishment and the Elimination of Responsibility* (New York: Athlone Press, 1962).

————. "Social Solidarity and the Enforcement of Morals," *University of Chicago Law Review* 35 (1966).

Hegel, Georg Wilhelm. *The Philosophy of Law* (London: Oxford University Press, 1969).

————. *Philosophy of Right* (Oxford: Clarendon Press, 1973).

Hentig, Hans Von. *Punishment: Its Origin, Purpose, and Psychology* (London: W. Hodge and Co., Ltd., 1937).

Hertz, Jerome (ed.). *The Pentateuch and Haf Torahs* (New York: Metzudah Publishing Co., 1941).

Hobbes, Thomas. *Leviathan* (New York: E. P. Dutton and Co., 1950).

Hobel, E. A. *The Law of Primitive Man: A Study in Comparative Legal Dynamics* (Cambridge, Mass.: Harvard University Press, 1954).

Hobhouse, Leonard T. *Morals in Evolution* (London: Chapman and Hall, 1951).

Holdsworth, Henry. *A History of English Law* (London: Methuen, 1966).

Holland, G. *Elements in Jurisprudence* (London: Methuen, 1971).

Jensen, Matthew. *The Articles of Confederation* (Madison, Wisc.: University of Wisconsin Press, 1940).

Kant, Immanuel. *The Philosophy of Law* (Edinburgh: T. T. Clark, 1887).

Kellner, Manachem (ed.). *Contemporary Jewish Ethics* (New York: Sanhedrin Press, 1978).

Kraft-Ebing, R. *Psychopathia Sexualis* (New York: F. J. Rebman, 1925).

Kroeber, Alfred L. *The Nature of Culture* (Chicago: University of Chicago Press, 1952).

Laslett, Peter (ed.). *Philosophy, Politics and Society* (Oxford: Basil Blackwell, 1967).

Laster, Robert E. "Criminal Restitution: A Survey of its Past and an Analysis of its Present Usefulness," *University of Richmond Law Review* 5 (1970).

Leibnez, Gottfried. *Theodicy* (New Haven, Conn.: Yale University Press, 1962).

Levi-Strauss, Charles. *Totemism* (Boston: Beacon Press, 1962).

Lewis, H. D. (ed.). *Contemporary British Philosophy* (New York: Macmillan Co., 1956).

Lindesmith, Arthur R. *The Addict and the Law* (New York: Random House, 1967).

Logan, C. H. "Sanctions and Deviance," *Law and Society Review* 7 (1973).

Maine, Henry. *Ancient Law* (New York: E. P. Dutton and Co., 1960).

Marx, Karl, and Engels, Frederick. *The Holy Family* (Moscow: Foreign Language Publishing House, 1956).

Matza, Darrell. "Techniques of Neutralization: A Theory of Delinquency," *American Sociological Review* 22 (1957).

McCloskey, H. J. "A Non-Utilitarian Approach to Punishment," *Inquiry* 8 (1965).

McCloskey, Ronald. *The American Supreme Court* (Chicago: University of Chicago Press, 1960).

McDonald, Forrest. *We the People: The Economic Origins of the Constitution* (Chicago: University of Chicago Press, 1958).

McDonald, William F. *Criminal Justice and the Victim* (Beverly Hills, Calif.: Sage Publishing Co., 1976).

McLaughlin, Andres. *The Confederation and the Constitution* (New York: Collier, 1962).

McPherson, Thomas, "Punishment: Definition and Justification," *Analysis* 28 (1967).

McTaggart, John E. "Hegel's Theory of Punishment," *International Journal of Ethics* 6 (1896).

Meiners, Roger B. *Victim Compensation* (Lexington, Mass.: Lexington Books, 1973).

Mill, James. "I Have Nothing to do with Justice," *Life Magazine*, March 12, 1972.

Millard, Martin, and Peter Bertocci. *Personality and the Good* (New York: David McKay, 1963).

Montagu, Ashley. *Man and Aggression* (New York: Oxford University Press, 1968).

————. *The Nature of Human Aggression* (New York: Oxford University Press, 1976.

Moore, George Edward. *Principia Ethica* (Cambridge: Cambridge University Press, 1903).

Morris, Herbert. "Persons and Punishment," *The Monist* 52, no. 4 (1968).

Morris, Norval. *The Future of Imprisonment* (Chicago: University of Chicago Press, 1974).

Mundle, Clarence, "Punishment and Desert," *Philosophical Quarterly* 4 (1954).

Myrdal, Gunnar. *Political Elements in the Development of Economic Theory* (Cambridge, Mass.: Harvard University Press, 1954).

Oppenheimer, Heinrich. *The Rationale of Punishment* (Montclair, N.J.: Patterson-Smith, 1975).

Packer, Herbert. *The Limits of Criminal Sanction* (Stanford, Calif.: Stanford University Press, 1968).

Piaget, Jean. *The Moral Judgment of the Child* (New York: The Free Press, 1965).

Pincoffs, Edmund L. *The Rationale of Legal Punishment* (New York: Humanities Press, 1966).

Pollock, Edward, and Maitland, Fredrick. *The History of English Law* (London: Oxford University Press, 1963).

Pound, Roscoe. *Social Control Through Law* (Hamden, Conn.: Anchor Books, 1968).

Quinton, Anthony M. "On Punishment," *Analysis* 14 (1954).

Ramsey, Paul. *Deeds and Rules in Christian Ethics* (New York: Charles Scribner's Sons, 1967).

Raphael, David. *Moral Judgment* (London: George Allen and Unwin, Ltd., 1955).

Rashdall, H. *Theory of Good and Evil* (Oxford: Clarendon Press, 1924).

Rawls, John. *A Theory of Justice* (Cambridge, Mass.: Harvard University Press, 1971).

————. "Two Concepts of Rules," *Philosophical Review* 64 (1955).

Read, B. "Crime and Punishment in East Africa," *Howard Law Journal* 10 (1964).

Reich, Charles. "Police Questioning of Law Abiding Citizens," *Yale Law Journal* 72 (1975).

Rosenthal, Erwin (ed.). *Judaism and Christianity* (London: The Sheldon Press, 1938).

Ross, William David. "The Ethics of Punishment," *Philosophy* 4 (1925).

————. *The Right and the Good* (Oxford: Clarendon Press, 1965).

Rossiter, Clinton. *Seedtime of the Republic* (New York: Harcourt Brace, 1953).

Round, Arthur. *Jurisprudence* (St. Paul, Minn.: West Publishing Co., 1959).

Schafer, S. *Compensation and Restitution to Victims of Crime* (Montclair, N.J.,: Patterson-Smith, 1970).

————. *Victimology: The Victim and His Criminal* (Reston, Va.: Reston Publishing Co., 1977).

Schorman, Frank. "The Enforcement of Matters of Customs and Morals," *Philosophical Studies* 30 (1976).

Schrey, Henry, H. H. Walz, and W. A. Waterhouse, *The Biblical Doctrine of Justice and Law* (London: SCM Press, 1955).

Schur, E. M. *Our Criminal Society* (Englewood Cliffs, N.J.: Prentice-Hall, 1969).

Scott, George R. *The History of Torture Throughout the Ages* (London: Luxor Press, 1938).

Sellers, Jerry. *Theological Ethics* (New York: Macmillan Publishing Co., 1966).

Seymour, Whitney. *Why Justice Fails* (New York: William Morrow Co., 1973).

Skolnick, Jerome H. "The Clearance Rate and the Penalty Structure," *Justice Without Trial* (New York: John Wiley and Sons, 1966).

Smith, K. J. *A Cure for Crime: The Case for the Self-Determinate Prison Sentence* (London: Duckworth Co., Ltd., 1965).

Spencer, Horace. "Prison Ethics," *Essays: Scientific, Political and Speculative* 3 (1892).

Spriggs, Timothy L. S. "A Utilitarian Reply to Dr. McCloskey," *Inquiry* 9 (1965).

Stanford, Peter. "A Model Clockwork Orange Prison," *New York Times Magazine*, September 17, 1972.

Stephen, Henry J. *A History of the Criminal Law in England* (London: Macmillan, 1883).

Szaz, Thomas. *Pain and Pleasure* (New York: Basic Books, 1975).

Turk, A. T. *Criminality and Legal Order* (Chicago: Rand McNally, 1969).

Vecchio, Giorgie Del. *Justice* (Edinburgh: W. Tait, 1952).

Walster, Edmund. "Legal Structures and Restoring Equity," *Journal of Social Issues* 27, no. 2 (1971).

Wasserstrom, Richard. "Strict Liability in the Criminal Law," *Stanford Law Review* 12 (1959-60).

Watson, Richard A. *The Promise and Performance of American Democracy* (New York: John Wiley and Sons, 1978).

Weiss, Paul. *Man's Freedom* (Carbondale Ill.: Southern Illinois University Press, 1950).

Williams, Robert M. *American Society* (New York: Alfred A. Knopf, 1970).

Wittgenstein, Ludwig. *Philosophical Investigations* (New York: Macmillan Publishing Co., 1968).

Wolfgang, Aaron. "Victim Compensation in Crimes of Personal Violence," *Minnesota Law Review* 50 (1975).

Wolin, Samuel. *The Politics of Punishment* (New York: Harper and Row, 1972).

Wooton, Barbara. *Crime and the Criminal Law* (London: Stevens and Sons, Ltd., 1963).

———. *Social Science and Social Pathology* (London: George Allen and Unwin, Ltd., 1959).

Wright, Erick Olin. *The Politics of Punishment: A Critical Analysis of Prisons in America* (New York: Harper and Row, 1973.

Wroth, C. K., and Zobel, Hiller B. *The Legal Papers of John Adams* (Cambridge, Mass.: Harvard University Press, 1965).

Zimring, Franklin E. *Perspectives on Deterrence* (Washington, D.C.: U.S. Government Printing Office, 1971).

———, and Hawkins, G. J. *Deterrence: The Legal Threat in Crime Control* (Chicago: University of Chicago Press, 1973).

Index

About the Authors

CHARLES F. ABEL is Assistant Professor of Political Science at Old Dominion University, Norfolk, Virginia. He has contributed to *Political Methodology*.

FRANK H. MARSH is Professor of Philosophy at the University of Colorado and Professor of Medicine and Medical Ethics at the University of Colorado Medical School in Denver. A practicing trial lawyer for 25 years, he is the author of *The Emerging Rights of Children in Treatment for Mental and Catastrophic Illnesses* and has contributed chapters to *Suicide and Euthanasia, The Hastings Center Report,* and *Ethics in Science and Medicine.* Additionally, he has published many articles in American and international journals.